REBEL WOMEN: STAGING ANCIENT GREEK DRAMA
TODAY

REBEL WOMEN

Staging Ancient Greek Drama Today

Edited by
John Dillon and S. E. Wilmer

Methuen

Published by Methuen 2005

1 3 5 7 9 10 8 6 4 2

First published in Great Britain in 2005 by
Methuen Publishing Limited
11–12 Buckingham Gate
London SW1E 6LB

Methuen Publishing Limited Reg. No. 3543167
A CIP catalogue record for this book is available from the British Library

ISBN 0-413-77550-X

Typeset by SX Composing DTP, Rayleigh, Essex
Printed and bound in Great Britain by
St. Edmundsbury Press, Bury St. Edmunds, Suffolk

Contents

Acknowledgements

The editors wish to acknowledge with gratitude a generous grant from the Programme in Mediterranean and Near Eastern Studies at Trinity College Dublin towards the publication of this work. They also want to thank Mairead Delaney, archivist at the Abbey Theatre, Dublin, and Dmitri Troubotchkin, Head of the Research Department at the Russian Academy of Arts GITIS, for help with providing photos and securing permission to use them, and Ms Svetlana Semikolenova, Director of Research of the Moscow Bakhrushin State Theatre Museum for her invaluable assistance. They also wish to thank Holly Maples for help with the index, Alice Coghlan for compiling the select bibliography and Mark Dudgeon of Methuen for advising on the preparation of the book.

Illustrations

Frontispiece: Marianne McDonald

Hall's article: Image from *Ariel* (Abbey Theatre)

Torrance's article: Three images: Electra and the Chorus, Greek country-women, and Greek Orthodox nuns

Macintosh's article: Image of Paquebot Poste Français by Dellepiane (copyright Pro-Artis Gendre Editeur-Diffuseur, Paris)

Kotzamani's article: Two images from Moscow Art Theatre 1923 production of *Lysistrata* (Moscow Bakhrushin State Theatre Museum)

Wilmer's article: Images from *Medea* (with Fiona Shaw) and *By the Bog of Cats. . .* (Abbey Theatre)

Foreword

Marianne McDonald, whose work and contributions to classical scholarship are being honoured in this volume, is a scholar of wide and varied achievement, to whom the topics being discussed here have a peculiar relevance. She is not, of course, a rebel in any violent sense – though she holds strong views on many subjects – but rather in the sense, let us say, that Euripides' Melanippe was a rebel, by taking a stand against the expectations arising from her station in life, and in favour of a life of scholarship.

In the circumstances into which she was born, especially when endowed with beauty and grace as well as wealth, it would have been all too easy for her to immerse herself in the life of high society and while away her life in expensive frivolities, to the delight of the gossip magazines. As things turned out, though, after a distinguished undergraduate career at Bryn Mawr, where she majored in Classics and Music – a combination which was to have a lasting influence on her subsequent career – she chose to continue with graduate studies in Classics. For this she turned to the University of California at Irvine, a good deal closer to her home near San Diego in Southern California. The area of study that attracted her was Greek tragedy, and particularly the tragic drama of Euripides.

This resulted in two achievements, the latter of which in particular has been of momentous importance for classical studies in general. First of all, she produced a fine monograph developed from her thesis, *Terms for Happiness in Euripides* (Göttingen: Vandenhoek & Ruprecht, 1978); but secondly, provoked by the problem of the difficulty of conducting word-searches in classical texts, when the technology was available to solve it, she initiated, with generous financial contributions, the project which has grown into the Thesaurus Linguae Graecae, and which now has captured the whole of ancient Greek literature on disk, with results from which all scholars in the field have greatly benefited. She herself, during the late 1970s and early 1980s, produced a series of semi-lemmatised concordances to the plays of Euripides, which remain a most useful tool.

However, since her graduate years, her main field of interest has become, not so much Greek tragedy in its historical context in the fifth century BC – though this does, of course, concern her – as the multifarious ways in which this art-form has impinged upon later European, and indeed world, culture. Already in 1983, she produced *Euripides in Cinema: The Heart Made Visible* (Philadelphia: Centrum), a delightful study of the uses made of classical tragedy by such figures as Pier-Paolo Pasolini (*Medea*), Jules Dassin (*Dream of Passion, Phaedra*), and Michael Cacoyannis (*Iphigenia at Aulis, The Trojan Women, Electra*). This was followed in 1992 by *Ancient Sun, Modern Light: Greek Drama on the Modern Stage* (New York: Columbia University Press), comprising illuminating studies of the work of Suzuki Tadashi, Peter Sellars, Tony Harrison, Theodoros Terzopoulos, and ending with a study of Tom Murphy's *The Sanctuary Lamp* and its connections with the *Oresteia*.

This trilogy of studies was completed in 2001 with a brilliant and deeply learned study of Greek tragic themes in opera, *Sing Sorrow: Classics, History and Heroines in Opera* (Westport, CT/London: Greenwood), in which her mastery of musical theory is used to good effect. Here she traces the origins of opera, as an attempt to return the musical element to Greek tragedy, from Monteverdi's *Il ritorno d'Ulisse in patria*, through works of Purcell, Mozart, Berlioz, Strauss and Stravinsky, to Lee Breuer's *The Gospel at Colonus* and Mikis Theodorakis' *Medea*. It is indeed a bravura performance, and confirms her position as the leading authority in the field of the reception of Greek tragedy.

In 2002, she co-edited, with Michael Walton, Professor of

Drama at Hull, and himself a major authority on the modern reception of Greek tragedy, a most valuable collection of essays (to which she herself contributed an important survey-article on 'The Irish and Greek Tragedy'), on Irish versions of Greek tragedy, *Amid Our Troubles* (Methuen), covering all the major contributions of Irish authors in modern times, and including essays by a number of them, such as Seamus Heaney (also a contributor to this volume) and Tom Paulin.

Her latest work, following on from these, is *The Living Art of Greek Tragedy* (Indiana University Press, 2003), a most entertaining and masterly study, which follows succinct accounts of the plots of the surviving plays of Aeschylus, Sophocles and Euripides with a fascinating survey, accompanied by perceptive and occasionally (justifiably) acerbic evaluations of modern productions of the various plays. The whole work serves well to illustrate how, indeed, Greek tragedy is a living art.

This succession of books has been accompanied, of course, by a ceaseless stream of articles and reviews, commenting on virtually all significant contributions to the field in the past quarter-century or so. She has herself, it should be said, translated quite a number of tragedies, either alone or in cooperation with others, and many of these translations have been successfully produced – *Antigone* in 2000; *Andromache* in 2001 (with Michael Walton); *Trojan Women*, 2002; and both Socrates' and Euripides' *Electra*s, 2004 (again, with Michael Walton).

This all adds up to an impressive scholarly achievement, and it is doubtless not over yet. Few, if any, people have done as much as Marianne McDonald over the past twenty-five years to ensure that Greek tragedy remains a truly *living* art, and this volume of essays stands as a modest tribute to that record.

John Dillon

LAUDES MARIANNAE MMV

Ἐνθάδ᾽ ἐπαινέομεν σοφίην κάλλος τε γυναικός
ἧς πολυιδρείη φαινέτ᾽ ἀριπρεπέως.
εὖ Διονυσιακοῖο νόμους δεδάηκε θεάτρου,
εὖ τε χοροῦ τέχνην ἔργα τε τῶν τραγικῶν.
ἦ ῥα Κλυταιμνήστρης χαλεπὴν ἠπίστατο ὀργήν,
Ἀντιγόνης τε δίκην, καὶ πάθος Ἀνδρομάχης.
ἑσπερίων σάφα οἶδεν ἀείσματα· δρᾶμα τ᾽ ἐναργῶς
δεῖξεν τῶν νοτίων εὔξενον Αἰθιόπων.
Ὠγυγίων δ᾽ ἄφενος νήσῳ νέμεν ὀλβοδότειρα·
Τῆσδ᾽ ἀρετὴν ὑμνεῖ μουσοφιλὴς θίασος.

G. L. H.

Introduction

S. E. Wilmer

One of the more perplexing statements that Aristotle makes in *The Poetics* concerns the role of women in Greek tragedy. He speaks of women in the same context as slaves: 'Goodness is possible in every type of personage, even in a woman or a slave, though the one is perhaps an inferior, and the other a wholly worthless being.'[1] He goes on to assert: 'It is not appropriate in a female Character to be manly, or clever.'[2] In suggesting that this is perplexing, I am not trying to imply that the position of women in Athens in the fifth and fourth centuries BC was not inferior to that of men. Athens was a patriarchal and androcentric society. Women were legally bound to their fathers until they married and then legally responsible to their husbands. If their husband died before them and they had a son, they would then be legally responsible to their son. However, Aristotle's statement seems perplexing because he was commenting on a corpus of Greek tragedy which included some of the great female roles in the history of Western theatre: Antigone, Electra, Alcestis, Medea, Clytemnestra, Phaedra, Hecuba, Helen, Cassandra and Andromache. As Helene Foley writes in *Female Acts in Greek Tragedy*: 'Leaving aside women's strikingly assertive and even rebellious behavior, the pervasive presence of female characters on the public stage in a society that preferred its own women to have as limited a public reputation as possible was even in antiquity something of a surprise.'[3]

Rebel Women examines the representation of ancient Greek heroines both in their original contexts and in the modern world. Many of the articles consider how such female characters have been portrayed in the twentieth century and in some cases have been transformed to enhance their relevance to topical and local situations and/or to strengthen and make more appealing their personalities and their actions. The book illustrates that in searching for appropriate strong female characters, both historical and mythological, who can speak to the current generation about the condition of women and the potential for women to be active in shaping their present and their future, contemporary theatre directors and dramatists have often turned to Greek tragedy and comedy. They have discovered that while Greek drama was written by men for a mainly (if not exclusively) male audience,[4] female characters in fifth-century drama often possess a strength of purpose, an ability to overcome male oppression, a sense of female solidarity and a commitment to higher values (than those of the men in that society) that are often lacking in theatrical figures from later centuries. While theatre scholars such as Sue Ellen Case have emphasised the misogynistic features underlying these plays and classicists such as Froma Zeitlin have argued that in their original social context the female characters' 'actions and reactions are all used finally to serve masculine ends',[5] modern productions have often exploited these dramas to serve female ends.

One serviceable aspect of the Greek heroines is their capacity for active intervention in events rather than simply displaying what Pomeroy calls 'normal female behavior'.[6] While some of the characters are docile and dutiful, such as Alcestis, Iphigenia and Ismene, others are capable of taking revenge for actions they will not tolerate. They take their fate into their own hands and plot a reversal in their fortune or in the fortunes of others. Clytemnestra in *The Oresteia* gains revenge by killing both Agamemnon and his mistress/slave Cassandra when he returns home from the Trojan War. Clytemnestra appears to the citizens of Argos after the double murder and gloats over her victory and the rightness of her actions. She is a dangerous and vicious woman who has sought and achieved revenge both for her husband's infidelity and for his murder of their daughter Iphigenia.

Sophocles' Electra equally plots revenge against her mother for her father's death and urges her brother Orestes to carry out her murder. Electra again succeeds in bringing about a brutal and vicious crime against nature and is exultant rather than apologetic in its execution. As Orestes strikes their mother, rather than cowering and feeling ashamed, Electra urges him to strike her again. She also recommends that the body of Aegisthus (Clytemnestra's lover) be thrown to the animals. Electra, whom Eugene O'Neill called the 'most interesting of all women in drama',[7] is, like her mother, vicious and unrepentant of her crime.

Medea is perhaps the supreme example of a woman plotting and executing an inhuman crime within the family. She not only kills the new bride and the new bride's father, but also, and more importantly, she kills her own children to punish her husband. Again she justifies her actions to the audience, as a woman who has made enormous sacrifices for her husband Jason, only to see him reject her. She has helped Jason steal the Golden Fleece, killed her brother, given up her customs and position at home to come to a foreign land where she is an exile, given birth to two sons and provided in every way for her husband, only to discover that he is prepared to reject her and marry another woman.

Antigone, on the other hand, is heroic in her willingness to sacrifice herself for the moral values in which she believes rather than the imposed values of the state. In order to preserve the dignity of her family and pay proper respect to her brother who lies unburied on orders from the state, she is willing to risk her own life to bury him. The Chorus attest to her heroic qualities even though they suggest that she should have obeyed the laws of the state. In Seamus Heaney's 2004 version, *The Burial at Thebes*, which he discusses in Chapter 8, this is expressed as follows:

> But someone as glorious
> In life and in death as you
> Can also seem immortal.[8]

It is worth mentioning that many of these Greek characters hold a special position in their society. They are normally from leading or royal families. They have distinguished family backgrounds and an important position of power. Clytemnestra, Alcestis, Phaedra and Hecuba are queens, and Antigone, Medea and Electra are princesses. However, Medea is an outsider in Corinth and, as Fiona Macintosh points out in her article (Chapter 3), she has been represented in twentieth-century versions as disenfranchised not only because of her gender but also because of her different background. Thus she has been represented as the Other, for example, in ethnic terms as an Asian princess in Lenormand's *Asie* (which Macintosh discusses) or in social terms as a Traveller in Marina Carr's *By the Bog of Cats...* which is the focus for Melissa Sihra's Chapter 5.

Another interesting and timeless feature is the power relationship that both Clytemnestra and Medea maintain with their husbands. They are women who will not allow themselves to be subjugated and mistreated. While in a position of dependence, they will not sit idly by while their husbands have a relationship with another woman. Equally, Medea, Clytemnestra and Antigone are not prepared to allow the decisions by men to stand unquestioned. They rebel against oppression, marginalisation and injury to their pride. They confront the values of the androcentric society and are prepared to risk reprisals against their actions for the sake of their own dignity and self-esteem. Likewise, in *The Suppliants* by Aeschylus, fifty women flee from Egypt from men who intend to marry them. On arriving in Argos, they seek protection from the gods and the local population against the men who pursue them, and in the lost part of the trilogy the women, after having been raped, ultimately kill all except one of their pursuers. Even in *The Trojan Women* (and especially in Brendan Kennelly's version, which Anthony Roche discusses in Chapter 7), the women who have been captured in the fall of Troy and turned into slaves convey a sense of rebellion against the social and military conventions imposed on them. Although Hecuba, Andromache and Cassandra are assigned as slaves or wives to the conquering heroes, they do not accept their fate meekly. They fight against their fate and underscore the iniquity of their plight.

A third feature that elicits an understanding of the female condition in modern society is the relationships among the female characters. As Rush Rehm illustrates in his article (Chapter 9), the expression of solidarity among women to overcome oppression is a common motif of Greek tragedy. In her hour of need, Medea calls on the complicity of the women around her to help in her campaign of revenge against her husband who has betrayed her. Although Medea does not gain explicit sympathy for her actions, there is a sense of female solidarity among the women against male oppression. The nurse and the Chorus-women do not agree with the nature of Medea's actions but, by their decision to keep silent and not interfere with her, they tacitly support her and become accessories to the crime. Just as in Susan Glaspell's play *Trifles*, where two female characters cover up the evidence of a third woman's murder of her husband, the nurse and the female entourage in *Medea* assist in the murders by remaining silent and taking no action that would alert others to Medea's intentions. Likewise, in the various versions of the Electra story by Aeschylus, Sophocles and Euripides, as Michael Walton points out in Chapter 10, the Chorus act in collusion with Electra. In *The Trojan Women*, a strong feeling of women's solidarity pervades as the imprisoned victims of male Greek authority discover their destinies together, and rant and rave and cry out in rage against their collective treatment. They also try to stand up for each other and protect each other, even though they are virtually powerless.

The theme of female solidarity is also touched on in *Antigone* between the two sisters Antigone and Ismene, as Ismene has to decide whether to support or condemn the actions of Antigone in burying their brother in contravention of Creon's decree. Antigone does not expect full solidarity from Ismene because of the risks involved. She allows Ismene to be released from her family obligations by carrying them out alone. Antigone argues that there is no need for both sisters to die for the honour of their family. Later, when Creon asks who is responsible for the deed, Ismene offers to act as an accessory but Antigone again exonerates her. Seamus Heaney renders this encounter as follows:

CREON: You helped her, didn't you?
Or are you going to claim you're innocent?

ISMENE: I helped her, yes, if I'm allowed to say so
And now I stand with her to take what comes.

ANTIGONE: I don't allow this. Justice won't allow it.
You wouldn't help.
We cut all ties.
It's over.

ISMENE: But now I'm with you. I want to throw myself
Like a lifeline to you in your sea of troubles.

ANTIGONE: Too late, my sister. You chose a safe line first.
The dead and Hades know who did this deed.

ISMENE: Antigone, don't rob me of all honour.
Let me die with you and act right by the dead.[9]

In many Greek tragedies, the offensive and unnatural actions of the women are provoked by male abuse. They are proud women who have been mistreated and the audience's sympathies are engaged because they can identify with that abuse and feeling of outrage. Euripides in particular calls attention to the 'double standard in sexual morality'.[10] In *Hippolytus*, Theseus remarks: 'I know young men who are no better than women at resisting Aphrodite's attacks on their immature minds. But their male status helps them out.'[11] Although portrayed by Aristophanes as a misogynist in such comedies as *The Frogs* and *Thesmophoriazusae* (being characterised by one of the women as having 'filled our husbands' minds with such awful ideas'),[12] Euripides often wrote from a female point of view and emphasised the plight of women in such plays as *Medea, Hippolytus, Iphigenia at Aulis* and *Trojan Women* (Bernard Williams suggests that Euripides could be considered both a misogynist and a feminist!).[13] Medea's rage is fully understandable to a modern audience because she has sacrificed so much to help her husband. The starting point for the play is a situation with which many married women can sympathise. The sense of abuse, shame and futility that turns to rage in a married woman who has sacrificed her life and career for a husband who then abandons her for another is a kind of rallying call for a feminist reaction. Medea is an icon for all women who are abused in this way, especially those suffering from the phenomenon of the successful businessman getting divorced to marry a trophy wife. The question of whether the actions Medea takes are appropriate to her sense of outrage is more problematic, but, certainly at the beginning of the play, the audience can sympathise with her as a victim of abuse who deserves redress.

The whole concept of marriage is called into question in Greek tragedy. The marriages of Clytemnestra, Medea and Deianeira end in homicide. Marriage is linked with slavery in *The Trojan Women* and self-sacrifice in *Iphigenia at Aulis*. Aeschylus's *The Suppliants* depicts marriage as hunt and conquest with the men chasing and subduing their prey. In Silviu Purcarete's celebrated production of *Les Danaides* (which attempted to complete the lost parts of the trilogy and which toured Europe and the USA in 1996), the sight of fifty men chasing fifty women to marry them against their will evoked memories of mass rape during the war in Bosnia. Marriage was portrayed as a type of violent action symbolised by its consummation. The subsequent scene in *Les Danaides* in which the fifty women take revenge was presented as a formidable act of female solidarity, excepting the one woman who took pity on her husband and let him escape.

Rather than festive occasions, marriage ceremonies are often transformed into funeral rituals in Greek tragedy, as Rush Rehm has illustrated in his book *Marriage to Death*, and modern productions often accentuate this feature. Thus, in the 2004 Abbey Theatre production of Seamus Heaney's *The Burial at Thebes*, Antigone wears a wedding dress as she goes to her death, and Hester Swane, the Medea figure in *By the Bog of Cats...*, is similarly clothed when she also committs suicide. Wedding ceremonies, such as that between Glauce and Jason in Pasolini's film of *Medea*, or between Iphigenia and Achilles, as Isabelle Torrance illustrates, in Cacoyannis's film *Iphigenia*, become fatal events with conflicting rituals, rather than the happy endings of renaissance comedy.[14]

By contrast, the disappearance of the husband can be represented as a liberating and empowering occasion for the wife. Clytemnestra boasts at the end of the original version of *Agamemnon*, in a significant role reversal, that 'her situation will be secure as long as her lover Aegisthus lights the fire on her hearth'.[15] Ruling the roost while Agamemnon has been away, Clytemnestra appeared as nine months pregnant in Purcarete's version of *The Oresteia* in 1998, as she proudly greeted him on his return from the ten-year Trojan War, before murdering him. Medea, as performed by Diana Rigg in London in 1993, seemed similarly liberated as she flew off triumphantly to a new life in Athens, leaving Jason in ruins.

These Greek tragedies, therefore, can become vehicles in modern production to highlight the power relationships between men and women in marriage and the right of women to rebel against patriarchal oppression. Some of the plays suggest that marriage equals enforced slavery, that the sexual act implies rape, and that the institution of marriage implies a patriarchal control of women. And so today a feminist construction is often placed on the adaptation of these plays. The characters of Clytemnestra, Medea, Electra and even Hecuba can be represented as women who have been victimised but who fight back, who empower themselves and are empowered by the support of other women, to take action to overturn their oppression. In the production of *Les Danaides*, Purcarete emphasised the image of the fifty women who are being pursued as innocent creatures unfairly victimised and unable to protect themselves. He presented the scene of revenge in a sympathetic and poetic mood, with the dresses of the women forming tents under which their new husbands slept on their wedding night, lit by candlelight, while the women quietly and unobtrusively dispatched them with domestic cutlery.

Greek heroines are also often represented as occupying the morally superior position and appealing to higher values which continue to resonate today. Sarah Pomeroy, in *Goddesses, Whores, Wives, and Slaves*, asserted: 'Many tragedies show women in rebellion against the established norms of society.'[16] Lysistrata argues that the men are destroying Athenian society through warfare and strives for a peaceful solution, which Marina

Kotzamani (Chapter 4) demonstrates as relevant to the modern day (and particularly to the Soviet Union in the 1920s Moscow Art Theatre production). Antigone maintains that the traditional rituals for the dead are more important to observe than an edict from a male dictator and, as Seamus Heaney indicates, her actions have a timeless quality that can be applied as usefully to current events as to earlier centuries. Hecuba pleads that the women in her court be treated with respect and dignity rather than being distributed like chattel. Medea upholds the sanctity of her marriage. Iphigenia pleads for her life before willingly sacrificing herself for the glory of Greece. And, as John Dillon observes (Chapter 12), Melanippe the Wise questions the theocratic under-pinning of the patriarchal state.

This book indicates that the problem of adopting female characters of Greek tragedy as feminist icons is not only their frequently tragic fates, but more importantly the exaggerated nature of their actions. There are, of course, a surprising number of females murdering males in Greek tragedy, some accidentally like Agave dismembering Pentheus and Deianeira poisoning Heracles, and others deliberately like Medea, Clytemnestra, Hecuba and her assistants in *Hecuba*, and the women in Aeschylus' *The Suppliants*. As previously mentioned, theatre and classics scholars have called attention to the misogynist values underlying some of the ancient texts.[17] Sarah Pomeroy has attributed the misogynist sentiments in Euripides' plays to his characters rather than to himself, suggesting that Euripides presented such opinions in order to raise important issues and represented 'women victimised by patriarchy in almost every possible way'.[18] The question that haunts the figure of Medea is: how can a mother justify killing her own children? Can an audience, even a feminist audience, maintain sympathy for a woman who acts contrary to the values of modern society and to the notions of motherhood, or is one forced to accept that the plays reflect the patriarchal values of Greek society and presented such characters as diabolical figures to men?

Because of this problem, modern productions often scale down or make palatable the egregious crimes of the women. As is illustrated in my chapter, it is noteworthy that Marina Carr, having based *By the Bog of Cats*. . . closely on the structure of Euripides' *Medea*, changed the ending so that the Medea character does not fly away triumphantly after killing her child but commits suicide. Similarly, Deborah Warner's production of *Medea*, which toured from Dublin to London, New York and Paris (2000–03), had Medea sitting quietly beside Jason at the end, both aghast at the turn of events. Likewise, Electra's conspiracy to kill her mother seems hard to justify in any way that would retain the sympathy of the audience. Thaddeus O'Sullivan's film *In the Border Country* (which updates the *Oresteia* to the Troubles in Northern Ireland) presents Clytemnestra's murder as partly accidental to make it more plausible and Electra more sympathetic. Clytemnestra's actions in the *Agamemnon* are equally problematic but can become more understandable to an audience when reminded that her husband sacrificed her daughter. Consequently, as Edith Hall argues in Chapter 1, many modern productions solve 'some of the problems of the *Oresteia*'s notorious sexism' by including parts of *Iphigenia in Aulis* in the performance, e.g. *Les Atrides* directed by Ariane Mnouchkine and *Ariel* by Marina Carr, or simply by including Iphigenia as a silent presence on stage, as in the 1999–2000 production by Katie Mitchell. (Conversely, Edith Hall also suggests that by incorporating Clytemnestra's revenge into productions of *Iphigenia in Aulis*, the play becomes less about victimised females, and more about females taking justifiable revenge for wrongful actions.) On the other hand, Clytemnestra's initial rage in the play, which might be easy to accept early on, is prolonged and grossly re-emphasised with her display of her victims on the *ekkuklema* at the end of *Agamemnon*. Depending on the production, the horror of the audience at her actions can be accentuated by this graphic display, and if the original structure of the play is preserved, it is rather difficult to sympathise with her when her hands are dripping with blood and the corpses lie at her side, as in the Peter Stein production of *The Oresteia* in 1980 at the Schaubühne in Berlin, that accentuated this by having blood running off the front of the stage into a gulley during her final speech. As James Diggle emphasises in

Chapter 11, Clytemnestra is an axe-murderer with a vengeance, exulting in Agamemnon's blood as if it were rain from heaven.

Initially, the audience might empathise with the hurt and rage that Medea, Electra and Clytemnestra feel but, without drastically rewriting the original or softening its impact through production techniques, it is difficult to maintain the sympathy of the audience for the characters by the end of the plays. We tend to be horrified by their actions. At the same time one could argue that the original versions of Greek drama provide an unusual respect for the power of women to rebel. While Edith Hall argues that the 'post-feminist Western liberal consensus can cope with the terrifying Clytemnestra of Aeschylus very much better if it is simultaneously offered the more sympathetic Clytemnestra of *Iphigenia in Aulis*', perhaps it is useful that these more outrageous characters can also serve, undiluted, as much as a warning to men as a role-model to women. Presumably it was because women had been represented on the fifth-century Athenian stage as a threat to an androcentric society that Aristotle later argued against female characters being portrayed as clever. As Creon observed in *Medea*, clever women are dangerous.

Although Froma Zeitlin has argued that Greek tragedy was not designed 'for woman gaining some greater entitlement or privilege for herself and not even for revising notions of what femininity might be or mean',[19] Greek tragedy outside of its original social context can do all of those things. This book shows some of the ways in which this has been possible. It combines studies of modern productions and essays on the original works, all in honour of Professor Marianne McDonald who herself has done a great deal for the study of the subject. It is divided into three sections that reflect some aspects of McDonald's scholarly interests:[20] international productions, Irish versions, and analysis of the original texts. The book arose out of a conference in Trinity College Dublin on *Rebel Women: Staging Ancient Greek Drama Today* in March 2003, and some of the articles herein were first presented as papers at that conference. The conference coincided with the 'pre-emptive' American and British invasion of Iraq and with the international protest against this invasion which, on 3

March 2003, took the form of thousands of readings and performances of *Lysistrata* occurring simultaneously throughout the world. Thus, the relevance of Greek drama to current social and political issues held a special significance at that time and is evident in many of the chapters. Although Froma Zeitlin, in her book *Playing the Other*, asserts that, in their original context, the female heroines of ancient Greek drama 'play the role of catalysts, agents, instruments, blockers, spoilers, destroyers . . . for the male characters',[21] these figures often attain greater autonomy and more sympathy from the audience in modern productions. Moreover, in today's society, for women who question and rebel against patriarchal structures, the Greek tragic heroines provide alternative models and have been frequently exploited in the twentieth and twenty-first centuries to focus on the position of women in society.

Notes

1. Aristotle, *On the Art of Poetry*, trans. Ingram Bywater (Oxford: Clarendon Press, 1920), pp. 55–6.
2. Ibid., p. 56.
3. Helene P. Foley, *Female Acts in Greek Tragedy* (Princeton, NJ: Princeton University Press, 2001), p. 6.
4. With regard to the academic debate about whether women attended the performances of ancient Greek drama, see Simon Goldhill, 'The Audience of Athenian Tragedy', in Pat Easterling (ed.), *The Cambridge Companion to Greek Tragedy* (Cambridge: CUP, 1997), pp. 62–6.
5. Froma I. Zeitlin, *Playing the Other: Gender and Society in Classical Greek Literature* (Chicago: Chicago University Press, 1996), p. 13. Sue Ellen Case in particular calls attention to the misogynistic attitudes in *The Oresteia*, especially evident in the characterisation of Clytemnestra in the *Agamemnon* and the judgment in *The Eumenides* 'establishing that the parental line is male. The mother is not the parent, but the nurse. The parent is defined as he who mounts.' See Sue Ellen Case, 'Classic Drag: The Greek Creation of Female Parts', *Theatre Journal*, 37 (3) (October 1985), pp. 317–327.

6. Sarah B. Pomeroy, *Goddesses, Whores, Wives, and Slaves; Women in Classical Antiquity* (New York: Schocken Books, 1975), p. 98.

7. Travis Bogard and Jackson R. Bryer (eds), *Selected Letters of Eugene O'Neill* (New Haven, CT: Yale University Press, 1988), p. 368.

8. Seamus Heaney, *The Burial at Thebes* (London: Faber and Faber, 2004), p. 38.

9. Ibid., pp. 24–5.

10. See Pomeroy, *Goddesses, Whores, Wives, and Slaves*, p. 110.

11. Euripides, *Hippolytus*, lines 967–70, as translated by Helene Foley in *Female Acts in Greek Tragedy* (Princeton, NJ: Princeton University Press, 2001), p. 107.

12. Aristophanes, *The Poet and the Women*, trans. David Barrett (London: Penguin, 1964), p. 113.

13. Bernard Williams, *Shame and Necessity* (Berkeley: University of California Press, 1993), p. 119.

14. Froma Zeitlin has shown the mythic origins of the overlap between marriage and death in the relationship between Demeter, Hades and Persephone (Zeitlin, *Playing the Other*, p. 10).

15. See Pomeroy, *Goddesses, Whores, Wives, and Slaves*, p. 98. Pomeroy explains: 'The double entendre is especially shocking because a woman traditionally lit the fire on her father's or husband's hearth.'

16. Ibid., p. 97.

17. Ibid., pp. 97–110; Zeitlin, *Playing the Other*, pp. 87–119; Foley, *Female Acts in Greek Tragedy*, pp. 12–13; Case, 'Classic Drag'.

18. Pomeroy, *Goddesses, Whores, Wives, and Slaves*, p. 110.

19. Zeitlin, *Playing the Other*, p. 347.

20. Unfortunately, there is not the space to represent all areas of Professor McDonald's interests, such as operatic and Asian versions of Greek tragedy. On the other hand, we have been able to include as a kind of an appendix, and a most welcome one, an extract from a forthcoming play by Athol Fugard on Hildegard of Bingen, a notable rebel woman, not from the classical world but from the medieval period.

21. Zeitlin, *Playing the Other*, p. 347.

International Adaptations

1. Iphigenia and Her Mother at Aulis: A Study in the Revival of a Euripidean Classic

Edith Hall

They will sing that here was a hero who was ready to shoulder his responsibilities, ready to set his private feelings aside for the sake of his country. They will call him the conqueror of Troy. They will call him the founder of Greater Mycenae. They will celebrate his return from the war, Agamemnon, Sacker of Cities, loaded with slaves and plunder, a five-star general, clasped in the welcoming arms of his queen Clytemnestra.

Barry Unsworth, The Songs of the Kings, p. 100

From the Renaissance to the Twentieth Century

Since the late 1990s, Euripides' *Iphigenia in Aulis* has enjoyed a sudden revival in the cultural arena; this essay asks what the reasons for this rediscovery might be. Its particular focus is on some recent Irish productions and versions by Irish writers. The argument proposes that what they have in common is less a shared stance on Ireland, religion, gender or even theatrical aesthetics, than a conviction that mendacious political rhetoric has in recent years become more effective, and that the rise of spin-doctoring has been made possible only by the epistemological and metaphysical vacuum situated at the centre of the Western collective psyche. The essay also suggests that thinking about the reasons for the recent stage rediscovery of this particular play can illuminate some of the special qualities it displayed in its original performance context in

Athens in 405 BC, especially the instability of its characters and the unparalleled bleakness of its evocation of religious and moral *aporia*. But some more recent historical context is required in order to appreciate the significance of the play's revival.

One of Euripides' last and most sombre plays, *Iphigenia in Aulis* exerted a profound influence on Greek and Roman antiquity, since it was the canonical dramatisation of what became a favourite theme in painting and narrative poetry.[1] The Euripidean version of the sacrifice at Aulis was also replayed consistently in the performance arts, from the Hellenistic tragic stage and concert hall to the Roman balletic dance medium of chorally accompanied pantomime.[2] Yet, since the Renaissance, the career of *Iphigenia in Aulis* has been extremely uneven: popularity in the sixteenth to eighteenth centuries was followed by a spectacular fall from favour which lasted from the French revolution until nearly the end of the twentieth century.

In comparison with most other Greek tragedies, the play certainly made a major impact on Renaissance Europe after it was first printed, in the Aldine edition of all seventeen Euripidean plays, at Venice in 1503. It was almost immediately translated by Erasmus into Latin (1506), along with *Hecuba*, with the result that for the whole of the sixteenth century these two tragedies were the most read and adapted of all Euripides' works.[3] *Iphigenia in Aulis* was Italianised by Ludovico Dolce (1543–47);[4] it also became the earliest Greek tragedy to receive a translation into English, Lady Jane Lumley's *The Tragedie of Iphigeneia*, a version on which this young aristocrat worked during the restoration of Catholicism under Mary Tudor; Lady Jane then presented it, apparently without irony, to her father (1553–58).[5] Subsequently, the Greek play's political potential was realised in a Dutch satire composed by Samuel Coster (1617).[6] Once Racine's *Iphigénie* had achieved its immediate success in 1674, *Iphigenia in Aulis* became one of the most popular theatrical archetypes of the late seventeenth and eighteenth centuries.[7] The marriageable maiden's graceful obedience to her father, the wielding of his absolute patriarchal authority, the motif of human sacrifice – all these were more than

4

congenial to the Christian, indeed dominantly Catholic, culture and unequal gender ideas of pre-revolutionary Europe; it is revealing to note how starkly the popularity of the story in Catholic Italy and France contrasts with the absence of revivals or new dramatic versions to emerge from Whiggish, Anglican, anti-Catholic mainland Britain, at least after the French Huguenot exile Abel Boyer's English-language *Achilles* (1700), an unsatisfactory attempt to render the myth palatable to Protestant taste and ideology.[8]

Yet the Aulis Iphigenia of the Renaissance, early modern and neoclassical periods was big business on the European Continent. Between Erasmus' Latin version of 1506 and the outbreak of the Greek War of Independence in 1821, the theme inspired at least thirty-seven paintings (mostly by Italians), two tapestries, and a ceramic plaque.[9] There were several Spanish plays about Iphigenia's sacrifice, many French, a few in German, and a satirical burlesque in Greek by Petros Katsaïtis (1720). Half-a-dozen *Iphigenia in Aulis* ballets of this period are attested, and from the time of Aurelio Aureli's 1707 *L'Ifigenia*, probably first performed in Venice, no fewer than thirty-nine operas.[10] These were predominantly Italian, and included compositions by such great names as Scarlatti, Porpora, Traetta, Cherubini and Simone Mayr in addition to the most famous *Iphigenia in Aulis* opera of them all, the lyrical French-language masterpiece by Christoph Willibald Gluck. In 1757, eight years before the première of Gluck's opera, Diderot even argued, during the course of a discussion of his own play *Le Fils naturel*, that the sacrifice of Iphigenia was the *ideal* subject for opera.[11]

In contrast with this long-standing and consistent high status, the almost total disappearance of *Iphigenia in Aulis* from the nineteenth-century stage, at least after 1820, is distinctly noticeable. With the exception of fairly steady revivals of Gluck's exquisite version in the opera house, the tragedy was almost entirely ignored for many decades. This period produced hardly any new translations intended for performance, or even staged theatrical productions other than occasional revivals of Racine's *Iphigénie*. There was one peculiar exception, which took place in Ireland in 1846. It is worth dwelling on not only because of the importance of Ireland in the subsequent, twentieth-century revival of Greek theatre,[12] but also because it demonstrates the reasons why *Iphigenia in Aulis* was not in tune with the mid-nineteenth-century *Zeitgeist*.

In 1845, John Calcraft, the manager of Dublin's Theatre Royal, persuaded the lovely English tragedienne Helen Faucit to travel to Ireland and perform 'Mendelssohn's *Antigone*' (a version offered in English ultimately deriving, via German, from Sophocles, with music composed by Mendelssohn to accompany the choruses and a few of the actor's speeches). This had been performed on a raised Greek stage, complete with Ionic pillars, 'authentic' tripods, and a set containing no fewer than five doors.[13] The inflated tone of the reviews indicates that Faucit's performance as Antigone was a triumph.[14] She excited all who watched her by managing to convey both a cool, abstract sense of the apprehension of a mournful destiny, and a tactile, loving intimacy. The consistent theme in the ecstatic Dublin press is her reconciliation of the formal, classical and ideal with warm humanity and emotion. Faucit's 'Grecian' poses and gestures, her elegant limbs framed in flowing drapery, were captured in the portrait created by Sir Frederick Burton, the Director of the National Gallery in Dublin, and impressed every commentator.[15] She seems to have been an acceptable object of male sexual desire.[16]

It is scarcely surprising that Faucit and Calcraft attempted, in November 1846, to build on this lucrative triumph by staging a second Greek tragedy featuring a persecuted virgin, Euripides' *Iphigenia in Aulis*. This time the play was proudly (although inaccurately) billed as offering the first *original* production of a Greek tragedy in Ireland.[17] Calcraft composed an English translation by synthesising several different versions, and cast himself as Agamemnon. Faucit successfully extracted the maximum pathos out of Iphigenia's predicament, without succumbing to sentimentality, when (as the *Freeman's Journal* for Monday, 30 November put it) she appeared 'a suppliant at her father's feet, shuddering with horror at that gloom and dark uncertainty that awaited her'. The symphony orchestra and oratorio-style chorus performed an original score (unusually not an adaptation of Gluck), composed by the theatre's musical director, Richard Levey. Like many directors before and since, Calcraft ameliorated the psychological harshness of the play by using the more comfortable (and almost certainly post-Euripidean) alternative denouement in which Iphigenia is replaced by a deer and whisked off to safety by the goddess Artemis, thus exonerating her father.[18] Calcraft offered his audience what the *Freeman's Journal* described as 'a magnificent tableau', involving Agamemnon's departing galley and 'the Grecian fleet wafted by a favouring gale from the winding bay of Aulis'. But despite all Calcraft's efforts, the audiences were not as enthusiastic as they had been the previous year, and plans to take the play to Edinburgh never materialised.

Calcraft had failed to see that while both Antigone and Iphigenia conform to strict models of ideal womanhood, Antigone displays moral strength as she stands up to male authority in order to defend her family's interests, while Iphigenia *accedes* to a male assault on her family's interests. In the ideological climate following the British Infant Custody Act of 1839, which had begun, at least, to undermine the almost total power nineteenth-century British men had previously wielded over their wives and families, the simple obedience to male authority displayed by Iphigenia was no longer the unquestioned ideal it once had been. The fate of the Dublin *Iphigenia in Aulis* thus heralded this tragedy's inability to strike resonant social and emotional chords throughout the entire Victorian period. Neither the supernatural, fantastic ending chosen by Calcraft, nor the (at that time still intolerable) horror of the text if performed without the miraculous substitution, was remotely congenial to the rational but sentimental subjectivity of that era. Neither Iphigenia's warlike rhetoric, nor Clytemnestra's veiled threats to Agamemnon (on which see further below), conformed to the contemporary idealisation of responsible maidenhood, gentle wifehood and sanctified maternity.

This relative lack of interest in the play was to continue to prevent it finding significant theatrical realisation, at least outside Greece, more or less throughout the first eight decades of the twentieth century. This near-absence from public stages stands in stark contrast to the rediscovery of many other Greek tragedies as performance texts, and the canonisation of their important place in the standard repertoire. The early twentieth century rediscovered such Euripidean heroines as Medea (for example, in Gilbert Murray's famous translation, directed by Harley Granville Barker at the Savoy Theatre, London, in 1907), and 'anti-war' plays such as *Trojan Women* (first revived by Granville Barker at the Royal Court Theatre in 1905, but consistently revived thereafter).[19] *Iphigenia in Aulis*, on the other hand, almost completely failed to recover a presence in performance (outside the opera house) during almost all of the twentieth century. And this was despite the brilliance of Michael Cacoyannis' film version (1976), widely regarded as his finest cinematic realisation of Euripides, and brought to the attention of classicists by Marianne McDonald and Kenneth MacKinnon.[20] This presentation of the ancient play, which offers an uncompromising critique of Agamemnon's motives, presenting them as inextricably bound up with a violently patriarchal ideology, had been hermeneutically and ideologically made possible only by (and appeared bang in the middle of) the feminist revision of patriarchy led intellectually by Kate Millett and Germaine Greer; their respective books *Sexual Politics* and *The Female Eunuch* had both been published in 1970.[21]

Iphigenia in Aulis Rediscovered

Cacoyannis' film, however original and inspiring, did not immediately unleash a stream of imitations in the theatre in the way that his versions of the Euripidean *Electra* and *Trojan Women* undoubtedly did; this was despite one memorable performance, when *Iphigenia in Aulis* constituted the first of seven abridged Euripidean plays included in Kenneth Cavander's ten-part *The Greeks* (1979), an account of the Trojan War and its aftermath premièred in the UK by the Royal Shakespeare Company.[22] The dearth of significant free-standing stage productions of *Iphigenia in Aulis* in the late 1970s and 1980s is also striking in comparison with the prominent use of other Greek tragedies addressing patriarchal authority, inter-ethnic conflict or atrocities bred by war. During the years when the anti-nuclear, civil rights and feminist movements were at their most active and culturally engaged, *Medea, Antigone* and *Trojan Women* were never far from the public stage.[23] Moreover, one of the most important reasons why Greek tragedy as a medium had since the 1960s begun to prove so attractive to directors was an increased interest in ritual performance styles, fed by the postcolonial theatrical critique of Western naturalism, especially through an engagement with Asiatic and African performance traditions. This (crucially) coincided with enhanced interest in the anthropology of ancient ritual within the discipline of Classics.[24] In academic circles this interest was particularly expressed in studies of the relationship between Dionysiac literature (including drama) and ritual. *Iphigenia in Aulis,* it could be argued, really *should* have attracted more directors given that it is fundamentally structured by two contrasting but isomorphic rituals (marriage and sacrifice), and that it includes both extensive funereal motifs, and choral odes featuring quite different ritual genres, including elements of paean, cultic-aetiological narrative and propemptikon.[25] But there were still hardly any Aulis Iphigenias, and none of much cultural significance, in the late 1970s or 1980s.

It is essential to grasp this background in order to make sense of the more recent explosion of interest in the play. For at some point in the 1990s, and more particularly in the early third millennium, everything changed. Iphigenia's experiences at Aulis have lately been enacted in a huge number of diverse productions. This point can be amply illustrated by a tiny selection of examples: in 2003 the tragedy was produced, in Friedrich von Schiller's recently rehabilitated verse translation of 1790, at the Deutsches Theater in Göttingen, and (in an English translation of Schiller) also in the Bay Area Parks production of the Shotgun Players in San Francisco.[26] In early 2001 *Iphigenia in Aulis* was performed at the Pearl Theater Company, New York, and the Dutch company Teater Aksiedent staged *Iphigeneia: Koningskind,* directed by T. Lenaerts, in March of that year.[27] Without even considering the new efflorescence of productions of Racine and especially of Gluck, or even the relevant third play of John Barton's 2001 epic cycle *Tantalus,* the

Euripidean Iphigenia was in 2002 prepared for sacrifice in quite separate productions in Vicenza in September, at the Teatro Olimpico by the Teatro Stabile di Catania, and both Frankfurt and Basel in November.[28] The play swiftly became a favourite on the US academic stage, performed at Denver (2001), Yale, Kansas (January 2003), and Colby College, Maine,[29] among many other venues. It began to be echoed in contemporary fiction, for example Ann-Marie MacDonald's story of child murder in a mid-twentieth-century military base, *The Way the Crow Flies*.[30]

There was also an intriguing cluster of performances or performed adaptations of *Iphigenia in Aulis* in the professional theatres of England and Ireland between 1999 and 2004, a cluster complemented by Barry Unsworth's novel based on *Iphigenia in Aulis*, entitled *The Songs of the Kings* (2002). Colin Teevan's stage adaptation *Iph. . .* was first performed at the Lyric Theatre, Belfast, on 2 March 1999, and has subsequently been twice broadcast on BBC Radio. Three years before her acclaimed 2004 production at London's Royal National Theatre, Katie Mitchell first directed Euripides' own *Iphigenia at Aulis*, in the English translation by Don Taylor, at the Abbey Theatre, Dublin, opening on 28 March 2001. A month after Unsworth's novel was published, Marina Carr's *Ariel* premièred at the Abbey Theatre, Dublin. And on 5 February 2003, Edna O'Brien's *Iphigenia* opened at the Sheffield Crucible. This cluster of plays (most of which I was fortunate enough to see) represents a noteworthy cultural phenomenon. Taken together, these versions and adaptations offer a promising intellectual context for investigating why this particular Greek tragedy has suddenly become so attractive to writers and directors, especially those associated with Ireland.

Interconnected Revivals

It is clear that all the instances of international interest in the play – whether in Germany, the USA, Britain, Ireland or elsewhere – are profoundly interconnected. Three important strands in the

Iphigenia tapestry recently have been constituted by the rediscovery of Schiller's translation of the play in German-speaking theatres, Michel Azama's 1991 *Iphigénie ou le péché des dieux*, produced, for example, in Quebec in 2003,[31] and, in the English-speaking world, the second part of Neil LaBute's *Bash*, entitled *Iphigenia in Orem*, in which a businessman chillingly relates the circumstances surrounding the death of his infant daughter. *Bash* was first staged in 1999 and filmed in 2000; LaBute's interests in *Medea* (the first part of *Bash* is *Medea Redux*) and in *Iphigenia in Aulis*, both plays about male power (underscored by religious authority) over the family, may or may not have anything to do with his commitment (which has since lapsed) to the Church of Jesus Christ of Latterday Saints. *Bash* is still performed with some regularity, recently in the UK at Oxford University in January 2004, and in 2005 in both Montreal and in Salem, Minneapolis.[32] And when it comes to the recent spate of Irish and English theatrical Iphigenias, there is no doubt that they have significant bearings upon each other. Three of the playscripts are by Irish writers from south of the border (Colin Teevan, Marina Carr, Edna O'Brien); three of them were first performed in Ireland (Teevan's *Iph. . .* in Belfast, Katie Mitchell's and Marina Carr's both at Dublin's Abbey Theatre); Edna O'Brien has a long-standing relationship with the Abbey Theatre.

In 1999–2000, Katie Mitchell had produced the *Oresteia* at London's Royal National Theatre, in Ted Hughes's translation; in that production Iphigenia had entered into the action in the form of a tiny actress, who visibly haunted the emotional and domestic landscape of both *Agamemnon* and *Libation-Bearers*. It was only a matter of time, it must have seemed to anyone who saw Mitchell's Iphigenia-focused production of the *Oresteia*, before she attempted *Iphigenia in Aulis* itself. When she did first stage the Euripidean tragedy, she chose to set it in the context of 1930s fascism, which was the logical retrospective extension of her mid-century, indeed clearly Second World War vision of the *Oresteia*. For Mitchell's Dublin production it was the Irish playwright Marina Carr who wrote a programme essay, and this commission may have stimulated Carr, even though she had already been drawn to the women of Greek tragedy, above all to Medea; it is the Euripidean Medea who lies behind the child-killing Hester Swane of her *By the Bog of Cats. . .* , first produced in October 1998 at the Abbey Theatre.[33] Colin Teevan, on the other hand, was introduced to *Iphigenia in Aulis* as a sixteen-year-old at school in Dublin, by an octogenarian Jesuit;[34] the play is indeed often used for pedagogical purposes. But Teevan has also recently discussed the impact made on him in the early 1990s by Ariane Mnouchkine's production of *Les Atrides*, in which the plays of the *Oresteia* were preceded by Euripides' *Iphigenia in Aulis* (a directorial decision of Mnouchkine's to which this argument will soon return). Edna O'Brien, meanwhile, is an old friend of Peter Hall and has implied that it was the Royal National Theatre *Oresteia*, in Tony Harrison's translation (1981), which suggested this play to her, although Part III of John Barton's *Tantalus* (2000–01) may have provided the more immediate impetus. O'Brien says that she also seems to have considered *Electra* and *Medea* and to have decided that they were overdone in comparison to the little 'foundling', as she has described *Iphigenia in Aulis*.[35]

Shared Aesthetics

Neither the professional theatrical grapevine nor aesthetic fashion can alone explain why any particular ancient play returns with such power into the contemporary consciousness. Nor does the 'ritual' argument work with *Iphigenia in Aulis* as it does with, for example, the several recent productions of *Hecuba* and Katie Mitchell's own RSC *Phoenician Women* (1995), where the opportunity to explore Balkan and Georgian singing traditions and funeral customs has been fundamental to the attractiveness of the texts.[36] Not one of these Anglo-Irish *Iphigenias* has been particularly interested in ritual, or musically experimental; indeed, they have been surprisingly conservative in the naturalism of their visual designs, costumes, acting and performance styles. Another 'aesthetic' feature of *Iphigenia in Aulis* which might help to explain its recent appeal might, rather, be its unusually novelistic features; O'Brien treats the play as might be expected of a writer who is primarily a novelist, adding (to my mind) superfluous extra narrators in the form of Agamemnon's concubine, the old witch woman and Iphigenia's nurse. A particularly 'novelistic' element in the Euripidean play is the device of the letter Agamemnon has sent to invite Iphigenia to Aulis, since the mendacious epistle, as in Euripides' *Hippolytus* and his lost *Palamedes*, always underscores the capacity of language for deceit.[37] *Iphigenia in Aulis* does indeed contain considerable explicit epistemological commentary on the nature of truth and fiction, appearance and illusion. But it must be conceded that cognitive issues have not been made prominent in any of the productions (although, as we shall see, they have been preoccupied with the science of persuasion).

Another aesthetic dimension which needs considering is the play's pronounced 'intertextuality'; within the Classics academy, at any rate, late twentieth-century literary taste increasingly appreciated Euripides' allusive, inter-mythical playfulness.[38] And in *Iphigenia in Aulis* almost all the characters provide narratives from the past or predictions of the future, thus often elaborately alluding to other texts in the mythical and dramatic tradition. Some of the self-conscious literariness which lends *Iphigenia in Aulis* such a distinctively 'modern' (if not 'postmodern') tone engages with the *Iliad*:[39] Euripides, for example, dangles before us the possibility of an entirely new, pre-Iliadic, 'wrath of Achilles', by creating a whole new dispute between Achilles and Agamemnon.[40] But the category of intertextuality leads the argument back ineluctably to the importance of the play's relationship with the *Oresteia*, for Euripides wrote this tragedy (as all his plays about the children of Agamemnon, including *Electra* and *Orestes*) partly in reaction to the Aeschylean trilogic archetype which had caused such a sensation in his youth. It was through the *Oresteia* that theatre audiences of the late fifth century had developed familiarity with the Atridae (knowledge of the trilogy is required by the audience of Aristophanes' *Frogs* [1124, 1128], first produced in 405, the same year as *Iphigenia in Aulis*). They would therefore have been equipped to take pleasure in the specifically proleptic features of *Iphigenia in Aulis* such as the stage presence of the baby Orestes.[41] Similarly, third-millennium audiences, who have become increasingly well acquainted over the last two decades with the *Oresteia*, can now appreciate the dialectical relationship between that mainstay of the repertoire and the neglected 'foundling' *Iphigenia in Aulis*.[42]

Gender Issues

Unlike some other Greek tragedies, above all *Medea* and *Oedipus*, *Iphigenia in Aulis* was rarely associated with the feminist movement or the often frantic discussion of gender inequality that characterised Western culture in the 1970s and 1980s.[43] Yet any performance or adaptation of a play in which a father authorises the killing of his daughter, in the face of desperate protests from his wife (and her mother), will inevitably find itself implicated in contemporary debates about patriarchy and its residues. There is a whole set of interlocking ways in which *Iphigenia in Aulis* could be used to explore the contemporary patriarchal status quo – above all in Eire, where the experiences of women, attitudes to female sexuality, and controversies over family legislation have taken forms different from those experienced in much of Northern Europe and the USA, mainly because of the country's overwhelmingly Catholic inheritance. The *patria potestas* which the established Catholic Church has for centuries exerted over its congregation in Ireland – especially through its continuing opposition to contraception, abortion and divorce – could with little difficulty be symbolised by the paternal power Agamemnon exerts over his family. Agamemnon can make arbitrary choices about when and whom his daughter is to marry; he can also take arbitrary decisions over when and why she is to die. The young woman's body is not her own, whether in sex or in death.

In Ireland the policing of women's bodies, their sexuality and their reproductive capacity has been particularly controversial:

some rural areas have been slow to modernise their attitudes towards women, and even slower to acknowledge just how terrible the plight has been of those judged immoral by their communities.[44] Witness the outraged reaction to Peter Mullan's devastating recent film *The Magdalene Sisters* (2002), which portrayed the mid-twentieth-century incarceration in laundries, sometimes for life, of girls who showed any signs of sexual independence. Yet it is difficult to read any of the recent productions of *Iphigenia in Aulis* as an attack on Catholicism. Even O'Brien's version, which contained some distinctively Catholic vocabulary, such as 'ripe for beatitude', was more interested in the similarities between pagan superstition and some features of Catholic worship than in making any serious theological arguments against the Catholic Church's positions on women, sex and the family.[45] Indeed, the rights of neither the Church nor individual fathers to control women have been particularly emphasised in any of these recent productions, despite the controversy surrounding the domination of women by their children's fathers as well as by the Church in Ireland. The 1988 Adoption Act sparked a vitriolic debate about fathers' rights even over non-marital and non-biological children.[46] The notion of parental struggle over children, and the exposition of the competing claims of the father and the mother, are indeed apparent in Marina Carr's *Ariel*, but this is generally in the later sections, drawing on the *Oresteia* and Sophocles' *Electra* rather than in the earlier, *Iphigenia in Aulis*-derived portion. Moreover, even the parental conflict in *Ariel* is overshadowed by Carr's interest in the mother–daughter relationship (Carr lost her own mother in her teens), and the true emotional climax is the heartrending final confrontation between Frances/Clytemnestra and Elaine/Electra (see fig.1).

There was, however, a suggestion in Edna O'Brien's version that Agamemnon was sexually attracted to Iphigenia (underscored by the introduction of the idea that he had committed adultery with a very young woman long before even leaving for Troy); child abuse, physical and sexual, is of course a red-hot issue in Ireland, where allegations of endemic pederasty have rocked the Catholic Church to its foundations. In 1992, on a notorious episode of *Saturday Night Live*, Sinead O'Connor tore up a picture of the Pope and denounced the prevalence of the sexual abuse of children in Ireland, routinely covered up, she alleged, by Catholic authorities. She was dressed in white robes, with head shorn, sitting beside a table of candles, looking for all the world (as a reporter in the *Los Angeles Times* of 6 October put it) like 'a sacrificial virgin'. Yet, besides the O'Brien version, none of the productions of *Iphigenia in Aulis* under discussion here has emphasised this potentially explosive dimension of the play.

What is more pertinent is the interest in *wife* abuse. The scale of the problem of marital violence against women in Ireland, especially in rural areas, is rarely admitted.[47] And the mistreatment of Clytemnestra by Agamemnon seems to have caught the attention of all three Irish adaptors: Teevan, Carr and O'Brien. More particularly, they all focus on the dimension of *Iphigenia in Aulis* which functions as offering a crucial aetiology for the vengeful Clytemnestra of the *Oresteia*. This is certainly the case in Marina Carr's *Ariel*, the most radically adapted of the versions. Frances has numerous grievances against her husband Fermoy, including her belief that he was responsible for the death of the son born to her in a previous marriage (a detail Carr has adopted from Clytemnestra's memory of Agamemnon's slaughter of her son by Tantalus at *Iphigenia in Aulis [IA]* 1151–2). But it is only when Frances overhears the information that the man responsible for the death of her daughter was none other than Fermoy that she is precipitated into attacking him lethally.[48] All the other variable motives which the theatrical tradition from Seneca to Eugene O'Neill has attributed to Clytemnestra – sexual passion for Aegisthus, desire for political power, fear for her own life, retaliation for Agamemnon's adultery – are almost completely effaced in *Ariel*.[49]

This element of psychological aetiology for the Aeschylean murderess is undoubtedly already present in the Euripidean text. There is emotional horror in the revelation that Agamemnon killed her first baby by smashing his head on the ground, and there is subtle menace in the way that the desperate mother, trying to dissuade her husband from the sacrifice, implicitly threatens him with the plot of the *Agamemnon*:[50]

Think about it. If you go off to war, leaving me behind at home during your long absence over there, how do you think I will feel every time I catch sight in our house of one of the chairs she used to sit in, now standing empty, and the girls' quarters empty, while I sit alone with nothing to do but weep, forever singing this dirge for her: 'The father who created you has destroyed you, my child. He killed you himself. . .' It will require only the slightest of excuses before the other girls you have left behind and I receive you back as it is fitting that you should be received (*IA* 1171–82; my translation)

What is striking about the recent modern versions is that they uniformly see this passage as of central importance to the impact of the play as a whole. Teevan and O'Brien's plays, which are much more lightly adapted versions than the first act of Carr's highly original *Ariel*, both extract the Euripidean passage, expand it significantly, add material actually taken directly from the Aeschylean *Agamemnon*, and place it in a significant position at the end of the play. Both thus negotiate the 'problem' of the Euripidean conclusion by reassuring their audiences that Iphigenia will not long remain unavenged, for the action dramatised in the first play of the *Oresteia* is imminent.

Teevan's play actually concludes with a 'flash forward', introduced by the stage direction '*Ten years later. Night. The roof of the palace at Mycenae, the evening of* AGAMEMNON's *return from Troy*'. The Euripidean Old Man appears, suggesting the Aeschylean watchman, while Klytaimnestra attacks Agamemnon backstage. His death cries are heard, and Klytaimnestra enters, to conclude the play by reporting that 'All the dead, they whisper revenge'.[51] Euripides' moral bleakness, in leaving Agamemnon unpunished (except by a subtle implication that something unpleasant will befall him far in the future) is thus replaced by a straightforward reciprocal killing. The doer suffers. More importantly, he is *seen* (and heard) to suffer *now*, rather than at some remote point in the future. This fundamentally transforms the ethics, and the gender alignment, of the Euripidean play. Although presenting her closing scene as the enactment of a prophecy, O'Brien, similarly, makes her Clytemnestra stand in twin pools of light and blood, and chillingly deliver lines from the Aeschylean Clytemnestra's triumphant speech over the corpse of her dead husband.[52]

These new finales reveal that one of the most important reasons for the revival of *Iphigenia in Aulis* as a free-standing drama is its crucial relationship, via Clytemnestra, to the *Oresteia*, the revival of which, since the landmark productions of Koun, Stein, Serban, Harrison–Hall and Mnouchkine, was one of the most remarkable features of the resurgent interest in Greek drama of the 1980s and 1990s.[53] The presence of *Iphigenia in Aulis* in recent productions of the *Oresteia* has been well described by Michelakis.[54] The argument inevitably returns to the legendary Théâtre du Soleil's production, *Les Atrides*, directed by Ariane Mnouchkine (1990), the first great female director of the *Oresteia* in theatre history, who famously preceded the trilogy with a performance of *Iphigenia in Aulis*.[55] This 'prologue' arrangement has had a huge impact on the way that people think about the *Oresteia*, for it solves some of the problem of the trilogy's notorious misogyny (a problem which emerged in the row about the 'sexist' use of all-male casts in Tony Harrison's version of the *Oresteia* in Peter Hall's direction in the early 1980s). If a production offers reasons why Clytemnestra, an abused wife and bereaved mother, turns into a vitriolic murderer, then it inevitably alters and modifies the impact of her violent characterisation in *Agamemnon*, and of the triumph of patriarchy in *Eumenides*. *Iphigenia in Aulis* functions like a speech delivered by a counsel for the defence of Clytemnestra: the text relates what she went through at her husband's hands, how terrible and long-standing had been his abuse of her and her children, and what the emotional circumstances had been under which he departed for Troy. The post-feminist Western liberal consensus can cope with the terrifying Clytemnestra of Aeschylus better if it is simultaneously

offered the more sympathetic Clytemnestra of *Iphigenia in Aulis*.
The reverse, I would like to suggest, also holds true. The
portrayal of male power over wife and daughter in Euripides'
Iphigenia in Aulis, the apparent glorification of a young female role
model who agrees to die with fervour just because her father tells
her to (a role model felt to be problematic to Western sensibility as
early as the mid-nineteenth century, let alone by the late twentieth
century), are both made palatable to post-feminist audiences by the
perceived implementation of the punishment of Agamemnon.
What seems to be troublesome to the contemporary world is the
idea that *both* Iphigenia and Clytemnestra suffer passively, without
assuming moral agency or putting up any appreciable resistance. By
extracting the murder of Agamemnon from Aeschylus, and fusing
it with the Euripidean version, Clytemnestra is rescued from
victimhood, and transformed into a responsive moral subject and
autonomous agent. Thus can *Iphigenia in Aulis* finally be reclaimed
for the modern stage.

Politics

Katie Mitchell's productions were both set against identifiably fascist
backgrounds,[56] but the Irish provenance of the versions under
discussion might be expected to lend local resonances to the play.
Does *Iphigenia in Aulis* address with special force the history of
twentieth-century Irish politics? I confess that I originally expected
adaptations of this particular drama, if written by Irish authors, to
reverberate with the theme of the blood sacrifice to the goddess Eire
(Danu), a theme formulated by the Irish Republican martyr and
mystic Patrick (Padráic) Pearse, whose own execution after the 1916
uprising became a potent sacrificial symbol. Drawing on the gospels'
presentation of the crucifixion, as well the ancient Irish *Táin*'s
narrative of the death of the warrior Cú Chulainn, Pearse's fusion of
Catholicism with nationalism and Gaelic revivalism produced the
heady conception of the redemptive sacrifice of youthful Irish blood:
as he said in 'The Coming Revolution' (November 1913): 'Bloodshed

is a cleansing and a sanctifying thing, and a nation which regards it as the final horror has lost its manhood.'[57] MacDara, the self-immolating nationalist hero of Pearse's 1915 play *The Singer*, celebrates the 'feminine' destiny of suffering: 'to be a woman and to serve and suffer as women do is the highest thing'. Both the language of sacrifice for the national ideal, and the pointedly gendered categories of thought, are startlingly similar to the overblown idiom adopted by some of Euripides' characters in *Iphigenia in Aulis*. Pearse's own rhetoric swiftly penetrated to the core of the romanticised picture of Irish revolutionary endeavour, especially his aestheticised presentation of the heroic corpse: as MacDara's lover Sighle puts it in *The Singer*, 'they will lie very still on the hillside – so still and white, with no red in their cheeks, but maybe a red wound in their white breasts, or on their white foreheads'.[58] Above all, Pearse's own poetry put centre stage the figure of the lamenting Irish universal Mother, whose children must be sacrificed on the altar of the nation's freedom: in the poem he is said to have written on the actual eve of his execution, entitled *The Mother*, the narrator comforts herself with the knowledge that although she has lost her children, 'In bloody protest for a glorious thing, / They shall be spoken of among their people'.[59]

In recent years, at least, Pearse's rhetoric has been increasingly criticised not only as evidence of a narcissistic psychopathology, but also as fanning the flames of fanaticism and violence in Ireland's youth for nearly a century. It was, therefore, a legitimate expectation that any contemporary Irish treatments of *Iphigenia in Aulis* would explore the dangers inherent in the glorification of the idea of blood sacrifice motivated by enthusiasm for a patriotic war. Yet this was not the case. Not one of the versions made any noticeable attempt to evoke the mythology and rhetoric of Irish republicanism. Although *Ariel* satirises the role played by corruption in parliamentary career-building within Eire, the one version with any noticeable 'topicalisation' in terms of religious factionalism, paramilitary violence, or the conflict between Ulster loyalists and republicans is also the only one to have premièred north of the Irish border.[60] In Teevan's *Iph. . .* the poetry speaks, occasionally, of the 'ghetto', the

'Grandmaster' and 'ghettomen'.[61] Teevan, indeed, has pointed out that *Iph*. . . was developed at the time of the worst post-war loss of Irish civilian life in the Omagh bombing of August 1998, and that the play transplants to contemporary Ireland the barbarous story of the politically motivated killing of an innocent youngster.[62] The Irish connection of *Iph*. . . has also been stressed in a production by *Tir Ná Nóg*, an Irish theatre group formed in Denver, Colorado, in 1998 and specialising in plays by Irish playwrights including Frank McGuinness, Samuel Beckett and J. M. Synge. The Denver group actually advertised *Iph*. . . as a 'modern-day variation of the classic Euripidean morality story . . . updated to reflect the situation in present-day Northern Ireland'.[63]

Yet the reason why readings of *Iphigenia in Aulis* are being performed so often has less to do with Ireland than with the new global (dis)order. The collapse of the Soviet Union and the fall of the Berlin Wall in 1989 may now feel like a long time ago, but it was the 1990s that saw the replacement of a Cold War waged by the West against the Soviet Union, a superpower actually led by white Europeans, with ongoing actual war with Islam, an enemy perceived very differently.[64] The transformation reached a climax during the first presidential election of George W. Bush, which precipitated the return of the American hard right to US foreign policy. This macro-political background is surely connected with the renaissance of staged productions of *Iphigenia in Aulis*. For, of all Greek tragedies, it is the one which at greatest extension and with the greatest clarity casts doubt on the legitimacy of an international (as opposed to civil) war, declared by the West on a 'barbarous' eastern foe. The question the play really asks is how the heroine can find a way 'to die nobly for an ignoble cause'.[65] The best 'cause' anyone in the play can produce is that laying siege to Troy will stop barbarians 'raping' Greek women (1379–82) – a crime the play is not even clear has actually been committed, since Helen's departure is earlier portrayed as a seduction and elopement (71–9). The one other ancient Greek play which undermines the justification for the Trojan War to a comparable degree is *Helen*, where the dramaturgical ruse of the chimerical Helen-*eidōlon* exposes the reason for which Greece had gone to war as a fabrication. But *Helen* does not involve anything like the same degree of suffering as *Iphigenia in Aulis*, where the impact of Clytemnestra and Iphigenia's pain is emotionally overwhelming. So is the tragedy's surgical exposure of the mindsets that can make people go to war. These include not only machismo 'posturing' by the men, but the way that women collude in such machismo by eroticising it, as the swooning chorus do in their admiration of the handsome soldiers assembling at Aulis (164–302).

It is no mere chance that the recent revival of *Iphigenia in Aulis* coincided with George W. Bush's 2000 election campaign and arrival in the White House; the relevance of the situation in Aulis to the run-up to the 2003 Iraq War was trenchantly expressed by the president of Colby College in Maine, himself a Vietnam veteran.[66] The Pearl Theater Company in New York produced their transparently political version in 2001, several months before 9/11, in the slightly stilted 1978 translation by Merwin and Dimock.[67] Edna O'Brien's *Iphigenia* opened in February 2003, in the last tense weeks before the outbreak of war as it grew increasingly inevitable; no spectator could help feeling the topical reverberations, which are prominent in virtually all the reviews.[68] O'Brien has denied that she *deliberately* set out to provide a commentary on the increasing likelihood of US–Iraq conflict. But when dealing with apparently unplanned, spontaneous and arbitrary 'topical relevance' in performance history, it is important to remember that contemporary concerns can act on a writer's psyche in the absence of either intention or self-consciousness. An old play can seem newly apposite at a purely intuitive level.

Spin Game

Gender relations, mediated through the modern audience's knowledge of the *Oresteia*, and their awareness of the international political situation leading up to the 2003 Iraq War, are thus both factors in the recent spate of *Iphigenia in Aulis*. But for a play to attract directors like Mnouchkine and Mitchell, let alone novelists of the calibre of Unsworth and O'Brien, there must be something more cerebral, more intellectual and more specific going on here. A clue lies in the penetrating insight formulated by the classical scholar Karl Reinhardt in his famous article 'Die Sinneskreise bei Euripides' (1957), in language that shows him responding to an existentialist tradition traced explicitly through Kafka and Sartre, and which reveals the profound influence of Samuel Beckett's dramatic universe. The term 'absurd' is prominent: Euripides' Medea is no longer the 'uncanny Undine' of earlier legend, but has 'dwindled into absurdity'; *Iphigenia in Aulis* teeters on the brink of 'the sheerest absurdity'. Reinhardt argued that Euripides is less a poet of direct protest than a nihilist, an existentialist practitioner of the theatre of the absurd, dedicated to revealing the hollowness of the intellectual and linguistic strategies by which humans struggle to comprehend their situation; by the last years of the Peloponnesian War, moreover, Reinhardt saw Euripides as reacting to a sense of loss and meaning in the world, which he thought must have felt similar to the catastrophic context of 1944, when Sartre wrote his existentialist theatrical masterpiece *Huis Clos* (the origin of the famous phrase 'Hell is other people').[69]

The politics of the revival of *Iphigenia in Aulis* are related to this tradition of Euripidean interpretation. The third-millennial spectator's experience of recent productions confirms that some of the most powerful moments (measured unscientifically in terms of apprehended audience tension and reaction) were not those times when problematic masculinity or militarism were the central focus. They were those times when characters on stage, unable to extricate themselves from absurd situations, were resorting to transparently hollow justifications, 'spinning' an argument, or attempting to make sense of their circumstances by conspicuously employing (in ancient terminology) the science of rhetoric. One example was Iphigenia's volte-face speech in O'Brien's adaptation (when, after electing to go to her death voluntarily, she enumerates the 'advantages' of her decision); another was the posturing of Agamemnon (brilliantly acted by Ben Daniels) to the Chorus during his encounter with Menelaus in Katie Mitchell's 2004 RNT production. Daniels conveyed a sense of thinking up lies at incredible speed under the pressure of public scrutiny. The most revealing example is Fermoy Fitzgerald's television interview scene in Carr's *Ariel*, which begins humorously but becomes more sinister as the scene is retrospectively 'edited' at its conclusion: Fermoy is advised to play his daughter's death as his 'trump card'. What people want, he is told, are the details of his personal life. He must, at all costs, not admit that he enjoys power, but work instead on his image as bereaved father.[70]

What is encouraging about this aspect of the revivals being considered here is that it shows Greek drama being treated as an intellectual art-form. Over the last three decades, Greek tragedy has all too often been seen as a primitive and unsophisticated medium, whose undeniable polemical power is fundamentally a naïve one, connected with its archaic ritual origins. Yet Aristotle rightly argued in his *Poetics* that 'the representation of intellect' (*dianoia*) through speechmaking is the third most important constituent element of tragedy, overshadowed only by plot and character (1450b). The inclusion in several of the productions of the contemporary technologies by which ruling groups communicate with their public, using the modern equivalents of ancient oratory – Carr's television cameras and Mitchell's loudspeaker systems – reveals one of the most sophisticated up-to-date resonances now being heard in the ancient play.

In an article the poet and classicist Anne Carson wrote in the persona of Euripides, the discussion centred on the self-deluding Phaedra rather than the self-deluding Iphigenia. But Carson argued that the talent for 'veiling' a truth in a truth could be described as feminine: 'As if truths were skins of one another and the ability to move, hunt, negotiate among them was a way of finessing the terms of the world in which we find ourselves. Skin game, so to speak.'[71] In the case of *Iphigenia in Aulis*, the finessing of the truth is by no means a female monopoly, and the game enacted in that tragedy relates not to 'skin' but to 'spin'. Barry Unsworth has certainly seen the awful actions represented in *Iphigenia in Aulis* as a tragedy created by 'spin'. His novel presents Iphigenia's death as necessitated solely by the activities of spin-doctors (especially Odysseus) encamped at Aulis, manipulating the psyche of Agamemnon as much as that of the assembled forces in order to serve their own sinister purposes.[72] The 'songs' of their kings are the epic lays created as part of a process of archaic public relations; the song of Iphigenia's death, Odysseus suggests to Agamemnon, will only ever be sung to his glory (see the epigraph at the beginning of this chapter). In *Ariel*, similarly, Fermoy kills Iphigenia in order to achieve his political ambitions, and he is seen using 'negative' PR to destroy his political rival's reputation and career even as he uses the 'pity' card after the apparently tragic loss of his eldest daughter in order to advance his own.[73] These two powerful realisations of the myth, which both appeared in late 2002, show two different authors, in disparate genres, sensing that it is in the power and dangers of spin-doctoring that lies the vivid contemporary immediacy of Euripides' play; it is, after all, a dramatic explanation of how a father persuaded himself to do something as absurd as kill his own daughter, and how she argued herself into applauding his decision.

To put a 'spin' on an argument, as one puts a spin on a baseball, is to attempt to inflect information in such a way as to exert complete control over other people's reactions to it. The verbal idiom entered public discourse in the USA in the 1980s, but only became truly part of popular currency, along with the terms 'spin-doctor', and 'spin-machine', in the following decade.[74] In Britain 'spin' is intimately associated with the strategies of the Labour Party, the leadership of Tony Blair, and the brilliant PR exercises conducted by his two latterday clones of Odysseus, the Labour lieutenants Peter Mandelson and Alastair Campbell, before, during and subsequent to the general election of 1 May 1997. More recently it became even more closely associated with the propaganda battle over the justifications for going to war with Iraq, and with the death of the civil servant Dr David Kelly, who apparently committed suicide under pressure of orchestrated rumours in the media: one newspaper headline alleged that he had been 'spun to death'.[75]

The general public's sensitivity to the activities of 'spin-doctors' provides a revealing answer to the sudden and intense resonance of the *Iphigenia in Aulis* since the late 1990s. Of all Greek tragedies it is the one most clearly about Big Lie theory, about politicians' ability to spin into existence the justification for a war, almost from nothing, but also about humans' tragic inability to use their own vast intellectual potential in order to protect themselves from doing inexcusable things to each other. The Hawks in Britain and America could teach the Sicilian sophist Gorgias a thing or two about defending the indefensible. Although *Iphigenia in Aulis* is not the Euripidean tragedy that most explicitly criticises the science of rhetoric taught by the sophists (that is probably another tragedy involving a virgin sacrifice, *Hecuba*),[76] it is the one that most clearly shows *in practice* the potential of rhetoric to persuade individuals to do things even quite contrary to their own best interests and in defiance of their strongest affective ties. It offers the type of examples of rhetoric in practice that led an ancient 'spin-doctor', Quintilian, to proclaim Euripides of much more use to the trainee orator than Sophocles (*Institutio Oratoria* 10.1.67). This point is brought over shockingly in Teevan's *Iph. . .*, where the sweet-voiced Iphigenia, in her death-wish speech, starts regurgitating aggressive slogans such as 'Smash Troy and all those stinking Trojans', bellicose phrases created in foul mouths quite other than her own.[77]

The role of spin/rhetoric within *Iphigenia in Aulis* is underscored by the manner in which almost everyone changes his or her mind, under rhetorical pressure, about the issue of the sacrifice. Euripides was fascinated by the factors which condition moral choices, and his tragedies repeatedly explored the dangers attendant upon precipitate decision-making. In *Hippolytus*, for example, the hero's death is caused by his father's over-hasty decision to curse and exile him. Athenian history provides numerous examples of similar decisions, especially in time of war: one notorious incident was the Athenian assembly's angry vote summarily to execute all the men of Mytilene (427 BC), a decision they revoked the very next day after a 'sudden change of heart' (Thucydides 3.36). This resulted in a desperate race against time as one trireme chased another across the Aegean Sea. In 406, the year before the first production of *Iphigenia in Aulis*, the

Athenians had precipitately executed no fewer than six of their generals, after an unconstitutional trial, as punishment for the great loss of life at the Battle of Arginusae; by 405 many must have regretted the whole tragic sequence of events.

Iphigenia in Aulis uses its myth to explore peremptory life-and-death decisions by showing how, during a military crisis, several members of the same family took and rescinded decisions about the life of an innocent girl. Agamemnon has summoned her to be sacrificed, changes his mind, but is incapable of sticking to the better moral course out of fear for his own army. Menelaus changes his mind, emotionally rejecting his earlier 'logical' justifications of the atrocity when he sees his brother's distress. Even Achilles allows himself to be persuaded that Iphigenia really wants to die. Indeed, the morally unstable universe of the play seems to have encouraged ancient actors to edit the roles they played more than usual, thus making even more changes to the text of *Iphigenia in Aulis* than were suffered by most Euripidean tragedies: not only were there alternative prologues and conclusions, but the individual speeches were extensively trimmed and elaborated.[78] The lines delivered by and about Achilles seem often to have been remodelled in ancient performances. The condition of the text suggests two discrete ancient readings of his character locked in textual combat.[79] And Iphigenia herself, far from being the inconsistent character Aristotle alleged,[80] or driven virtually into psychosis as has more recently been claimed,[81] proves herself a typical, well acculturated Argive: she has internalised her community's behavioural patterns, becoming as morally unstable and vacillating in the face of well tricked-out arguments as the strongest men in the Greek army, her father and uncle included.

Spin works best in a world with few external moral reference points, and insecurity about the nature or requirements of divinity. One strand in the play's reception since ancient times has been the view that it shows the evil effects of religious zealotry or superstition. This interpretation has an aetiology extending back to Lucretius, the ancient Epicurean polemicist, who after narrating the sacrifice at Aulis famously pronounced, 'so much evil can religion bring about' (*de Rerum Natura* 1.80–101). The increasing religious fanaticism, whether Islamic or Christian, at the heart of the third-millennial international crisis, might lead one to expect *Iphigenia in Aulis* to be used to condemn religious ardour. Yet none of the productions under discussion suggests that Iphigenia was being sacrificed primarily for a reason of faith (although religion is a secondary motivation in the case of Marina Carr's Fermoy Fitzgerald, who has a pagan and decidedly Nietzschean set of metaphysical convictions, unaligned with any identifiable species of modern monotheism).

The world depicted in *Iphigenia in Aulis*, relative even to the confused and disturbing metaphysical environments of most Greek tragedy, is in fact astoundingly *irreligious*, as well as remarkable for its lack of consensual ethical standards. Very little happens except that an oracular demand for human sacrifice, which was received, accepted and put into motion before the beginning of the play, is actually carried out after the two key agents – the sacrificing father and the sacrificed daughter – talk themselves into it. The crucial transformations do not take place on the level of action, or weather, or even Iphigenia's body, but exclusively in the minds of the leading characters. *Peithō* of a particularly sinister kind (spin) is seen to take effect. There is little emphasis on the oracle delivered by Calchas (indeed it is only summarised in *oratio obliqua* at 89–91), no discussion of it, no further omen, no angry bird, no inspection of entrails. There is no guidance from any priestly figure, no divination of the will of heaven. There is no new communication from the gods during the course of the entire play (a point well brought out in Foley's analysis).[82] Agamemnon even criticises all seers as frauds, while failing to contest Calchas' faintly recalled pronouncement. This presentation of the myth implies that the suffering Iphigenia must undergo is not only *entirely avoidable*, but that it remains so until the eleventh hour.

A Tragedy for the Third Millennium

In Terry Eagleton's new study of tragedy, *Iphigenia in Aulis* is presented as a play of intellectual significance. Eagleton argues that it tantalises the audience with the possibility that the disaster can be averted, and in possessing this quality it must be grouped with *Othello* and two of Ibsen's late plays: *The Wild Duck* (1884), and *When We Dead Awaken* (1899).[83] The play is used to support Eagleton's repudiation of the claim made by some respected theorists of tragedy, that the genre always and generically must claim that suffering is *ineluctable*.[84] The characters in *Iphigenia in Aulis* may be stranded in an ethical and metaphysical vacuum, with no way of discerning any meaning in their universe, but this does not mean that they need to *choose* to perform and suffer an inhumane atrocity. This is a play which will always speak loudest to an audience themselves characterised by intense, secularised moral *aporia*. No character can find a moral framework to help them identify and then adhere to their instinctive ethical reactions to what is happening – even Clytemnestra is ultimately persuaded out of her proposal to take a defiant last stand against Iphigenia's sacrifice (1459–60).[85] The one exception is the old slave, an impressive individual who does seem to be capable of independent ethical intuition and steady resolve. It is very nearly true that in the world portrayed in *Iphigenia in Aulis* nobody does wrong with any great willingness (in ancient philosophical terms, half-heartedly demonstrating the truth of the Socratic principle that *oudeis hekōn hamartanei*), since, after reflection, both Agamemnon and Menelaus do think better of the sacrifice scheme.[86] But they do not possess the moral vertebrae which would enable them to jeopardise their generalships in order to prevent it.

The environment inhabited by the characters in *Iphigenia in Aulis*, according to Eagleton's definition, is tragic precisely *because* it is morally fragile and metaphysically unknowable. This apprehension is expressed in Michael Billington's response to Carr's *Ariel*: 'it emerges as more than a modernised Greek myth . . . it confirms Carr's status as a writer who, in an age of ironic detachment, believes in the enduring possibility of tragedy'.[87] In the course of his new definition of the 'tragic', Eagleton proposes that this ancient and troublesome art-form has the potential to offer a significant living presence in the theatres of the third millennium, but only if it combines three essential elements: representation of hardcore suffering, open-ended metaphysics and aesthetic beauty. It is difficult to think of any tragedy – ancient, Renaissance, early modern or more recent – that more brilliantly exemplifies these three characteristics.

No other play has metaphysics so open-ended that, on top of a psychic environment that is presented as virtually devoid of either gods or moral certainties, any aspiring director can choose between two different endings: arbitrary, random and unexplained salvation by suddenly intrusive divine intervention, or unmitigated misery centred entirely in the human domain. Eagleton himself sees *extreme* qualities in the play: Iphigenia is one of the three characters he identifies (along with Shakespeare's Desdemona and Ibsen's Hedwig Ekdal) as being deprived by their authors of any free-will, any control whatsoever over their fates.[88] *Iphigenia in Aulis* also qualifies as a third-millennial tragedy on Eagleton's criterion of unmitigated suffering, since it is impossible to think of psychological pain worse than Iphigenia's, or bereavement more agonising than that undergone by Clytemnestra (movingly portrayed by Susan Brown in Edna O'Brien's production, as well as by Ingrid Craigie's Frances in the première of Carr's *Ariel*). And in terms of aesthetic beauty, *Iphigenia in Aulis* not only contains some of Euripides' loveliest lyrics, especially in the Chorus's proleptic account of the fall of Troy and in Iphigenia's *thrēnos* (751–800, 1475–531), but one of his greatest poetic monologues: this is Iphigenia's appeal to Agamemnon (1211–52), 'If I had the voice of Orpheus . . .', which well deserves its place as a hardy perennial in anthologies of Greek verse. The most beautiful poetry in the play is reserved for a rare moment of authentic emotion and moral conviction. Here Iphigenia for once fails to 'finesse the truth' at all.

A Posthumous Rebellion

Iphigenia is no rebel woman: she is perhaps the most tractable of Greek tragic heroines. She willingly accepts – indeed, embraces – the fate of victim of male authority, the *patria potestas*. And yet her play has re-emerged lately as important in the performance repertoire partly because it lends her mother's descent into the rebellion and murderous rage of the *Oresteia* not only credibility, but a kind of legitimacy. The very performance text of Iphigenia's play has thus rebelled against the manner in which its ancient form silences the pain of the childlike victim and her mother. This recent rebellion is demonstrated in the way the text has been consistently altered to reveal the future legacy left by Agamemnon's war crime at Aulis, and especially Clytemnestra's revenge. The play has also re-emerged because it speaks to a world where innocent victims of international war – many still children and teenagers – have no power even to protest against their fates; they are at the mercy of international wars justified by the sophisticated orchestration of public opinion in both domestic politics and global news enterprises. Iphigenia has suddenly become important because, like so many victims of conflict in the modern global village, she could not rebel and was, almost literally, 'spun to death'. This obedient Greek tragic woman persuaded herself into dying in order to acquire immortal *kleos*: by a strange paradox, she has indeed won fame in recent years by serving rebellious purposes posthumously. As John Wilkinson puts it in his poetic chapbook *Iphigenia*, a visceral reaction to the Iraq War, her conspicuous cultural presence forces us to an important question:

> . . . does the blood-red garland
> decked in thorns like spurs,
>
> manifest the crowning dream of a virgin
> wading through blood.[89]

Notes

This essay began life as a paper delivered at the Archive of Performance of Greek and Roman Drama in Oxford as one of a seminar series arranged by Avery Willis and Kathleen Riley. It was subsequently delivered at a conference in May 2004, organised by Pantelis Michelakis, at the University of Bristol, and in December of the same year in association with the University of San Diego, CA, at the home of Professor Marianne McDonald. I am extremely grateful to all my hosts for their comments and criticism, as well as to Marina Carr, Fiona Macintosh, Christopher Rowe, Colin Teevan, Barry Unsworth and the editors of this volume.

1. See e.g. Aristotle, *Poetics* 1454a 32; Lucretius, *de Rerum Natura* 1.84–103; Ovid, *Metamorphoses* 12.1–38, 13.182–95. The most famous visual image is the first-century AD Roman copy, discovered at Pompeii, of a lost fourth-century BC painting of the sacrifice of Iphigenia by Timanthes. It is now in the Naples Archaeological Museum.

2. An *Iphigenia* by Euripides (probably the Aulis play) was revived at the Athenian Dionysia in 341 BC (*Inscriptiones Graecae* II² 2320, translated in Eric Csapo and William J. Slater, *The Context of Ancient Drama* [Ann Arbor: University of Michigan Press, 1995], p. 229). It was also imitated by other dramatic poets: see Bruno Snell and Richard Kannicht (eds), *Tragicorum Graecorum Fragmenta*, vol. ii (Göttingen: Vandenhoeck and Rupecht, 1981), fr. 663. A lively performance tradition is confirmed by a papyrus (Leiden inv. 510) on which are preserved small portions (lines 784–92 and 1499–1502) of lyrics from *Iphigenia in Aulis*, with musical annotation, transcribed in M. L. West, *Ancient Greek Music* (Oxford: Clarendon Press, 1992), pp. 286–7. The papyrus seems to constitute a libretto for a professional tragic singer, from which he could learn excerpted lyrical highlights from the play to perform at a recital: see Edith Hall, 'The Singing Actors of Antiquity', in P. Easterling and E. Hall (eds), *Greek and Roman Actors: Aspects of an Ancient Profession* (Cambridge: CUP, 2002), pp. 3–38, at p. 13. The story of Agamemnon and Clytemnestra provided themes for pantomime dancing at the time of Lucian (*On Dancing* 43).

3. *Euripidis tragici poet[a]e nobilissimi Hecuba et Iphigenia: Latin[a]e fact[a]e Erasmo Roterodamo interprete* (Paris: J. Badius, 1506).

4. *Ifigenia, tragedia* (Venice: Domenico Farri, 1551).

5. This version has been published conveniently in Diane Purkiss (ed.), *Three Tragedies by Renaissance Women* (London: Penguin, 1998).

6. *Samuel Costers Iphigenia. Treur-spel* (Amsterdam: Nicolaas Biestkins, 1617).

7. On Racine's play see Martin Mueller, *Children of Oedipus and Other Essays on the Imitation of Greek Tragedy 1550–1800* (Toronto, Buffalo and London: University of Toronto Press, 1980), pp. 39–45. More generally, see the fascinating and (fairly) comprehensive study by Jean-Michel Gliksohn, *Iphigénie de la Grèce antique à L'europe des Lumières* (Paris: Presses universitaires de France, 1985).

8. See E. Hall and F. Macintosh, *Greek Tragedy and the British Theatre 1660–1914* (Oxford: OUP, 2005), ch. 2.

9. See Jane Davidson Reid (ed.), *The Oxford Guide to Classical Mythology in the Arts* (New York and Oxford: OUP, 1993), vol. i, pp. 599–605.

10. Ibid. On the wider influence of *Iphigenia in Aulis* on operas see Marianne McDonald, *Sing Sorrow: Classics, History, and Heroines in Opera* (Westport, CT and London: Greenwood Press, 2001), p. 69. The Katsaïtis play has been republished in a modern edition of his works by Emmanuel Kriaras (Athens: Institut français d'Athènes, 1950).

11. Denis Diderot, *Entretiens sur 'le Fils naturel'*, published with his *Paradoxe sur le comédien*, with an introduction by Raymond Laubreaux (Paris: Garnier-Flammarion, 1967).

12. See Fiona Macintosh, *Dying Acts: Death in Ancient Greek and Irish Tragic Drama* (Cork: Cork University Press, 1994), Marianne McDonald and J. Michael Walton (eds.), *Amid Our Troubles: Irish Versions of Greek Tragedy* (London: Methuen, 2002); Des O'Rawe, '(Mis)translating Tragedy: Irish Poets and Greek Plays', in Lorna Hardwick, Pat Easterling, Stanley Ireland, Nick Lowe and Fiona Macintosh (eds), *Theatre: Ancient and Modern* (Milton Keynes: Open University Press, 2000), pp. 109–24; Oliver Taplin, 'Sophocles' *Philoctetes*, Seamus Heaney's, and Some Other Recent Half-rhymes', in E. Hall, F. Macintosh, and A. Wrigley (eds), *Dionysus since 69: Greek Tragedy at the Dawn of the Third Millennium* (Oxford: OUP, 2004), pp. 145–67.

13. For a full discussion of this remarkable production of *Antigone*, which began in Prussia and took Covent Garden, London, by storm in the late winter of 1845, see Hall and Macintosh (eds), *Greek Tragedy and the British Theatre*, ch. 12.

14. See Carol Jones Carlisle, *Helen Faucit: Fire and Ice on the Victorian Stage* (London: Society for Theatre Research, 2000), pp. 144–7.

15. See Hall and Macintosh (eds), *Greek Tragedy and the British Theatre*, ch. 12 with fig. 12.4.

16. See e.g. Thomas de Quincey, 'The *Antigone* of Sophocles as Represented on the Edinburgh Stage', in *The Art of Conversation and Other Papers*, vol. xiii (Edinburgh: Adam and Charles Black, 1863), pp. 199–233.

17. In the 1720s there had been productions of Greek tragedies, including *Hippolytus* and *Philoctetes*, at the school run in Capel Street, Dublin, by Thomas Sheridan (Richard Brinsley Sheridan's grandfather). See Hall and Macintosh (eds), *Greek Tragedy and the British Theatre*, ch. 9.

18. See John William Calcraft, *Iphigenia in Aulis: A Tragedy, From the Greek of Euripides, as Presented in the Theatre of Bacchus, at Athens, circa BC 430. Adapted to the Modern Stage*, 3rd edn (Dublin: 1847). Many thanks to Norma Macmanaway and Charles Benson, Keeper of Early Printed Books at TCD, for help with researching this production.

19. See Hall and Macintosh (eds), *Greek Tragedy and the British Theatre*, ch. 17.

20. Marianne McDonald, *Euripides in Cinema: The Heart Made Visible* (Philadelphia: Centrum Philadelphia, for the Greek Institute, 1983), pp. 128–91; Kenneth MacKinnon, *Greek Tragedy into Film* (London: Croom Helm, 1986).

21. See two essays in Hall et al. (eds), *Dionysus since 69*: Edith Hall, 'Introduction: Why Greek Tragedy in the Late Twentieth Century?', pp. 1–46, at pp. 9–18, 38–9; Helene Foley, 'Bad Women: Gender Politics in Late Twentieth-century Performance and Revision of Greek Tragedy', pp. 77–111.

22. John Barton and Kenneth Cavander, *The Greeks: Ten Plays Given as a Trilogy* (Heinemann: London, 1981). *The Greeks* recently received its first full production in New York by the Imua Theatre Company at the Manhattan Ensemble Theater: see Charlotte Stoudt, 'Wartime Myths', *Village Voice*, 20 July 2004.

23. See Hall et al. (eds), *Dionysus since 69*, especially chs 1, 3, 8, 11, and the chronological listing in ch. 15.

24. See Erika Fischer-Lichte, 'Thinking about the Origins of Theatre in the 1970s', in ibid., pp. 329–60.

25. See Helene Foley, 'Marriage and Sacrifice in Euripides' *Iphigenia in Aulis*', *Arethusa*, 15 (1982): 159–80, revised version in Helene Foley,

Ritual Irony: Poetry and Sacrifice in Euripides (Ithaca, NY and London: Cornell University Press, 1985), pp. 65–105; Rush Rehm, *Marriage to Death: The Conflation of Wedding and Funeral Rituals in Greek Tragedy* (Princeton, NJ: Princeton University Press, 1994), especially p. 102.

26. See the extensive review by Joe Mader, 'Iffy "Iphigenia"', in the *San Francisco Examiner*, 2 June 2003.

27. There are several photographs of the latter production archived at http://www.aksiedent.be/producties/iphigeneia/iphigen.htm

28. Schiller's translation was directed by Wolfgang Spielvogel at the Theater Prima Donna/Schwerzer Held, opening 14 November 2002; the Basel production constituted Part I of *Krieg am Troja* at the Theater Basel.

29. More recently, productions of *Iphigenia in Aulis* with explicit intentions of protesting against the continuing US aggression in Iraq have been staged by, e.g., Voices of Women at San Diego University's Institute for Peace and Justice (June 2004), and by the Thousand Things Theater Company (with puppets) in Minneapolis (February 2005).

30. Published in London by Fourth Estate (2003); see the review by Aida Edemarian, *Guardian*, 11 October 2003.

31. The production was at the Théâtre Niveau Parking, 23 September to 18 October 2003. The play is available as Michel Azama, *Iphigénie ou le péché des dieux* (Paris : Ed. Theatrales, 1991).

32. At the Théâtre-Ste-Catherine in Montreal, and the Minneapolis Caliban Co. The play is published in Neil LaBute, *Bash: Latterday Plays* (New York: Overlook Press, 1999).

33. Marina Carr, *By the Bog of Cats. . .* (Loughcrew, Oldcastle, County Meath: Gallery Press, 1998). *By the Bog of Cats. . .* is discussed in depth by Melissa Sihra, this volume, ch. 5. The 2004–05 London production at the Wyndham's Theatre won it a nomination for the Olivier Award for best new play.

34. See Colin Teevan, *Iph. . . After Euripides' 'Iphigeneia in Aulis'* (London: Nick Hern Books, 1999), 'Introduction', p. xiii.

35. Veronica Lee, 'The Anger of Heaven is Nothing to the Anger of Men', *Independent on Sunday*, *Life* section, 9 February 2003, p. 8. In the USA, where *Tantalus* premièred, there had been two composite performances including part or all of *Iphigenia in Aulis* that attracted attention in the 1990s: Ellen McLaughlin's *Iphigenia and Other Daughters* (1995), and

The Iphigenia Cycle directed by JoAnne Akalaitis (1997). *Iphigenia in Aulis*, however, remained only rarely performed as a free-standing piece in its own right. Barry Unsworth, like O'Brien, remembers the impression made upon him by the 1981 RNT *Oresteia*.

36. One the earliest performances to explore the Balkan style of *a capella* lamentation was Laurence Boswell's production of *Hecuba* at the Gate in Notting Hill (1992), for which the music was composed by Mick Sands. Sands also supplied the rather less dissonant music for Tony Harrison's new translation of the play, starring Vanessa Redgrave (Royal Shakespeare Company, 2005).

37. See Dale Chant, 'Role Inversion and Its Function in the *Iphigenia at Aulis*', *Ramus*, 15 (1986): 83–92.

38. See e.g. Froma Zeitlin, 'The Closet of Masks: Role-playing and Mythmaking in the *Orestes* of Euripides', *Ramus*, 9 (1980): 51–77, conveniently republished in Judith Mossman (ed.), *Oxford Readings in Euripides* (Oxford: OUP, 2003), 309–41; Robert Eisner, 'Euripides' Use of Myth', *Arethusa*, 12 (1979): 153–74 at pp. 157–8; A. N. Michelini, *Euripides and the Tragic Tradition* (Madison, WI and London, 1987), pp. 3–51.

39. See especially Pantelis Michelakis, *Achilles in Greek Tragedy* (Cambridge: CUP, 2002), pp. 84–143.

40. Wesley D. Smith, 'Iphigenia in Love', in Glen W. Bowersock, Walter Burkert and Michael C. J. Putnam (eds), *Arktouros: Hellenic Studies Presented to Bernard M. W. Knox* (Berlin and New York: de Gruyter, 1979), pp. 173–80, at p. 177.

41. See Karl Luschnig, 'Time and Memory in Euripides' Iphigenia at Aulis', *Ramus*, 11 (1982): 99–104.

42. See John Chioles, 'The *Oresteia* and the Avant-garde: Three Decades of Discourse', *Performing Arts Journal* 45 (1993): 1–28; F. Macintosh, P. Michelakis, E. Hall and O. Taplin (eds), *Agamemnon in Performance 458 BC to 2004 AD* (Oxford: OUP, 2005).

43. See Hall, 'Introduction', and Foley, 'Bad Women' in Hall et al. (eds), *Dionysus since 69*.

44. For further discussion see e.g. the essays in Anthony Bradley and Maryann Giulanella Valiulis (eds), *Gender and Sexuality in Modern Ireland* (Amherst: University of Massachusetts Press, 1997).

45. See Edna O'Brien, *'Iphigenia': Euripides, Adapted with an Introduction* (London: Methuen, 2003), p. 36; Edith Hall, 'Barbarism with Beatitude', *TLS*, 21 February 2003, p. 19.

46. See e.g. William Duncan and Paula Scully, *Marriage Breakdown in Ireland: Law and Practice* (Dublin: Butterworths, 1990); Geoffrey Shannon, *Divorce: The Changing Landscape of Divorce in Ireland* (Dublin: Round Hall, 2001).

47. E. Mahon, 'Women's Rights and Catholicism in Ireland', *New Left Review*, 166 (November–December 1986).

48. Marina Carr, *Ariel* (Loughcrew, Oldcastle, County Meath: Gallery Press, 2002), pp. 56–60.

49. See further E. Hall, 'Aeschylus' Clytemnestra *versus* Her Senecan Tradition', in Macintosh et al. (eds), *Agamemnon in Performance*.

50. See Smith, 'Iphigenia in Love', in Bowersock et al. (eds), *Arktouros*, p. 178.

51. Colin Teevan, *Euripides, Iph. . .*, 2nd edn (London: Oberon Books, 2002), pp. 75–6.

52. O'Brien, *Iphigenia*, pp. 43–4.

53. See Anton Bierl, *Die Orestie des Aischylos auf der modernen Bühne* (Stuttgart: M & P Verlag, 1997); Macintosh et al. (eds), *Agamemnon in Performance*.

54. In his review of Susanne Aretz, *Die Opferung der Iphigeneia in Aulis. Die Rezeption des Mythos in antiken und modernen Drama* (Stuttgart and Leipzig: B. G. Teubner, 1999), which was published in *Bryn Mawr Classical Review* (2002) and is available online at http://ccat.sas.upenn.edu/bmcr/2002/2002–01–05.html

55. See Evelyne Ertel (ed.), *La Tragédie grecque: les Atrides au théâtre du Soleil*, *Théâtre aujourd'hui*, no. 1 (Paris: CNDP, 1992).

56. Mitchell may well have been responding to the comments made by the author of the translation she used, the late Don Taylor, in an introduction he wrote to the play in 1990, printed in his *Iphigenia at Aulis* (London: Methuen, 2004), pp. vii–xviii, at p. xvi: 'We see the young girl transforming herself before our eyes into a fascist poster, or a Nazi statue of German womanhood sacrificed for the greater Reich.'

57. Quoted in Vivian Mercier, 'Irish Literary Revival', in W. E. Vaughan (ed.), *A New History of Ireland: Ireland under the Union II, 1870–1921*, vol. vi (Oxford: OUP, 1996), p. 377. On the blood sacrifice theme in Irish nationalist literature and culture more generally, see also Sean Farrell Moran, *Patrick Pearse and the Politics of Redemption: The Mind of the Easter Rising, 1916* (Washington, DC: Catholic University of America Press, 1994); Barbara Brodman, 'The Cult of Death in Irish (and Mexican) Myth and Literature: From

Fatalism to Fire of the Mind', in Bruce Stewart (ed.), *That Other World: The Supernatural and Fantastic in Irish Literature and Its Contexts* (Gerrard's Cross: Colin Smythe, 1998); Martin Williams, 'Ancient Mythology and Revolutionary Ideology in Ireland, 1878–1916', *Historical Journal*, 26 (2) (1983): 307–28.

58. See Patrick Pearse, *Collected Works* (Dublin and London: Phoenix Publishing, 1917), vol. i, p. 109.

59. 'The Mother' is printed in Patrick Henry Pearse, *Collected Works*, 5th edn (Dublin: Irish National Publishing Company, 1924), p. 333. See also his statement, 'I see my role in part as sacrifice for what my mother's people have suffered, atonement for what my father's people have done' (*Selected Poems: Rogha Dánta*, ed. Eugene McCabe, Dublin: New Island Press, 1993), p. 9.

60. Some people speculated – inconclusively – whether there was some point being made in the choice of a Northern Irish accent for the actor who played Menelaus in the 2001 Dublin production directed by Katie Mitchell: see e.g. Victor Merriman, 'Greek Tragedy Loses the Plot', *Sunday Tribune*, 1 April 2001; Emer O'Kelly, 'Tales of Greek Inevitability', *Sunday Independent*, 1 April 2001.

61. Teevan, *Euripides, Iph. . .*, pp. 19, 66.

62. See Hall, 'Introduction' in Hall et al. (eds), *Dionysus since 69*, p. 21; the comments were made in the interview cited ibid. at p. 30, n. 59.

63. See www.shamrocker.com/Tir%20Na%22Og%20PR5 (accessed September 2004).

64. See Edith Hall, 'Recasting the Barbarian', in *The Theatrical Cast of Athens* (Oxford: OUP, forthcoming), ch. 6.

65. Herbert Siegel, 'Self-delusion and the *Volte-face* of Iphigenia in Euripides' "Iphigenia at Aulis"', *Hermes*, 108 (1980): 300–21, at p. 301.

66. William D. Adams, 'Iphigeneia's Truth: Revisiting Classical Themes as War Looms', *Colby Magazine* (winter 2003). (Slightly altered from his earlier article, 'See the Tragedy of March to War', *Baltimore Sun*, 12 January 2003.)

67. W. S. Merwin and George E. Dimock, *Euripides, Iphigeneia at Aulis*, in the series *The Greek Tragedy in New Translations* (Oxford and New York: OUP, 1978). In the wake of the 2003 Iraq War and Aeschylus' *The Persians*, in Ellen McLaughlin's adaptation, at the National Actors Theater in New York City during June of that year, the same company produced a 'protest' *Persians* in January 2004. On the very recent efflorescence of productions of *Persians*, see Edith

Hall, 'Aeschylus, Race, Class, and War', in Hall et al. (eds), *Dionysus since 69*, pp. 169–97, and 'The Mother of All Sea-battles: The Reception of Aeschylus' *Persians* from Xerxes to Saddam Hussein', in E. Bridges, E. Hall and P. J. Rhodes (eds), *Cultural Responses to the Persian Wars* (Oxford: OUP, forthcoming 2006).

68. See e.g. John Peter, 'Making War, not Love', in *Sunday Times, Culture* section, 16 February 2003, pp. 18–19; Lee, 'The Anger of Heaven', *Independent on Sunday*, 9 February 2003.

69. Karl Reinhardt, 'Die Sinneskreise bei Euripides', *Eranos*, 26 (1957): 79–317, reproduced in his *Tradition und Geist* (Göttingen: Vandenhoek and Ruprecht, 1960), pp. 223–56, and included in an English translation by J. Mossman, as 'The Intellectual Crisis in Euripides', in J. Mossman (ed.), *Oxford Readings of Euripides*, pp. 16–46. The word 'absurdity' occurs with reference to Medea and *Iphigenia in Aulis* on pp. 27 and 29 of this translation respectively. Thereafter the German-speaking tradition of Euripidean scholarship has often continued to see Euripides as an absurdist playwright, a tendency expressed, for example, in the title of Walter Burkert's influential article, 'Die Absurdität der Gewalt und das Ende der Tragödie: Euripides' Orestes', *Antike und Abendland*, 20 (1974): 97–109. For a fascinating account of the dialectical relationship between Beckett's plays and Greek tragedy, see Katharine Worth, 'Greek Notes in Samuel Beckett's Theatre Art', in Hall et al. (eds), *Dionysus since 69*, pp. 265–83.

70. Carr, *Ariel*, pp. 45–6.

71. Anne Carson, 'Euripides to the Audience', *London Review of Books*, 5 September 2004, p. 24.

72. Barry Unsworth, *The Songs of the Kings* (London: Hamish Hamilton, 2002), pp. 90–1 (Palamedes' *curriculum vitae*), 126 (Macris' concern for establishing a reputation), 131 (Achilles' PR), 151 (Croton lauded by the Singer as champion of civil liberties), 155 (Odysseus' free indirect discourse on the pleasures of spinning falsehoods in order to make them look like responsible political concepts), 208 (the Blairite 'moral case' that Menelaus makes for launching the invasion of Asia).

73. One of the few reviewers to see the importance of political corruption to Carr's realisation of the ancient role of Agamemnon was Jean-Louis Perrier, in 'Le théâtre, apôtre de la diversité culturelle en Irlande', *Le Monde*, 14 October 2002.

74. Bernard Ingham, *Wages of Spin* (London: John Murray, 2003);

George Pitcher, *The Death of Spin* (Chichester: Wiley, 2002); Stuart Ewen, 'Changing Rhetorics of Persuasion', in his *PR! A Social History of Spin*, Part III (New York: Basic Books, 1996).

75. 'Spun to Death' was the front-page headline of the *Daily Mirror*, 19 July 2003. See also the leader 'Spinning to Death', *Sunday Times*, 20 July 2003, p. 18. At this time it became commonplace to encounter in the press the concept of spin appearing as an abstract noun, almost a personification, implying an active cosmic principle or even autonomous agent beyond human control: see, for example, the digest of the foreign press in 'Spin Exaggerated WMD danger', *Guardian*, 31 May 2003, p. 28.

76. On the prominence of the discussion of rhetoric in tragedy generally, see the exemplary discussion by R. G. A. Buxton, *Persuasion in Greek Tragedy* (Cambridge: CUP, 1982).

77. Teevan, *Euripides, Iph. . .*, p. 70.

78. See especially the fundamental study by Denys Page, *Actors' Interpolations in Greek Tragedy: Studied with Special Reference to Euripides' Iphigeneia in Aulis* (Oxford: Clarendon Press, 1934); the issue is also discussed in Gudrun Mellert-Hoffman, *Untersuchungen zur 'Iphigenie in Aulis' des Euripides* (Heidelberg: C. Winter, 1969). On the alternative prologues to *Iphigenia in Aulis*, see David Bain, 'The Prologues of Euripides' *Iphigenia in Aulis*', *CQ*, 27 (1977): 10–26.

79. This point is well demonstrated by Michelakis, *Achilles in Greek Tragedy*, p. 141.

80. *Poetics* 1454a26, a view with which A. W. Schlegel, who set the tone for most nineteenth-century criticism of Euripides, heartily concurred in *A Course of Lectures on Dramatic Art and Literature*, 2nd edn, trans. John Black, 2 vols (London: J. Templeman and J. R. Smith, 1840), vol. i, pp. 176–7.

81. See e.g. Siegel, 'Self-delusion', *Hermes*, no. 108, p. 321.

82. See Foley, *Ritual Irony*, pp. 66, 96–100.

83. Terry Eagleton, *Sweet Violence: An Essay on the Tragic* (Malden, MA and Oxford: Blackwell, 2003), pp. 35, 125.

84. For example, Jeanette King, *Tragedy in the Victorian Novel* (Cambridge: CUP, 1978), p. 16.

85. In my personal view it was one the few weaknesses of Katie Mitchell's production that Clytemnestra's ultimate acquiescence, as described in the Greek original, was written out in favour of a feisty and more admirable last-ditch struggle against Iphigenia's arrest.

86. See the insistence of both Agamemnon (1361) and Iphigenia (1456) that he is authorising the sacrifice unwillingly, with e.g. Plato, *Protagoras* 345d–e, and G. Vlastos, *Socrates, Ironist and Moral Philosopher* (Cambridge: CUP, 1991), p. 136, n. 26.

87. Michael Billington, 'Ariel', *Guardian*, 5 October 2002.

88. Eagleton, *Sweet Violence*, p. 125.

89. John Wilkinson, *Iphigenia* (London: Barque Press, 2004).

2. Resonances of Religion in Cacoyannis' Euripides

Isabelle Torrance

Religion is an integral part of ancient Greek tragedy. Drama in fifth-century BC Athens was performed as part of a religious festival in honour of the god Dionysus. The area in which it was performed was a religious sanctuary, and the Greek gods and religious rituals are a feature of every Greek play.[1] Tragedy as a genre also regularly perverts religious ritual with horrifying results. Such a religious undercurrent is arguably the most difficult element of Greek drama to translate for a modern audience, who are part of a generally monotheistic society with no experience of ancient ritual practice. However, religious ritual in Greek drama is one of its vital components, and to ignore this completely when presenting plays to a modern audience is to limit the full impact of the drama.[2] This paper will show how Cacoyannis' two Greek-language films of the so-called 'Trojan trilogy', that is *Electra* and *Iphigenia*,[3] are charged with images which echo modern religion, specifically the Greek Orthodox faith. Such images are extremely effective for retaining some sense of religion and ritual which was so important in the original, and is extremely difficult to reconstruct in modern terms.

As a cinematic interpretation of Greek tragedy, the films belong to what has been termed the 'realistic mode', that is, they are shot in naturalistic surroundings rather than being a film of a theatrical performance.[4] Cacoyannis is generally faithful to the original plots,[5] but he suppresses the role of the gods. For example, the Dioscuri, who appear as *dei ex machina* to resolve the action of Euripides' *Electra*, are completely absent from Cacoyannis' film, as are Poseidon and Athena who speak the prologue in Euripides'

Trojan Women.[6] When the gods are mentioned in Cacoyannis, they are referred to within their ancient context, but their presence is less important than in the original plays. However, I would like to draw attention to two patterns of religious imagery from Cacoyannis' films, involving two Euripidean women, Iphigenia and Electra. The religious echo is used very differently in the two but, each time, it serves to reinforce an integral element of the original Euripidean play, and contributes to the portrayal of the two female figures, allowing us to judge whether or not Iphigenia and Electra are indeed 'rebel women'.

Iphigenia's Wedding[7]

The conflation of death and marriage in Greek tragedy is a common motif,[8] but it is arguably nowhere more palpable than in Euripides' *Iphigenia in Aulis*, where the whole premise of the plot involves the lure of Iphigenia to her death through the false promise of an illustrious marriage to the most eligible bachelor of the Greek army, Achilles.[9] In a modern context, where marriage is still an important religious ritual, it is not difficult to create a pattern of imagery that will suggest marriage. However, through the medium of film, and with injections of images mostly extraneous to the original play, Cacoyannis is able to exploit wedding imagery to highlight the important tension between joy and doom, which is integral to the structure of the original. This creates a pathos which reaches its climax in the final scenes.

The era-defying continuity of traditional bridal attire from antiquity through the ages to modern Greek Christianity allows Cacoyannis to fuse the ancient wedding image with the modern in an unparalleled way.[10] The two essential elements of nuptial dress for the bride in the ancient wedding were her wedding veils/robes[11] and her wedding crown. The bridegroom also wore a crown, and these were made from natural vegetation (leaves and flowers).[12] Today, images of white, translucent, flowing robes and veils unmistakably evoke the Christian concept of a wedding, but in the Greek

Orthodox tradition, bride and bridegroom *still* wear bridal crowns as an important part of the wedding ceremony, and the crowns are still made from leaves and flowers.[13] The crowns are 'crowns of joy', but they are also 'crowns of martyrdom' representing the self-sacrifice as well as the happiness that any lasting marriage entails.[14] In this way, the modern connotations of the bridal crown also reinforce the tensions between joy and sacrifice which are present in the ancient play. The crucial crowning scene, which precipitates Iphigenia's slaughter in Cacoyannis' film, must strike strong emotional chords with a specifically Greek audience, or one familiar with modern Greek religious custom. It is a perversion of the marriage ritual.

The crowning scene comes after Iphigenia has decided to die for Greece and goes willingly to her sacrificial death. Having been lured to the Greek camp by her father through the pretence of a marriage with Achilles, she is a maiden ripe for marriage, but ultimately accepts, as she says in the film, that 'Death will be [her] marriage and children and fame'.[15] The image of Iphigenia going to her death is the young Tatiana Papamouskou dressed in the intended bridal apparel. Just twelve years old at the time of shooting, Papamouskou is gracefully tall and serene, yet has a natural air of innocence and vulnerability. Before walking to the sacrificial altar, she asks her handmaidens to fetch her her bridal outfit and her crown. The crown she mentions is clearly her intended wedding crown. They adorn her with a white flowing robe, but the crown is not produced until she meets her father who prepares her for sacrifice. He places the wedding crown on her head, and anoints her with lustral water as she kneels before him. Iphigenia's wedding crown is made of wheat sheafs and other dry-looking flowers and leaves. It is untrimmed, and the protruding stalks are clearly arid and dead, representing Iphigenia's barren and fruitless marriage to death.[16] In this context, we see that the wreathed Iphigenia is an extremely potent symbol of marriage conflating with death, not only according to the ancient play, but also in modern religious terms.

The fact that Agamemnon himself places the crown on Iphigenia's head, and anoints her with lustral water, as well as

Iphigenia's position, kneeling before him, very much cast Agamemnon in the role of the presiding priest over the ceremony for a modern audience. This is in spite of the fact that, in ancient terms, he is not a presiding priest since he does not hold the sacrificial knife. It is noteworthy that Cacoyannis chooses this particular sequence of events. In the original play, not only does Agamemnon not hold the sacrificial knife, he does not even place the crown on Iphigenia's head. This is done by Calchas, as reported by the Messenger at line 1567. Of course, the authenticity of the ending of Iphigenia is a vexed question, given that the play was quite probably not completed by Euripides before he died, and was produced posthumously.[17] In Euripides' earlier *Iphigenia in Tauris*, Agamemnon is certainly presented as having slaughtered Iphigenia himself.[18] Cacoyannis retains Agamemnon as an accessory to the crime rather than the actual perpetrator, who is the evil Calchas. However, he consolidates Agamemnon's guilt for a modern audience by casting him in this role reminiscent of a priest at a wedding ceremony.

This culmination of wedding imagery through the adorning of the sacrificial victim in her bridal attire is foreshadowed at various points throughout the film. Translucent white cloth is introduced into frames at strategic moments and serves as an important visual reminder of the hideous lure of marriage. Following news of the fictitious wedding reaching Argos, we are shown Agamemnon coming out of his tent and gazing in front of him with a sombre expression. The camera then focuses on a white veil hanging limp (there is no wind, of course) from the tall narrow tree stump at a short distance from the tent, implying that this is the focus of Agamemnon's gaze. He touches his head anxiously. This is followed by a close-up shot of Agamemnon's eyes, dark with worry, and once again we are guided to the end-point of his gaze, this time the protruding branch of a nearby tree. The branch looks dry and brittle, reflecting the dustiness and cragginess of the surrounding landscape, and the twigs which are focused on have sparse foliage in contrast to the bushiness of the main part of the tree.[19] The veil and the branch represent the two elements of

Iphigenia's bridal attire: her white bridal robes and her bridal crown which will be made up of such dry and brittle foliage. The series of silent shots is presented against the very faint background of a slow drum-beat, which helps to create a sense of unease. With the interlude over, we are transported back to Argos, where the retinue is setting off for Aulis. As they arrive at their destination, Cacoyannis once again exploits the image of the white veil. This time we look out from Agamemnon's tent through his eyes and through the white veil which is now hanging as a kind of screen at the opening of his tent. Then we see him slowly lift the veil giving him a clear view of the retinue arriving at Aulis. In this way, Cacoyannis uses the veil, and the suggestion of the crown, as images which haunt Agamemnon in his guilt and highlight the horror of his deed.

Simultaneously, the veil and crown are used to represent the excitement among the females (Iphigenia, her mother and her handmaidens) concerning her impending marriage. In the build-up of imagery towards the final climax, the veil is a more prominent image than the crown. We are given a very quick glimpse of a crown and white veils during the short scene in which Iphigenia is changing clothes before the arrival at Aulis.[20] But much more excitement is generated by the sight of the prospective groom Achilles in the Greek camp. He is seen by Iphigenia and her handmaidens through a white veil which screens their tent completely (unlike the veil in Agamemnon's tent which creates only a partial screen). Iphigenia herself is too modest to rush forward to the screen to get a better view. While Achilles then bumps into Clytemnestra and Agamemnon's deception begins to reveal itself, Cacoyannis inserts a shot of Iphigenia and her handmaidens in their tent. The young girls have draped white veils over Iphigenia and play by hiding her in the veils and then letting her out. All the while, they sing joyfully of stirring up winds 'so that we may take Troy'.[21] This scene creates a strong sense of unease in the viewer through its sharp contrast to the horrific reality of how winds will be raised to sail to Troy.[22] To heighten the tension even further, the camera then cuts back to Clytemnestra who has just been told the truth about the sacrifice. Her reaction is one of disbelief and confusion mingled with horror which then gives way to realisation and very vocal anguish.

When Iphigenia overhears her mother, and learns the true purpose of their visit to Aulis, she takes off in a panicked run in an attempt to escape. Mariane McDonald has well noted how the pathos of this scene is reinforced in that it mirrors the opening scene of the sacred deer desperately trying to escape the arrows of the Greek army.[23] In a different context, Cindy Benton has remarked that tragedy, like horror, can be seen as 'victim-identified', and that both horror and tragedy are ritualistic and formulaic genres.[24] In light of these parallels, and bearing in mind the growing popularity of the horror film in the 1970s, Iphigenia's desperate run, off the main path and down the rocky hillside until she finally falls down, takes on a new symbolism for a cinema-going audience. Against the model of Hitchcock's *Psycho*, with its single female victim,[25] Iphigenia's death is inevitable, and this is reinforced for us by the fact that the outer white veil which has been resting on her shoulders slips off and falls by the roadside as she runs. Not only is this a symbol of her lost marriage, it is a clear indication that the Greek soldiers will find her and bring her to her sacrificial death.

The final exploitation of the wedding imagery, before its culmination in the crowning scene, is a close-up of Iphigenia's bridal veil passing though Clytemnestra's hand, as the distraught mother watches her child walk resolutely to her death. The image is potently reflective of Iphigenia's life, now equated with her marriage, literally slipping through her mother's hands, and helps consolidate the terrible anguish of Clytemnestra's suffering. Clytemnestra's anguish is more important in Cacoyannis than in Euripides, because Cacoyannis is much more concerned with making us understand what drives Clytemnestra to kill her husband on his return from Troy. There are two particularly powerful scenes in his film which highlight the mother's raging agony at the death of her child: one when Clytemnestra first learns Agamemnon's plan, and the second, when Iphigenia sees no choice in her death and decides to die honourably.[26] Her fury is captured for the audience in the final image which shows Clytemnestra in her chariot gazing in seething anger at the Greek ships sailing away as the sun sets.[27]

As presented in Cacoyannis' film, Iphigenia's marriage is her own death, the doom of her father, and ultimately the destruction of her mother, for Cacoyannis firmly implies it is the crime which sets the cycle of vengeance in motion. In the first half of the film, he exploits wedding imagery to reflect the mounting tension between the joy of the female contingent at the prospective wedding, and the doom which Agamemnon knows his lies will entail. Once the secret is out, the wedding images become solely associated with anguish and vulnerability, and the perversion of a sacred ritual. One key aspect in the success of this system of imagery is its accessibility for a modern audience, with images particularly pertinent to modern Greek religious custom.

Electra's Virginity and Cacoyannis' Use of the Chorus

I have chosen to discuss *Electra* second, not because of the sequence of mythological events, but because the religious image which I wish to highlight in *Electra* is much more subtly embedded in the structure of the film than is the wedding imagery of *Iphigenia*. The use of wedding imagery in a representation of *Iphigenia at Aulis* is an obvious, indeed a necessary choice, though *the way* in which Cacoyannis has exploited it in his film is, in my opinion, extremely successful. The image I will be discussing from *Electra*, while similarly more potent for a Greek audience, is neither an obvious nor a necessary choice, and perhaps not even a completely conscious one. I will argue below that the group of women who accompany Electra in the play, the 'main Chorus' as I see it, are reminiscent of Greek Orthodox nuns and that their attire creates an ambiguity, which, for a modern Greek audience, serves as a visual parallel for *both* Greek country-women *and* Orthodox nuns. In a modern Greek context, both country-women who are in mourning for the loss of a relative, and Orthodox nuns wear black clothes with their heads covered by a black headscarf.[28] The similarity between Cacoyannis' main Chorus and Greek country-women is evident from Figures 3 and 4. However, when we compare the costumes of Cacoyannis' main Chorus with the habits of Greek Orthodox nuns, as shown in Figure 5, there is a striking correspondence.[29] In fact, we can observe in Figure 4 that the country-women's dresses are not quite full-length. For a contemporary audience, this makes the full-length robes of Cacoyannis' Chorus-women even more suggestive of Orthodox nuns, who do wear a full-length habit. Thus, while in the ancient context of Cacoyannis' film, the Chorus-women are clearly meant to be country-women, for a modern Greek audience they are also visually suggestive of nuns. This extra layer of imagery helps to confirm Electra's virginity, in spite of her technically married status.

The Chorus of Euripides' *Electra* is composed of local country maidens, who come to visit Electra to try to convince her to join them at the festival of Hera for unmarried girls. The arrival and request of the Chorus highlight themes of importance to the play. First and foremost, their presence and identity act as a foil through which the complexity of Electra's marital situation can be expressed. The fact that they ask her to join them at the festival, although she is married, reinforces for the audience that Electra's marriage remains unconsummated. Yet she *is* married. Electra's identity as a woman is in a state of liminal suspension, belonging neither among 'maidens' as a social group, nor properly among 'married women'.[30] Second, Electra's admission that she has no suitable attire to attend such a festival highlights her costume of rags and her poverty. She is certainly more wretched than the Chorus-maidens who offer to lend her a fine dress and gold jewellery (190–2). Thus the theme of poverty versus wealth is introduced, and this theme will be exploited to full effect towards the end of the play when Electra's rags act as a potent contrast to her mother's decadent finery.[31]

In his film of the play, Cacoyannis veers away from this single choral identity. Instead, he introduces different choral contingents which fulfil various functions of the original single Chorus.[32] Thus the group of maidens who come to urge Electra to the festival become a subsidiary contingent in Cacoyannis' film. But let us clarify this fractioning of the Chorus by tracing the construction of the various choral groups through the film. First, it should be noted that Cacoyannis' *Electra* is shot in black-and-white, and all the different members of the overall choral body are dressed in very similar costumes. All the Chorus-women wear a headscarf and long dark robes. However, on careful examination, we can identify distinguishing features, even among this seemingly homogeneously dressed group.

The first choral contingent we encounter is the group of women, standing in formation in the fields, who sing as Electra is driven in a wagon by her new peasant husband to her new home.[33] The woman who leads the lament (fitting in the context of a princess forced by her parents to marry a commoner) wears a grey headscarf and dark robes. The women on the hill in the background wear headscarves and robes of various shades (of grey and black). The song continues and the women's voices are joined by men's. Finally, the song is completed by the peasant himself. The main function of this first Chorus is to sing an interlude while Electra enters her new life. But the introduction of male voices in the song emphasises the male presence in the locality.[34] It also foreshadows the lack of male presence in Electra's new entourage. The only male in Electra's internal community (until Orestes and Pylades turn up) is her husband who, as is emphasised, does not sleep with her,[35] or even spend much time with her.

The next choral contingent is the group which greets Electra on her arrival at the peasant's house. At the end of the scene, the group will split into two different parties; the group that accompanies Electra, I will call the main Chorus. A variety of women involved in daily chores come to meet Electra as she arrives. One woman holds an infant and his cries provide the background noise for the scene. As Mariane McDonald has pointed out, this brief introduction of a baby serves to contrast with Electra's barren marriage, implied by her name.[36] It also foreshadows Electra's fictitious childbirth, which she uses as bait to lure her mother to her death. Although the women are all in similar dress, there are some important differences between them. The woman holding the baby wears a grey dress and darker headscarf, while the older women have altogether darker clothes and headscarves. Most of the younger women wear lighter-coloured headscarves, and all of them wear dresses with a low neckline,[37] in contrast to the older women who are all in black and completely covered up (see Figure 3, where the two distinct choral costumes are obvious). One of the black-scarfed women advises Electra: 'Do not sigh, my child. Pray to the gods and they will hear you.' The equivalent of these lines are spoken by the Chorus in Euripides as an attempt to coax Electra into participating at the festival of Hera.[38] But in the visual context of Cacoyannis' film, this first pious advice offered by the Chorus,[39] helps to sow the seeds for a visual parallel between these women and Greek Orthodox nuns. The advice in the film is delivered without the context of a religious festival, and is therefore a more general expression of faith in divine power.

When Electra asks to be shown to the grave of her father, most of the women leave the area. The young women with the low necklines disperse. The woman with the baby slinks off, and the baby is never seen again, confirming the childless state of the community once Electra has entered into it. A small group of women remains. These are all older women, dressed in the darkest robes, with the blackest headscarves, and covered completely from head to toe, with just their faces and hands visible; that is, the group whose attire is visually reminiscent of Greek Orthodox nuns. The woman in the blackest of the dark robes, who had first given Electra advice, leads the procession to Agamemnon's grave. These are the women who form the main Chorus. Their garb reflects Electra's own perpetual state of mourning (for Agamemnon, for Orestes' absence, for her wretched existence),[40] but it also reinforces the unconsummated status of Electra's marriage, a fact which in turn highlights the nobility of Electra's peasant husband, and simultaneously allows her to remain an untouched and therefore suitable wife for Pylades.

Cacoyannis' main Chorus of women receive Electra into their community and are witnesses to events during the course of the film. In the beginning, Electra is shown as the victim of an extreme injustice, with which the Chorus sympathise, and this sympathy in turn guides our own. Until the arrival of Orestes and Pylades, Electra's peasant husband is the only male in this otherwise exclusively female community. This is in spite of the fact that earlier scenes in the film show a significant male presence in the kingdom.

This main Chorus of country-women supersedes the original Chorus of Euripides' play, though this choral contingent is certainly represented in Cacoyannis' film. The young maidens who invite Electra to the festival of Hera rush down from the hillside as Electra and the main Chorus walk homewards after having gone some distance to collect water. They sing the final verse of the film's first choral song, originally sung by the peasant, but this time only female voices are heard, once again emphasising the absence of males. The young women, who hurry towards Electra and the main Chorus, are the same young women who had greeted Electra on her arrival but then dispersed when asked to lead her to Agamemnon's grave. They wear the same low-necklined dresses and lighter coloured clothes. When Electra declines to join these women at the festival, they join the back of the group which moves towards the peasant's house. The group encounters Orestes and Pylades, searching for Electra. Fearing for Electra's safety, the choral group (now made up of two contingents) forms a human shield around her, hiding her from view. It is clear that they are protecting Electra as one of their own. But as it becomes apparent that the men mean Electra no harm, the group of women parts (see Figure 3), and Electra then strikes up a conversation with Orestes.

The leader of the main Chorus has an instrumental role during this exchange, as she silently coaxes Electra to reveal her virginity by laying a reassuring hand on her shoulder.[41] The revelation of Electra's virginity precipitates the beginning of interaction between Electra and Pylades. In the original play, Castor, who appears *ex machina*, commands Orestes to give Pylades Electra as wife (1249), reaffirming that she is a virgin (1284). Cacoyannis is far less direct in his development of the relationship between Pylades and Electra. As noted by Mariane McDonald, Pylades' interest in Electra is subtly implied by a series of glances.[42] The close of the film shows Electra leaving in one direction and Orestes in the other. Pylades follows Orestes who silently motions him away when he catches up, and Pylades then follows in the footsteps of Electra as the credits roll. This is very different from the clear affirmation of their projected relationship at the end of Euripides' play. Cacoyannis leaves us with only an implication of a relationship, foreshadowed at various points in the build-up to the conclusion.

The first, and perhaps most important, sign of Pylades' interest is the close-up of his face as he glances in Electra's direction when she reveals her virginity in the presence of the Chorus-women. This is followed by a series of gazes exchanged between Electra and Pylades during the recognition scene. Later, as Orestes and Pylades set off to murder Aegisthus, Electra is overcome by a moment of anguish at the thought of possible failure. Pylades holds her for a moment without speaking, and she recovers. Thus the relationship develops from exchanged glances to actual physical contact. Following the matricide, Electra realises, to some extent, the horror of her deed and laments, 'What man will lead me to a bridal bed?' Immediately following Electra's query, we are once more shown a close-up of Pylades, and the implications are obvious if not actually explicit.[43]

During this time, the choral group, made up of the main Chorus, and the subsidiary chorus of maidens, fulfil a variety of functions. They tell a story as an interlude inspired by the 'Shield of Achilles' ode, which reminds the children of the calibre of their father, who was struck down by Clytemnestra. However, Cacoyannis omits the closing lines of the original choral ode, where the Chorus address the absent Clytemnestra saying: 'Therefore will the heavenly gods send the justice of death to you also, and the day will come when I will see the gory blood pouring forth from the sword at your throat' (482–6). By omitting these lines, Cacoyannis does not portray the Chorus as sanctioning the revenge, though it is a tribute to the director's effort to do justice to the original that he does include this ode, which has been repeatedly berated as irrelevant to the plot by scholars of the period.[44] The Chorus witness the recognition scene but are not privy to the murder plans. When Orestes, Pylades, Electra and the Old Tutor leave the peasant's house, the two choral contingents have once again separated. The maidens emerge from behind the house, and the main Chorus from the side. Both contingents of women follow the departing group with their gaze. They remain watching when Electra returns to her cottage, and then move away.

From the moment of Orestes and Pylades being welcomed into Electra's house, Electra stops being part of the main Chorus's internal group. The main Chorus now become completely outside observers. In terms of the Chorus' visual evocation of nuns, Electra's move away from their enclave also marks the beginning of her relationship with Pylades. But the Chorus's new distance from Electra also highlights their distance from the murders, from which they are dissociated. During the matricide, the main Chorus are shown outside the house in which it is being perpetrated, and their physical distress reflects nature's revulsion at the crime.[45] When Electra emerges from the house after the deed, the main Chorus have gathered into a group which parts to let Electra through as she leaves. This is a strong contrast to the physical protection the choral group had offered her when threatened by strangers (who turned out to be Orestes and Pylades). It represents the Chorus's final rejection of Electra.

The choral dynamic in Cacoyannis' film is complicated, but it is also extremely effective.[46] The precise identity of the main Chorus is never specified. This facilitates exploitation of the visual parallel with Greek Orthodox nuns for a modern audience. In turn, this extra layer of imagery expresses and confirms a significant element of Electra's identity, her virginity, and also helps to characterise Electra at different stages of the film. When Electra is part of the choral group, she inspires a certain amount of audience sympathy. But once distanced from the Chorus, she becomes a vile character, no longer a victim, but an abhorrent figure, capable of plotting and perpetrating a matricide.

The different choral contingents in the play work in harmony with each other to help reproduce the choral functions of the original play. One such effect is to create an atmosphere of ritual, and it has been noted that the Chorus of Cacoyannis' *Electra* is more stylised than is his use of the Chorus in later films.[47] The specific visual parallel of the main Chorus, as a group of women living alone in the Greek countryside, all wearing long dark robes with covered heads, reminiscent of nuns, makes Cacoyannis' use of a stylised Chorus particularly appropriate to the subject-matter of *Electra*.

Conclusion

Cacoyannis' strength has been seen in his Greek-language productions of Euripidean tragedies.[48] The success of his films lies in part with his ability to do justice to the original play while simultaneously tailoring his art, through the medium of film, for a modern audience. Cacoyannis' aim was to interpret Euripides,[49] and this effort, to understand a complex playwright thoroughly, is what comes across on screen. Some of his additions or omissions may not please all critics, but I hope to have shown that Cacoyannis' choice of images suggesting modern religious parallels, especially for a Greek audience, enrich his films while remaining faithful to the original plays.

Religious allusion is used very differently in the two examples discussed above. In the first, wedding imagery functions as a direct echo of the original ancient Greek ritual context. This echo is facilitated for a Greek audience and in a Greek production by the residue of ancient rituals and customs which have survived from antiquity to the present day. However, the specific choice of images and their positioning within the film are entirely directed by Cacoyannis. The medium of film also facilitates attention to such details as Cacoyannis has created, details which are not present in the original, nor could be introduced effectively into a stage production. The second image is also specific to Greek society.

However, the religious allusion has no direct counterpart in the original tragedy. It is a modern image, used to reinforce an integral feature in the ancient play. The religious image is also exploited to help re-create the atmosphere of ritual which was such an integral part of fifth-century performance.

But how does Cacoyannis' exploitation of religious imagery shape our understanding of these two heroines? Does it detract from or add to a reading of Iphigenia and Electra as 'rebel women'? It seems that a different conclusion must be reached in each case. In her contribution to this volume, Edith Hall concludes that the Iphigenia of modern productions of Euripides' *Iphigenia in Aulis* 'is no rebel woman', but 'one of the most accepting victims of male authority', and further, that directors have exploited this play to give meaning and 'near-legitimacy' to Clytemnestra's murder of Agamemnon in the *Oresteia*. Certainly, Cacoyannis is concerned to emphasise Clytemnestra's desire for revenge at the end of his film, and he depicts Iphigenia as a childish victim (rather than a woman), who adores her father. But the religious imagery also confirms Iphigenia's status as a victim rather than a rebel. The exploitation of the white veils highlights Iphigenia's purity and innocence, while the potent scene in which she is anointed for sacrifice by her father underlines his position of authority in front of which she, literally as well as metaphorically, bends. Agamemnon's own authority has been shown, in the film, to be ineffectual in the face of the evil scheming of Calchas and the will of the army. This is reflected in the final image of Iphigenia's sacrifice which reveals the physical violence of the seer, before which the young girl is helpless. Thus the power of each man reflects the degree of his responsibility for the sacrifice. Calchas is portrayed in Cacoyannis' film as ultimately more responsible than Agamemnon.

For the figure of Electra, the religious imagery reinforces her rebellion against nature by killing her mother. While Electra is not rebelling, the fact that the Chorus-women who accompany her look like nuns inspires a more sympathetic audience reaction to Electra's character. However, the Chorus-women become distanced from Electra when Orestes and Pylades arrive, and while the double murder plots are being hatched. When the murder of Clytemnestra is being committed, Electra's ultimate act of rebellion, the Chorus-women react violently, as if receiving the blows themselves. This represents the Chorus's ultimate rejection of Electra and her rebellion, and serves as a guide for audience response. The negativity of Electra's rebellion is reflected in the lack of explicit provision for her marriage to Pylades in Cacoyannis' film. Although there are clear implicit suggestions concerning their relationship, the close of the film leaves matters much more open-ended than does Euripides' play. Electra *is* a 'rebel woman', but her departure from the virginal choral enclave portrays her rebellion in an entirely negative light.

Notes

I am grateful for the comments of those who attended the original presentation of this paper in Dublin, and I especially thank Lynn Kozak, Judith Mossman and Steve Wilmer for their insightful comments on earlier drafts of this article. It is indeed appropriate that this article on Cacoyannis should be included in a Festschrift for Marianne McDonald, who has been instrumental in bringing his films to the attention of classicists. I also acknowledge, with appreciation, the financial support of the Irish Research Council for the Humanities and Social Sciences, during the period in which this article was researched and written.

1. See e.g. R. Seaford, *Reciprocity and Ritual: Homer and Tragedy in the Developing City-State* (Oxford: OUP, 1994); C. Sourvinou-Inwood, *Tragedy and Athenian Religion* (Lantham: Lexington Books, 2003). Even if one agrees with S. Scullion's 'Nothing to Do with Dionysus: Tragedy Misconceived as Ritual', *Classical Quarterly*, 52 (2002): 107–37, in his recent and controversial argument that Greek tragedy is not necessarily derived from Dionysiac cult, and that tragedy itself is not essentially a ritual activity, nevertheless it cannot be denied that ritual activity (for example laments, prayers to the gods, burial rites, sacrifices, libations etc.) takes place in all Greek tragedies, as Scullion himself acknowledges (pp. 136–7).

2. Cf. T. Eagleton in *Sweet Violence: The Idea of the Tragic* (Malden, MA and Oxford: Blackwell, 2003), pp. xvi–xvii, who draws attention to the fact that 'religion is the most important symbolic form which humanity has ever known . . . Yet those eager to study popular culture pass embarrassedly over this global, longest-lasting, most supremely effective mode of it.'

3. For those who are unable to consult the films themselves, the synopses compiled by M. McDonald will be most helpful, in *Euripides in the Cinema: The Heart Made Visible* (Philadelphia: Centrum Philadelphia, for the Greek Institute, 1983). The films are a trilogy only in the loose sense that the events in *Iphigenia* are a mythical precedent for the Trojan War, the aftermath of which is depicted in *Trojan Women*, which itself predates the events of *Electra* in terms of mythical history. However, the films were shot achronologically, *Electra* first in 1961, *Trojan Women* ten years later in 1971, and *Iphigenia* last in 1978. (On the reception through the ages of Euripides' *Iphigenia in Aulis*, on which Cacoyannis' *Iphigenia* is based, see Edith Hall's contribution to this volume, Chapter 1.) *Electra* and *Iphigenia* are in Greek, *Trojan Women* is in English. Furthermore, since they are based on the Euripidean plays which were not a trilogy, it is not surprising that the films seem only superficially connected to each other; cf. K. MacKinnon, *Greek Tragedy into Film* (London: Croom Helm, 1986), p. 75.

4. MacKinnon, *Greek Tragedy into Film*, uses the terminology of J. J. Jorgens in *Shakespeare on Film* (London: Indiana University Press, 1977), on which see also L. Hardwick, *Reception Studies* (*Greece and Rome: New Surveys in the Classics*, no. 33) (Oxford: OUP, 2003), pp. 72–3.

5. Cacoyannis is not completely faithful to the original plays. Notably, he imports mythical elements from external sources in order to contextualise his films. The opening of his *Iphigenia* includes the slaughter of the sacred deer which causes Artemis' anger and explains her demand of the sacrifice of Iphigenia. This version is based on the *Cypria*, and is used in Sophocles' *Electra*, though in Cacoyannis' film, Agamemnon himself does not shoot the deer. Similarly, the beginning of his *Electra* shows the murder of Agamemnon by his wife and her lover which spawns the hatred of the children and their thirst for revenge.

   He also directs our sympathies with much more certainty than Euripides towards particular characters. While Euripides complicates issues of blame in his *Electra* and *Iphigenia in Aulis*, Cacoyannis delineates clearer villains and victims; see further on Cacoyannis' *Iphigenia*: McDonald, *Euripides in the Cinema*, pp. 156–81; McDonald, 'Cacoyannis and Euripides' *Iphigenia*: The Dialectic of Power', in M. Winkler (ed.), *Classics and Cinema* (Lewisburg, PA: Bucknell University Press, 1991), pp. 127–41; and M. McDonald, 'Eye of the Camera, Eye of the Victim: *Iphigenia* by Euripides and Cacoyannis', in M. Winkler (ed.), *Classical Myth and Culture in the Cinema* (Oxford: OUP, 2001), pp. 90–101. On Cacoyannis' *Electra*, see McDonald, *Euripides in the Cinema*, pp. 284–307, and K. MacKinnon and M. McDonald, 'Cacoyannis vs. Euripides: From Tragedy to Melodrama', in N. W. Slater and B. Zimmermann (eds), *Intertextualität in der griechisch-römischen Komödie* (Stuttgart: M&P Verlag für Wissenschaft und Forschung, 1993), pp. 222–34, esp. pp. 226–8.

6. In the film, the voice-over of a narrator delivers the prologue.

7. All line numbers of Euripides' *Iphigenia in Aulis* and *Electra* are quoted from J. Diggle, *Euripidis Fabulae: Tomus III* (Oxford: OUP, 1994) and *Euripidis Fabulae: Tomus II* (Oxford: OUP, 1981), respectively. Any translations aim at clarity rather than poetic merit.

8. See esp. R. Rehm, *Marriage to Death: The Conflation of Wedding and Funeral Rituals in Greek Tragedy* (Princeton, NJ: Princeton University Press, 1994), who discusses the motif in eight tragedies.

9. On the conflation of wedding and sacrificial imagery in Euripides' *Iphigenia in Aulis*, see esp. H. Foley, 'Marriage and Sacrifice in Euripides' *Iphigenia in Aulis*', *Arethusa*, 15 (1982): 159–80, and *Ritual Irony: Poetry and Sacrifice in Euripides* (Ithaca, NY and London: Cornell University Press, 1985), pp. 68–78, 84–92.

10. Compare the continuity of traditional lament in Greece through the ages, traced in detail by M. Alexiou in *The Ritual Lament in the Greek Tradition* (Cambridge: CUP, 1974), and more recently by G. Holst-Warhaft in *Dangerous Voices: Women's Lament and Greek Literature* (London: Routledge, 1992). Cacoyannis himself sees connections between women in ancient and modern Greece in M. McDonald and M. Winkler, 'Michael Cacoyannis and Irene Papas on Greek Tragedy', in Winkler (ed.), *Classical Myth and Culture in the Cinema*, p. 75. Cf. also the concept of 'cinematic attitudes towards space which entail a sense of shared values and a concept of common history and culture' developed by P. Michelakis in 'The Past as a

Foreign Country? Greek Tragedy, Cinema and the Politics of Space',
in F. Budelmann and P. Michelakis (eds), *Homer, Tragedy and
Beyond: Essays in Honour of P. E. Easterling* (London: Society for the
Promotion of Hellenic Studies, 2001). See esp. pp. 242 and 244–5,
where this is discussed particularly in the context of Cacoyannis'
Electra.

11. Ancient bridal robes may have been white (see Rehm, *Marriage to
Death*, p. 156, n. 14), but there is also strong evidence to suggest that
the colour purple was an important element of the bride's attire (see
J. H. Oakley and R. H. Sinos, *The Wedding in Ancient Athens*
[Madison: University of Wisconsin Press, 1993], p. 16).

12. According to Oakley and Sinos, *The Wedding in Ancient Athens*,
p. 16, some vase paintings seem to depict metal crowns, though their
shape still imitates a crown of woven plants.

13. That the crowns are made of leaves and flowers is particular to the
Greeks. The Russian Orthodox tradition uses crowns of silver and
gold. In spiritual terms, the coronation ceremony is 'the outward and
visible sign of the sacrament [and] signifies the special grace which the
couple receive from the Holy Spirit, before they set out to found a new
family or domestic Church' (T. Ware, *The Orthodox Church*
[London: Penguin, 1993], pp. 294–5).

14. Ibid., p. 295.

15. In the play, she says (1398–9): 'Sacrifice me, and sack Troy; this will be
my monument, and my children and my marriage and my fame for all
time.' It is important in the ancient context that Iphigenia agrees to die.
An animal destined for sacrifice was sprinkled with water as a gesture
which forced it to 'nod' in agreement to its own sacrifice, as a good
omen (R. Parker, 'Sacrifice, Greek', in S. Hornblower and A. Spawforth
[eds], *The Oxford Classical Dictionary* [Oxford: OUP, 1996], p. 1344).

16. The image of Iphigenia in her crown has been chosen by Cacoyannis
as the final image of the film in his '*Iphigenia*: A Visual Essay' in
Winkler (ed.), *Classical Myth and Culture in the Cinema*, pp. 102–17.
His caption reads simply (117): 'Crowned with a wreath of flowers,
Iphigenia walks to her death.'

17. See Diggle's scheme of probable authenticity of lines in his *Euripidis
Fabulae: Tomus III*, and Diggle, *Euripidea: Collected Essays* (Oxford:
OUP, 1994), pp. 490–507 for defence of his readings.

18. Though Iphigenia is ultimately saved by Artemis, unbeknown to the
Greeks, Agamemnon is described as killing Iphigenia at *Iphigenia in*

Tauris, 8, 211–13, 360, 366, 784, 853–4, 1083; lines quoted from Diggle, *Euripidis Fabulae: Tomus II*.

19. It is noteworthy that the barren landscapes in Cacoyannis' films have been interpreted as evoking the bleakness and suffering of Greece in the context of military dictatorship (see Hardwick, *Reception Studies*, p. 82, discussing Michelakis, 'The Past is a Foreign Country', in Budelmann and Michelakis [eds], *Homer, Tragedy and Beyond*), and the military is a very potent force in *Iphigenia*.

20. Interestingly, the crown shown briefly in this scene is smooth, unlike the bridal crown of the final scenes whose protruding stalks are unmistakable. This may suggest the corruption of a smooth transition which instead becomes an uncivilised act of aggression.

Although we do not actually see Iphigenia being sacrificed, we witness the violence of Iphigenia being grabbed from behind (by Calchas) as she stumbles blindly through the mist, and we see the horror in Agamemnon's face as he gazes on what must be his slaughtered child.

21. For some reason, this song is not translated in the subtitles.

22. In Euripides' play, Iphigenia's sacrifice will raise the winds, but the implication of Cacoyannis' film is that the winds are rising anyway without her sacrifice, and that Iphigenia dies because of Calchas' wish to settle a personal score with Agamemnon; see B. Knox ,*Word and Action: Essays on the Ancient Theater* (Baltimore: Johns Hopkins University Press, 1979). p. 353.

23. McDonald, 'Eye of the Camera . . .', in Winkler (ed.), *Classical Myth and Culture in the Cinema*, pp. 90–1.

24. C. Benton, 'Split Vision: The Politics of the Gaze in Seneca's *Troades*', in D. Fredrick (ed.), *The Roman Gaze: Vision, Power, and the Body* (Baltimore: Johns Hopkins University Press, 2002), pp. 31–56, at p. 33 with n. 11. On the ritualised and formulaic nature of the horror film, see C. Clover, *Men, Women, and Chainsaws: Gender in the Modern Horror Film* (London: BFI Press, 1992), pp. 9–11, quoted in part by Benton.

25. Clover (1992), *Men, Women, and Chainsaws*, notes (pp. 24–5) that *Psycho* (1960) is the 'appointed ancestor of the slasher film' and that its enormous success 'prompted a flood of imitations and variations'. The difference between *Psycho* and the later variant formula for slasher films is that rather than just having one female victim, there are several victims, usually with one final girl who survives (see ibid., pp. 35–41).

26. Both these moments are captured in the stills in Cacoyannis, '*Iphigenia*: A Visual Essay', in Winkler (ed.), *Classical Myth and Culture in the Cinema*, pp. 111 and 115.

27. Earlier, Clytemnestra had warned Agamemnon that if he went through with the sacrifice, she would be waiting for him on his return from Troy. Interestingly, Cacoyannis omits from this exchange Clytemnestra's recollection of Agamemnon's murder of the child from her previous marriage, which features in the original play. This is one way in which Cacoyannis detracts from Agamemnon's villainy, while portraying Calchas and Odysseus as the real villains.

28. On Greek country-women wearing black as a sign of mourning, see L. M. Danforth and A. Tsiaras, *The Death Rituals of Rural Greece* (Princeton, NJ: Princeton University Press, 1982), p. 39 and *passim*; on Greek Orthodox nuns donning a black habit after their novitiate since Byzantine times, see C. A. Frazee, 'Greece', in W. M. Johnston (ed.), *Encyclopedia of Monasticism* (Chicago: Fitzroy Dearborn, 2000), pp. 543–50, at p. 545.

29. The monastery to which these nuns belong was founded in 1991; see further P. Riches, 'A Taste of Strawberries: Pilgrimage to the Two Monastic Dependencies of Simonopetra in Southern France 14–17 June 2002', in *Friends of Mount Athos: Annual Report 2002* (2002), pp. 61–6, at pp. 64–6.

30. On Electra's characterisation, and the role of the Chorus in this play, see F. Zeitlin, 'The Argive Festival of Hera and Euripides' *Electra*', in *Transactions of the American Philological Society*, 101 (1970): 45–69, republished in J. Mossman (ed.), *Oxford Readings in Classical Studies: Euripides* (Oxford: OUP, 2003), pp. 261–84.

31. It is impossible to say for certain what the original Chorus wore. It has been suggested by M. Kubo in 'The Norm of Myth: Euripides' *Electra*', *Harvard Studies in Classical Philology*, 71 (1966): 15–31, that (23) the Chorus were actually dressed in festive finery from their first entrance. This may be true, but the Chorus announce that the festival will take place in two days' time (171–2), which may be an indication that they are not dressed in festive attire. On the theme of wealth versus poverty and its ambiguities in *Electra*, see M. J. O'Brien, 'Orestes and the Gorgon: Euripides' *Electra*', *American Journal of Philology* (1964): 13–39, at 34–6.

32. These functions are to sing interludes (from a structural point of view), to introduce and develop themes pertinent to the drama, and to

provide a possible guide for audience sympathy by expressing their own.

33. On the significance of the landscape in Cacoyannis' *Electra*, as consolidating the relation between Greek countryside and folklore, and incorporating an archaeological site (i.e. the palace at Mycenae in the prologue of the film), see Michelakis, 'The Past is a Foreign Country', in Bundelmann and Michelakis (eds), *Homer, Tragedy and Beyond*, pp. 244–5.

34. There is a strong male presence in the crowd of locals that greets Agamemnon on his return from Troy at the very beginning of the film. Later, at the revel organised by Aegisthus, there are large numbers of male harvesters and some male dancers. There are also various shots of men working in the fields throughout the film, and a strong male contingent in the group of locals who gather outside Electra's house after the matricide.

35. This is reinforced by a shot of Electra alone in bed, just after Orestes and Pylades have arrived still unbeknown to all.

36. McDonald, *Euripides in the Cinema*, pp. 266 and 314, n. 7. The word '*alectra*' which literally means 'without a marriage-bed' can be used as a pun on Electra's name. Sophocles exploits this in his *Electra*, at line 962.

37. It is possible that the young women's dresses contain a white panel at the top rather than a low neckline. I have watched the various scenes in which they feature repeatedly, but have been unable to ascertain which is the case. Whichever it is does not alter my argument. The younger women's dresses are distinct from the older women's. For the sake of simplicity, I call these 'low-necklined dresses' throughout this paper.

38. Euripides, *Electra*, 195–7: 'It is not through groans, child, that you will gain happiness, but by honouring the gods with prayers.'

39. This is the second choral utterance, the first being an exclamation of pity at Electra's fate.

40. Indeed, when her mother and Aegisthus marry off Electra to the peasant (incorporated into the action at the beginning of the film), Cacoyannis shows Electra laying her shorn hair, a potent sign of mourning, at her mother's feet.

41. This is part of a system of hand imagery in the film which was brought to my attention by Lynn Kozak. The prologue of the film, which shows Agamemnon's murder, focuses at certain points on his hand

writing in the throes of death, creating an association between hands and violence. In the scene where Electra reveals her virginity, we are shown a positive, supportive and comforting hand gesture, which suggests the potential for an ultimately positive outcome, supported by the Chorus. Later, we are shown Electra with her hand on top of Orestes' inside the hut, here an image of unity after the recognition. But there will be no positive outcome and this image will ultimately be associated not only with violence, but with perversion and pollution. After the matricide, Electra and Orestes clasp each other's hands only to realise that their hands are covered in their mother's blood. At this realisation, they let each other's hands go, a symbol of the awful finality and horror of their deed.

42. McDonald, *Euripides in the Cinema*, pp. 268, 271.

43. Ibid., p. 276.

44. It was three years after the release of Cacoyannis' *Electra* that O'Brien's influential article ('Orestes and the Gorgon', 1964) defended the relevance of this ode to the play as a whole.

45. Compare the barbarian Trojan slaves who stand absolutely still in their fine and brightly patterned attire as the matricide is being perpetrated. Cacoyannis also barbarises Clytemnestra by making the costumes of the Trojan slaves echo her own. They are similarly bright and adorned with the same types of geometric patterns.

46. Cf. Knox, *Word and Action*, p. 351, who calls *Electra* 'a film remarkable for . . . its imaginative handling of the chorus'.

47. MacKinnon, *Greek Tragedy into Film*, p. 76; McDonald, 'Cacoyannis and Euripides' *Iphigenia*', in Winkler (ed.), *Classics and Cinema*, p. 129.

48. Cf. Knox, *Word and Action*, p. 351, who calls *The Trojan Women*, filmed in English, 'a wooden affair' and 'a disappointment'.

49. Cacoyannis, '*Iphigenia*: A Visual Essay', in Winkler (ed.), *Classical Myth and Culture in the Cinema*, p. 79.

3. *Medea* between the Wars: The Politics of Race and Empire

Fiona Macintosh

The numerous anti-racist productions of Euripides' *Medea* in Britain in the 1980s appeared at the time to be very much a product of the relatively new attitudes to ethnicity and 'otherness' that had been gleaned from both theory and practice.[1] From the academy had come postcolonial theory; and from ethnic minority groups themselves, who were just beginning to find their voices in local government (and especially in the capital through the conduit of the Greater London Council), came new empirical evidence that regularly underpinned the 1980s' *Medea*s.

However, as with many things proclaimed 'new', antecedents are not hard to find; and in the case of the 1980s' anti-racist configurations of *Medea*, we can readily identify startling prefigurations in the interwar period in both Europe and the United States. One of these *Medea*s was the 1926 German version by Hans Henny Jahnn; and revivals of Jahnn's play in the 1960s, 1970s and the very early '80s brought a black Medea back once again to the radical stages of Europe.[2] But the fact that Jahnn's *Medea* had enjoyed a comeback was not necessarily due to its adroit handling of inter-racial tension alone; it was as much its risqué medley of sadism, paedophilia and homo-eroticism that gave it a contemporary flavour.

Jahnn's play becomes far more interesting, however, if it is seen within its original context, at a time when the politics of race and empire was becoming increasingly highly charged in the Europe of the late 1920s. In this article, however, I do not wish to focus on Jahnn's version, which has already received considerable attention from wide quarters;[3] instead, I wish to concentrate on a slightly later and lesser-known version of Euripides' play by the French avant-garde playwright, Henri-René Lenormand. Lenormand's *oeuvre* has largely been forgotten both in France and elsewhere, even though he worked very closely with those who are now central to histories of the modern theatre (notably Georges Pitoëff, Gaston Baty, Firmin Gémier). It was Lenormand, moreover, and not Antonin Artaud, who coined the phrase 'theatre of cruelty'.[4]

Leno rmand's version of *Medea*, entitled *Asie*, was first performed at the Théâtre Antoine in December 1931; and it went on to enjoy an international profile in the 1930s, being performed in Italy, Greece and Austria after a successful run in Paris. But it has never been revived (as far as I know) since the war and it has rarely received critical attention.[5] This neglect, moreover, is surprising for not only did *Asie* inspire (directly and indirectly) two important American versions of *Medea* – the first in 1935 by the poet and playwright Countee Cullen (the 'poet laureate' of the Harlem Literary Renaissance) and the second, the much better known play by Maxwell Anderson, *The Wingless Victory* of 1936[6] – it was also written at a critical juncture in France's colonial history, and it goes further than any other contemporary reworking of Medea in its use of the myth to explicate the iniquities and the perils inherent in the colonial experience.

Greek Myth, Primitivism and the French Avant-garde

Lenormand in *Les Confessions d'un auteur dramatique*, written some years after *Asie*, explains that the seeds of his version of the *Medea* were planted during a visit to Athens in 1930, when he went to see a revival of two of his plays written in the early twenties, *Le Simoun* and *Râtés*.[7] During his stay, Lenormand was taken to Delphi by the husband of the famous Greek tragedienne, Marika Kotopouli (who took the lead in both plays), to see the second Delphic Festival organised by the poet Angelos Sikelianos and his

American wife, Eva Palmer.[8] In his *Confessions*, Lenormand recalls watching a rather amateur rendering of *Prometheus Bound*, during which he was overwhelmed by the open-air setting, which he felt was able to afford far greater special effects than anything on offer in the commercial theatre. Indeed, as was characteristic of the French avant-garde in this period as a whole, Lenormand's passion is less for the technological advances of his age; it is really the 'primitive' that captures his imagination and shapes his creative aesthetic.[9] His visit to Delphi that summer, together with an intensely passionate relationship with a Greek married woman referred to only as Ismene (whom we are told provided him with the model for his figure of Medea), made Lenormand determined to write his own tragedy based on Greek myth.[10]

There were, of course, other reasons why Lenormand should have turned to Greek myth in general and to the myth of Medea in particular at this time. Cocteau's recent adaptations of Sophoclean drama in Paris of the 1920s – his condensed *Antigone* (1922) and his Latin libretto for Stravinsky's opera-oratorio *Oedipus Rex* (1927) – had already shown the French avant-garde that Greek tragedy was fertile territory for modernist theatrical experimentation. But whereas Cocteau's experiments in the twenties are essentially formal, Lenormand's concern (as with Jahnn's recent *succès de scandale*) was to update the myth for political purposes. For Lenormand in 1931, Euripides' *Medea* enables him to enter into an important and highly charged debate on French colonial policy in Indochina.

Lenormand had already tackled France's colonial conduct in two earlier plays – in both *Le Simoun* (1920), which is set in the Sahara, and in *A l'ombre du mal* (1924), which is set in equatorial Africa; and in these early plays, he explores the deleterious effects of a change of climate on the European mind and body, and exposes the fatal consequences that these entail for the indigenous population. *Le Simoun* enjoyed considerable success not only abroad (as in Athens in 1930) but also at home. However, as had been the case with *A l'ombre du mal* in 1924, *Le Simoun* met with the strictures of the Comédie-Française; it was withdrawn after only thirty performances, in 1937, after ministerial pressure had been exerted to put a stop to the presentation of a play in which French colonial settlers appeared in a bad light.[11] *Asie* was thus Lenormand's third play about France and its territories, and, after French North Africa and the Central African colonies, Lenormand turned his attention to France's most important colonial conquest, Indochina.[12]

L'Exposition Coloniale and French Indochina on Display

When *Asie* opened at the Théâtre Antoine in December 1931, it was especially timely. Earlier in the year – from May to November – Paris had hosted the spectacular Exposition Coloniale Internationale in the Bois de Vincennes. During six months, the exhibition had attracted nearly 34,000 visitors, who had come to see '*la plus grande France*' on display, with Indochina at the centre of the spectacle.[13] For not only was the centrepiece of the exhibition a reconstruction of the temple of Angkor, there were dancing girls from the palace of Phnom Penh, decorously arranged on the running boards of cars, to provide added attraction for the flocks of male visitors. It was here too that Antonin Artaud first encountered Balinese dance-drama, which was to prove such a powerful determinant in shaping his aesthetic.[14] The aim of the exhibition was to make each citizen feel part of '*la plus grande France*' – metropolitan France being only one twenty-third of the French empire, as the Colonial Minister, Paul Reynard, reminded his audience at the opening of the exhibition.[15] In a very real sense, the exhibition served as an enormous confidence booster for the French nation, still reeling from the devastation of the First World War. Now with 100 million citizens in total, France could with pride and confidence resume her former role as a key player on the international stage.

Paul Reynard spoke of the grandeur of France's expansion '*d'outre-mer*' (usually translated as 'overseas' but literally 'beyond the seas') – a carefully chosen phrase, implying voluntary unity between the 'old' metropolitan centre and the 'new' France of the colonies.[16] In many ways, the exhibition attempted to capture the sentiments expressed in an important study of French colonialism published that year by the liberal-leaning, former governor of Indochina, Albert Sarrault. In *Grandeur et servitude coloniales*, Sarrault explains the colonial process not in terms of market forces, but as the collective work of European solidarity working towards scientific, moral, political and economic progress.[17] However, the blatant propaganda of the exhibition did not go unnoticed. That same year the counter-view was amply provided by Louis Roubaud's exposé of French duplicity in the Far East, provocatively entitled (since the designation Vietnam was at that time proscribed) *Viet-Nam, la tragédie indochinoise*. Journalists from the left-wing newspapers, notably the Communist Party's daily, *L'Humanité*, denounced the exhibition as '*Cette apothéose [qui] est celle du crime*' (This apotheosis that is founded on crime).[18] And when Lenormand's play opened at the Théâtre Antoine in the immediate wake of the exhibition, it was to provide no less a critique of official government policy.

There was, of course, considerable irony in making Indochina the focus of l'Exposition Coloniale Internationale. Despite being the most developed and the wealthiest of all French territories, it was most recently – as Roubaud's study of Vietnamese history had shown – the site of one of France's bloodiest confrontations with its colonial population. With the frustrations attendant on an increasingly highly educated population being denied the reforms they had anticipated in return for the considerable help they had given the metropolitan centre during the First World War, nationalist fervour began to spread throughout Indochina. Tension was high from the start of 1930 and the situation came to a head with the mutiny of fifty soldiers from Yen Bai garrison in Tonkin (in the north) in January, followed by bloody reprisals and no fewer than 10,000 fatalities as chaos ruled throughout the whole region during the remaining months of the year.[19]

In France there was a general feeling that reform was necessary, but there was equally the view that the problems in Indochina were part of the vast Leninist revolutionary strategy. Indeed, since 1920 and the Second International Communist Congress, revolution in the East had been deemed vital by the communists to the revolutionary cause in order that colonial peoples could unite with European workers in the overthrow of capitalism.[20] And up until 1935, when Hitler began to appropriate much anti-colonial terminology and intervened on behalf of nationalist movements in the colonies, the communist parties of Europe were active in their support of the colonial struggle. For *L'Humanité*, the mutiny at the garrison at Yen Bai was '*une grande revolution anti-impérialiste et agraire*' (a great anti-imperialist and agrarian revolution).[21]

Asie and the Colonial Encounter

Lenormand's play, like the products of other dissident voices within France, is written in militant opposition to the 1931 colonial exhibition; and it uses Euripides' tragedy in order to tell an alternative version of France's colonial history. The 'Asie' of the title refers both to the continent of Asia and to the Medea figure herself, Princess Katha Nahum Moun, whose father was a descendant of the sun and king of the Sibang peoples. Also in keeping with what is now understood as the standard colonial trope of Woman as Nation, the Glauke figure, here called simply Aimée (Beloved) is deliberately cast in contradistinction to the Princess. When Lenormand's Jason begins his seduction of Aimée on board the steamer bound for France, he refers to her meta-phorically as Europe: '*Vous êtes l'Europe vers qui je me précipite à la vitesse de deux cent milles par jour*' (You are the Europe I'm rushing towards at the rate of 200 miles per day).[22]

Although for the Jason-figure, Aimée may have a soul chiselled like the fleur de lys (38), she in fact represents liberal Europe at its worst: both pitying the plight of her rival and, at a later point in the play when she defends the Princess who is threatened with deport-ation from Marseilles (Act II, tableau VI, 89ff.), also seemingly speaking on her behalf, exactly as the organisers of the colonial exhibition in Paris had claimed to be doing for their colonial subjects. But in reality, Lenormand's representative of liberal Europe is merely patronising (for her, the Princess is a 'poor wild animal separated from her skin' [40]); and she is ultimately prepared to benefit from the misery of those whose fate troubles her conscience (93).

Jason/de Mezzana in Lenormand's version is translated into a forty-year-old war veteran-turned-adventurer, who after emerging from an expedition in the jungle had joined the Sibang people in their struggle with their neighbours. The Princess was seduced by this white demi-god who had miraculously appeared alone from out of the jungle, and went on to save him from certain death at the hands of the king's soldiers, by killing both her father and her brother.

The first act takes place on board a steamer bound for Marseilles from Saigon via Cambodia (see figure 6). When asked by Aimée to explain how he came to live with a barbarian wife and rule over the Sibang people for eight years, Lenormand's Jason explains his own seduction in terms of a fascination with unknown dark territories: the years with the Princess constituted a perilous and enticing voyage into the depths of the earth from which he is now thankfully re-emerging into the light (38). While he can only be circumspect in his account of his fascination with the Orient in his conversations with Aimée and her colonial administrator father (de Listrac, the Creon-figure), in exchanges with the Princess later on in the first act (48ff.), it becomes clear that this *soi-disant* anthropologist (like other colonial adventurers and, most famously, Kurtz in Conrad's *Heart of Darkness*) is really fascinated by the Nietzschean will to power: both over others and increasingly over other worlds.

In a fascinating scene towards the end of the first act on board the steamer, the Princess reminds her treacherous husband of the time when he urged her to take him to the edge of the forest to consult the spirits of the other world in a magic pool (48ff.). Terrified but driven by the desire to possess hidden secrets, this Jason clearly wanted to have power over both present and future; and he could only ever enjoy such power through the considerable skills of his Asian wife. Even earlier in Act I, when asked by de Listrac why his rule over the Sibang had ended, Lenormand's Jason clearly concedes the power of other worlds, albeit in a suavely enigmatic response. He explains that you could say (in colonial terms) that his rule ended on account of a conspiracy; but that it was in reality the ancient gods who had chased him out of the country by blowing hatred into the souls of the Sibang people (17).

It is no doubt significant that this Jason figure, de Mezzana, is not entirely French, being the son of a Catalan mother and a Corsican father who was brought up in Barcelona. He is very far from being the colonial functionary like de Listrac; and with his pioneering (Corsican-corsaire, piratical?) spirit he is clearly representative of the first nineteenth-century phase in the French colonial process. But after his marriage to Aimée between the first and second acts and his alliance with the colonial class, he joins forces with the capitalists who are now in the throes of buying up Sibang and (at de Listrac and de Mezzana's suggestion) seeking to appoint the Princess as their puppet dictator. From fascination with the barbaric 'other', de Mezzana has now moved towards gross economic, political and social exploitation of that other, all in the spurious names of progress and security.

If Lenormand employs the relationship between Medea and Jason to reflect France's exploits in Indochina since the 1860s, he uses the children, whose role is greatly enhanced in the play, in order to comment upon the rather more recent troubles there. From the first act in the play, the children's mixed race is deemed to be a deficiency – from the hideous eugenicist point of view expressed both by the white Europeans and the Princess herself, who sees her sons' inability to withstand the disease of the jungle (that necessitates their repatriation to a missionary in Cambodia) to be a direct consequence of their hybridity (28–9). Wooed as they are by both Western religious practices and increasingly by Western symbols of progress – the children's fascination with technology is constantly encouraged during the course of the play by their father and de Listrac – they find it difficult to relate to their barbarian mother. She in turn experiences what Frantz Fanon (the Antillean psychiatrist) identified as the 'psycho-existential problem' of colonial inter-relationships,[23] being denied in her case recognition by her own children on grounds of her ethnicity (47). But her anxieties for her sons' future in a white society clearly relate equally to broader concerns over French–Indochinese relations.

In the second act, after de Mezzana (the Jason figure) has married into the colonial class, he cynically seeks to reforge a pact with his estranged wife in order to exploit Sibang's economic potential. He visits the Princess in the hotel to which she has been confined in Marseilles and explains that he and his new father-in-law will provide her with letters to help her return to Indochina. The Princess disdainfully retorts: *'Je n'ai pas besoin de ton aide, pour régner!'* (I have no need of your help to return to power) (82). As with the Indochinese rebels who had begun their resistance movements in the late 1920s, the Princess refuses to deal with the treacherous imperialists whose promises of progress really mean a denial of self-determination.

When the Princess realises at the very end of the second act that the children are more important to de Mezzana than his new wife, Lenormand is implying that for the capitalist West the territories are in a very real sense of more intrinsic value than its European heartland. With this realisation, as in Euripides' tragedy, infanticide becomes the most obvious form of revenge. But here in the French version, Medea will kill her children in order to avenge not only her father and her brother, but also her people, who have similarly been betrayed by Jason, whose cynicism has led him to sell them out to the forces of Western capitalism.

When the Princess has made up her mind to kill her children, she realises that her children's fate was sealed long ago. At the start of Act III, when she is in the newly wedded couple's large villa on the outskirts of Marseilles, she again recalls (now in conversation with her faithful servant) the time when she assisted her adventuring husband in his communion with the other world: what they had both seen (but neither understood) when they went to the heart of the forest was two bloodstained corpses floating in the stream (113). Now she understands the omens for the first time: as with liberation from the coloniser, separation from her European husband necessarily entails bloodshed. As she sits with her children in their bedroom at the top of the house in the final scene of the play, soothing them as they fall into the fatal sleep that the mango jelly she has given them brings upon them, she assures them that when they wake they will be free of the blight of industry (142) – the obverse realities of the colonial dream that dominate the Western world and are about to engulf Asia as well.

In these final moments of the play, we realise that Lenormand's Medea has been seduced, then schooled and finally betrayed by Western ways, just as the French-educated, Indochinese rebels have been. And now, like them, she is seeking a terrible revenge on her enemy by destroying the 'European' side of herself at enormous personal cost. But unlike Euripides' protagonist, Lenormand's Medea has (like the continent she embodies) no unequivocal victory over her enemy: following her children's death, she opens the window, salutes her ancestor, the sun, proudly declaring her independence ('*J'ai trouvé mon royaume* . . .' [I have found my realm], 142), only to take a fatal leap from the ledge in the mistaken belief that she is about to be ushered away in the chariot of the sun. The French Indochinese Medea and her people, as we know too well and as Lenormand so presciently prefigures here in his play, will have to wait many more years to escape the imperialist forces of the Western world.

Medea today is regularly understood as an outsider, but this has not always been the case. Since the Renaissance she has been represented in turn as a witch, an abandoned wife and a proto-typical feminist.[24] The contemporary stress on Medea's ethnic difference dates back to the first part of the nineteenth century. As early as 1821 her ethnicity was of central concern in the theatre in Franz Grillparzer's trilogic version of the myth, *Das Goldene Vließ*, which was written and performed against a background of violently anti-semitic riots in Austria.[25] But it was not until the twentieth century that Medea, the ethnic 'other', became a dominant concern in dramatic treatments of the myth.

When the actress Sybil Thorndike toured South Africa in the part of Medea in Gilbert Murray's version of the play in 1928–29, she recorded what can now be seen as a representative shift in response to Euripides' tragedy at that time. Thorndike recalls how the management of the theatre in Johannesburg (after considerable pressure from the company) had agreed exceptionally to allow black people (albeit segregated in the dress-circle) to join the audience. Thorndike comments:

Until now it had been for me a war cry for all oppressed people – now it was the blacks, as Medea, crying out against the civilised whites in the person of Jason, the Greek. And they felt it. You heard sort of deep-breathing sounds coming from the dress-circle, and it was absolutely thrilling.[26]

If the South African context afforded the English actress a new perspective on the play, Lenormand's version some two years later went on to develop those insights further. The audiences who saw *Asie* in Paris in 1931, and then two years later in Italy, Austria and Greece, were being shown just how readily Euripides' play can lend itself to a fully developed allegory of the modern colonial struggle. Here in Lenormand's play, Medea, cast in the role of Asia herself, is wooed and exploited for European gain, but ultimately and defiantly refuses the trappings of the capitalist West.

Notes

This article was originally delivered as a paper at the conference on 'Classics and Colonialism', organised by Barbara Goff, on 11 May 2001 at the Institute of Classical Studies, London. I am grateful to both the organiser and members of the audience for their helpful comments.

1. From April to July 1986 alone there were two major anti-racist productions of *Medea* in London with multi-racial casts: Theatre Clwyd at the Young Vic (trans. J. Brooke, dir. Toby Robertson) in April, with a white woman exiled among blacks; the Lyric,

Hammersmith (trans. P. Vellacott, dir. Mary McMurray) May to July, with Madhur Jaffrey as Medea. For the relatively late arrival of postcolonial theory within the British academy, see Bart Moore-Gilbert, *Postcolonial Theory: Contexts, Practices, Politics* (London and New York: Verso, 1997), pp. 5–11.

2. Fiona Macintosh, 'Introduction: The Performer in Performance', in Edith Hall, Fiona Macintosh and Oliver Taplin (eds), '*Medea' in Performance 1500–2000* (Oxford: Legenda, 2000), p. 21.

3. W. Kleinhardt, '*Medea* – Originalität und Variation in der Darstellung einer Rache', Ph. D. dissertation, Hamburg University, 1962; Lillian Corti, *The Myth of Medea and the Murder of Children* (Westport, CT: Greenwood Press, 1998), pp. 180–6.

4. The only full-length study of Lenormand is Paul Blanchart's *Le Théâtre de H.-R. Lenormand: Apocalypse d'une société* (Paris: Masques-Revue Internationale d'Art Dramatique, 1947). For a highly informed background to the period, see Dorothy Knowles, *French Drama of the Inter-War Years 1918–1939* (London: Harrap, 1967).

5. For European tours in Italy, Greece and Austria, see Henri-René Lenormand, *Les Confessions d'un auteur dramatique*, vol. 2 (Paris: Michel, 1953), pp. 240–54. For critical attention, see Angela Belli, 'Lenormand's *Asie* and Anderson's *The Wingless Victory*', *Comparative Literature*, 19 (1967): 226–39; and E. van Zyl Smit, 'Contemporary Witch – Dramatic Treatments of the Medea Myth', D. Litt. dissertion, Stellenbosch University, 1987, pp. 154–79.

6. Corti, *The Myth of Medea*, pp. 190ff.; Macintosh, 'Introduction', in Hall et al. (eds), '*Medea' in Performance*, pp. 21–2.

7. Lenormand, *Les Confessions*, pp. 247 ff.

8. Ibid., p. 249. For the Delphic Festivals organised by Sikelianos, see Fiona Macintosh, 'Tragedy in Performance: Nineteenth- and Twentieth-century Productions', in P. E. Easterling (ed.), *The Cambridge Companion to Greek Tragedy* (Cambridge: CUP, 1997), pp. 305–6; and Gonda Van Steen, '"The World's a Circular Stage": Aeschylean Tragedy through the Eyes of Eva Palmer-Sikelianou', *International Journal of the Classical Tradition*, 8 (Winter 2002): 375–93.

9. Cf. Christopher Innes, *Avant Garde Theatre 1892–1992*, rev. edn (London and New York: Routledge, 1993), p. 3.

10. Lenormand, *Les Confessions*, p. 255.

11 Ibid., pp. 79–81 for the censorship of *A L'ombre du mal* in 1924; and

Knowles, *French Drama of the Inter-War Years*, pp. 94–5 for the withdrawal of *Le Simoun* from the repertoire of the Comédie-Française.

12. For the pre-eminence of French Indochina, see Albert Sarraut, *La mise en valeur des colonies françaises* (Paris: Payot, 1923): '*A tout point de vue [l'Indochine] est la plus importante, la plus développée et la plus prospère de nos colonies . . .*' cited in Jean Martin, *L'Empire Triomphant 1871–1936*, vol. 2 *Maghreb, Indochine, Madagascar, îles et comptoirs* (Paris: Éditions Denoël, 1990), p. 183.

13. For an excellent account of the ideological context, see Raoul Girardet, *L'Idée Coloniale en France 1871 à 1962* (Paris: La Table Ronde, 1972), pp. 175ff.

14. Innes, *Avant Garde Theatre*, p. 12.

15. Girardet, *L'Idée Coloniale en France*, p. 185.

16. Ibid., p. 186.

17. Ibid., pp. 192–3.

18. Ibid., pp. 218, 209. All translations from the French are my own unless indicated otherwise.

19. Martin, *L'Empire triomphant*, pp. 260–4.

20. Girardet, *L'Idée Coloniale en France*, pp. 195ff.

21. Cited in ibid., p. 209.

22. Henri-René Lenormand, *Théâtre Complet*, vol. IX (Paris: G. Crès, 1936), Act I, Tableau III, 38. All subsequent references to the play will appear in brackets after the citation.

23. Frantz Fanon, *Black Skin, White Masks*, trans. Charles Lam Markmann (London: Pluto Press, 1986); *Peau noire, masques blancs* (Paris: Éditions du Seuil, 1952).

24. Macintosh, 'Introduction', in Hall et al. (eds), '*Medea*' *in Performance*, pp. 7–31.

25. Ibid., pp. 12–14.

26. Cited by Elizabeth Sprigge, *Sybil Thorndike Casson* (London: Gollancz, 1971), p. 186.

4. Lysistrata Joins the Soviet Revolution: Aristophanes as Engaged Theatre

Marina Kotzamani

Aristophanes' Lysistrata is the rebel woman par excellence of classical Greek drama. The heroine's intervention to stop the Peloponnesian war between the Athenians and the Spartans is a rebellious act of revolutionary magnitude. Lysistrata successfully organises and leads a great popular mobilisation, which is in fact a women's mobilisation. A supreme political strategist, the comic heroine is effective in forcing the men to end the war by rallying support from women all over Greece. Lysistrata's pressure tactics on the men are boldly original. The women withhold sex from men until they conclude peace. Moreover, they occupy the Acropolis, to prevent men from obtaining money for the war from the treasury. By choosing the Acropolis as the site of their protest they transgress on a traditionally male space, emblematic of Athenian democracy.

The recent war of the USA against Iraq has highlighted the significance of *Lysistrata* as a classic: an open-ended work that can be shaped to respond to cultural concerns across time and geography. As part of the *Lysistrata* Project, over 1,000 readings of the play were organised in fifty-nine countries around the world on 3 March 2003, to protest the war that was then imminent. Indeed, whatever the meaning of the play in antiquity, the women's rebellion has exerted strong fascination on modern audiences. *Lysistrata* is by far the most popular Aristophanic play in the stage history of Attic comedy since the nineteenth century.

On the ideological level, a striking feature of modern productions is that they have tended to focus exclusively either on the sexual or on the political import of the women's rebellion. Thus, we can clearly distinguish between sexual and political interpretations of the play. While today it is unproblematic that women may have a strong interest in both sex and in momentous social issues such as war, this was certainly not the case before the Second World War. Interpretations focusing on the strike, such as Maurice Donnay's notorious Belle Époque version (1892), undermine the occupation of the Acropolis and use the play as a springboard for the exploration of female sexuality.[1] By contrast, interpretations emphasising women's concern to end the war, such as Laurence Housman's feminist version (1910), downplay the sexual element and demonstrate women's aptitude for politics.[2]

Perhaps the most remarkable political interpretation of *Lysistrata* in the twentieth century was a Soviet production directed by Nemirovich-Danchenko for the Moscow Art Theatre's Musical Studio in 1923. In the spirit of its rebellious heroine, the production presented a highly original interpretation of the Attic comedy, directly reflecting the experience of the October Revolution. No less a figure than Anatoli Vassilievitch Lunacharsky, the first People's Commissar of Education of the newly founded Soviet Union, singled out the *Lysistrata* production in 1925 as 'an achievement of very great importance', adding: 'The *reviewers* on our daily newspapers did not fully comprehend its importance, but of course it will be understood by the historians of our contemporary theatre.'[3]

Modern Western scholarship on the Soviet theatre has generally ignored this production without apologies. In this article, I show that *Lysistrata* was an innovative project, which thoroughly challenged theatrical tradition. Nemirovich-Danchenko's interpretation has a unique place in the stage history of Aristophanes' plays as the first modern interpretation of Attic comedy as *théâtre du peuple*. At the same time, *Lysistrata* is significant to the development of the Soviet theatre in the 1920s. I discuss the production as an exemplary model of the new revolutionary theatre, especially as envisioned by Lunacharsky, the official representative of state policy on culture at the time. I also argue that *Lysistrata* should receive greater attention in the West as the Moscow Art Theatre's

(MAT) first successful attempt to respond to the aesthetic and ideological concerns of the early post-revolutionary period.

Rehearsals for *Lysistrata* started in the autumn of 1922. Stanislavsky and the main company of MAT had already left, in September, on the celebrated tours to Europe and the United States, which would keep them abroad until August 1924. Nemirovich-Danchenko, the co-director of the theatre, had stayed behind in Moscow with only the apprentices of the studios. The MAT was in dire straits. Five years had elapsed since the October Revolution and it had still not managed to secure its position as a significant force in Moscow's cultural life. Critics of all leanings mercilessly attacked its ideological and artistic principles, which now seemed dated and irrelevant. As the director of the Theatre Section of Narkompros, V. E. Meyerhold had launched the 'Theatrical October', threatening to close down academic theatres as reactionary. Meyerhold scorned the MAT's naturalism as petit bourgeois and anti-theatrical, and warned that it 'contaminated' the audience of workers, peasants and soldiers.[4] Even though generally supportive of the theatre, Lunacharsky, too, had expressed concern that its offerings 'were too refined for a proletarian audience . . . [who] perhaps have reason to be dissatisfied'.[5] The Narkom thought it essential for the MAT to unburden its art of meticulous attention to detail. In 1922, Jury Sobolev, a critic traditionally loyal to the MAT, still could not see any signs of progress:

A revolution occurred in Russia, it swept by in blizzards and storms . . . but the Art Theatre remained just as it was under the pressure of the theatrical waves. It gave very few signs of its participation in revolutionary contemporaneity. Too quickly it has become a sort of museum, a monument to past culture, carefully preserved and protected.[6]

Nemirovich-Danchenko's correspondence in the early 1920s affords a vivid inside view of the demoralised spirit that characterised the MAT in the early post-revolutionary period. In January 1923, when *Lysistrata* was already in rehearsal, the director wrote a letter to V. Kachalov, reviewing the course of the MAT in the post-revolutionary period. He stated the problems lucidly and honestly, and at the same time conveyed a sense of confusion, even despair about the future:

Five years, it is now the sixth year we have been disoriented. Five years ago, we thought that in two or three years . . . we would adapt to life's novel circumstances. And yet, the sixth year is now running and we are still a long way from having clear plans of even our most immediate future conduct. Apparently, we are now standing more firmly on our feet, yet frequently, we still attach everlasting value to what has run its course or take the ephemeral sensation for a new goal.[7]

Indeed, a central problem of the MAT in the post-revolutionary period was the forging of a new artistic identity. Nemirovich-Danchenko was eager to study how other directors responded to the novel circumstances. In April 1922 he had been strongly impressed by the solutions E. Vachtangov had adopted in the *Princess Turandot*. In his congratulatory letter to the director he wrote: 'The director of this production knows exactly what to discard from the old and what is to remain intact and knows how to do it. Yes, the gentle and bold hand is here functioning instinctively, confidently fleshing out the course of tomorrow's theatre.'[8]

The *Princess Turandot* was part of a string of comic productions that flooded the theatre in 1922. Meyerhold's *Magnanimous Cuckold*, A. Granovsky's *The Sorceress* and A. Tairov's *Giroflé-Girofla*, which all appeared in that year, celebrated theatricality and delighted audiences with their optimism and humour.[9] The civil war had ended and the fiercely polemical attacks of 'Theatrical October' against the academic theatres had died out. Summing up the more relaxed, optimistic mood in 1922, Lunacharsky wrote:

We are experiencing a period of some relaxation after the nervous fit in which everyone lived during the heroic years of the revolution . . . People want to laugh and seek relief in impressions far removed from that which has disturbed, tormented and enraptured them. Russian citizens have a basic right to a pleasant, cheerful hour of light, carefree amusement.[10]

Nemirovich-Danchenko's decision to mount *Lysistrata* appears to have been partly influenced by the cheerful theatrical atmosphere of 1922. In October of that year, he noted in his correspondence the turn of theatres towards lighter offerings, shrewdly remarking: 'Academic theatres are responding to the audience's wishes to see cheerful productions, with Lunacharsky's approval.' Even though at the lowest ebb of despair, confessing, 'I am ready to quit', Nemirovich-Danchenko was far from giving up. In the same letter he revealed: 'I will probably produce Aristophanes' *Lysistrata*, for which I will write chorals and songs.'[11]

From the earliest post-revolutionary period, Aristophanes had been claimed as an agitational writer, whose plays could be directly related to contemporary political and social circumstances. In 1917, Lunacharsky had expressed the wish that 'timely Aristophanic comedy will find its place in the workers' theatre'.[12] Indeed, in 1919, there appeared a new edition of a late nineteenth-century adaptation of *Plutus* by D. P. Averkiev, entitled *The Golden Grandfather*. In this text, the original characters have been replaced by Russian peasants and the action takes place in a village near Moscow. The editors recommended this version as appropriate for performance on the amateur stages of Russian villages and hoped that Aristophanes could reconquer in modern times an audience of peasants.[13] The Attic dramatist had also attracted the attention of Meyerhold. As director of the First Theatre RSFSR, he had announced in 1920 the inclusion of *Women in the Assembly* in the repertory's programme. However, he never staged this or any other play by Aristophanes, even though he had expressed a high regard for the political and artistic value of his comedies.[14]

In accord with revolutionary ideology, Nemirovich-Danchenko saw Aristophanes in political terms. Even if he had been partly encouraged to stage *Lysistrata* by the general tendency towards cheerful productions in 1922, he was certainly determined not to mount a frivolous comedy. From the first readings of the play, he emphasised that the ancient dramatist was 'a great popular poet', making references to his 'relentless, healthy and highly moral sarcasm'.[15] *Lysistrata* impressed him as 'a brilliant' comedy, of exceptional social, moral and political relevance. Nemirovich-Danchenko opted for an interpretation that would limit the erotic element, characterising the play as a 'popular and heroic comedy'.[16]

Lysistrata is a popular play primarily on account of its characters and theme. In his rehearsal notes to actors, Nemirovich-Danchenko clarified that 'the characters of this comedy are the people', as distinct, on the one hand, from individuals and, on the other, from the aristocracy: 'The life of individuals is of no concern here and it is significant that there is an emphasis on the popular, not on the aristocratic element.'[17] He described the women as 'vendors of grain, onions, fruit, poultry', clearly indicating their humble origins.[18] Thematically, the play deals with a mobilisation of the people to achieve a worthy political and social cause. Nemirovich-Danchenko's synopsis of the play, printed in the production's programme, leaves no doubt as to his reading. There is considerable refinement and variety in the description of the play's action in agitational terms, presenting it as an organised political uprising: for example, 'The women . . . under the command of Lysistrata conspire to save Greece.' To this end, they are 'united in a pan-Hellenic confederation of peace and love'. Their 'revolt is not only of an emotionally passive character but is also active', as they seize the Acropolis. In the negotiations with the Athenian and Spartan envoys, men 'listen' to Lysistrata's 'ardent, patriotic plea and conclude peace'.[19]

Far from adopting an objective perspective, Nemirovich-Danchenko's interpretation is biased in favour of the women mobilising for peace, idealistically described in rehearsal as 'healthy, strong, life-loving'.[20] By contrast, the old men represent the reactionary establishment who have a vested interest in the continuation of the war. The central axis of Nemirovich-Danchenko's *Lysistrata* is the conflict between the two Choruses, symbolising conservatism and progressive change. Analogies with the contemporary Soviet Union in the early twenties are inescapable. In the aftermath of the bloody strife between communists and whites, Nemirovich-Danchenko had decided to mount a play directly relevant to recent events by virtue of its theme (civil war) and politically correct, as it would celebrate the victorious forces of the revolution.

Nemirovich-Danchenko's reading of *Lysistrata* signified a bold and important change of policy. In sharp contrast to his own and Stanislavsky's earlier post-revolutionary statements in defence of the MAT's apoliticism, Nemirovich-Danchenko now clearly declared that theatre must be political. In his letter to Kachalov of 17 July 1921, he had interpreted Meyerhold's removal from the directorial post of TEO as confirmation that 'The course we decided on while you were here finally prevails on all fronts. That is, to stay away from politics . . . to firmly believe that only real art is necessary, even in the most extreme moments of revolutionary imperatives.'[21] The autumn of 1922 Nemirovich-Danchenko's views had in fact moved closer to Meyerhold's. In the rehearsals of *Lysistrata* he asserted:

Academic theatres are frequently reproached for being backward, for not responding to the times. Justifiably so. We should not keep away from life, nor claim we are apolitical. Total apoliticism, what absurdity! . . . Withdrawing into oneself is pure conservatism. The artist lives with his time. Moreover, it is interesting to respond to the demands of a new audience.[22]

Lysistrata also offered an excellent opportunity for Nemirovich-Danchenko to distance himself from the MAT's stigmatised approach to *mise-en-scène*, projecting naturalistic detail and sombre psychologism. As he explained, he had partly chosen to mount the play for its apt exemplification of contemporary artistic values. *Lysistrata* could not be associated with the company's traditional offerings, as it completely 'lacked sentimentalism and the petit bourgeois mentality'. Nemirovich-Danchenko's characterisation of the play as a popular comedy, then, also applies to its form. *Lysistrata* is rich in 'eternal ideas' such as 'nature, war, peace',[23] clearly and boldly, even crudely represented. Ambiguity and subtlety are swept away by exuberant gaiety, colourfulness and optimism.

Nemirovich-Danchenko commissioned a new version of *Lysistrata* from the dramatist Dmitry Smolin, which accurately expressed his popular interpretation of the play.[24] However, this version departs significantly from the Greek original. Aristophanes presents the women's scheme as a comic utopia. The sexual instinct is the overriding, compelling reason to conclude peace. Urgency is comically emphasised with the insistent presence of raised phalluses, forcing the course of events towards resolution. Aristophanes is playful and deeply ironical in identifying the achievement of peace with sexual satisfaction. The conclusion of the treaty between Athenians and Spartans is metaphorically presented as negotiation over the sexual possession of Peace, personified as a beautiful, tempting maiden. In Aristophanes' utopia the sexual instinct reigns, annulling the possibility of political deliberation.

Smolin toned down the emphasis on sexual deprivation as a driving force of the plot. Sexual jesting runs the risk of distracting attention from the struggle for peace or of trivialising it. Smolin's decision to avoid it strengthens the emphasis on the political interpretation of the play's action. In the Russian version the resolution is the outcome of meditated and carefully implemented political scheming. Far from falling prey to instinct, characters display admirable reticence and a clear, controlling head. Smolin tightened the plot and recast it in almost realistic terms, placing central emphasis on the presentation of an effective political struggle.

In the Russian version, the personification of Peace as a sexual incitement to negotiation has been removed. Smolin presents the meeting of the delegations in lofty terms, alien to the Aristophanic spirit. Spartan and Athenian warriors are welcomed to the negotiations as heroes: 'Welcome gallant sons of Sparta / Favoured land of mighty Zeus / Worthy sons of your fore-fathers, / Bold, audacious and defiant.' Athenians sing as they enter: 'With our spears aslant / With our shields on our arms, / With our daggers prepared, / Fearless we come / In the thick of the battle!'[25] This is in marked contrast to the picture of warriors in the original: 'Behold our local Sons of the Soil, stretching / their garments away from their groins, like wrestlers.'[26] Towards the end of the play, the Athenians and Spartans are eager to conclude the peace treaty because they claim to have realised the value of peace. Rather than allude to urgent sexual need, in an interpolated moral sermon they assure Lysistrata that: 'Our woes have made a unit of us. / We are all parts of one large body, / Aching and crying for peace and love.'[27] The women's mobilisation has served a distinct didactic purpose.

Smolin's adaptation of the choral passages also strongly supports the political interpretation of the play. There is a marked distinction in the treatment of the male and the female Chorus. While Smolin almost left the old men's line assignment intact, he redistributed the women's choral lines throughout the play to various speakers.[28] In this way he constructed a biased picture of the choral battle, presenting it, as it were, from the women's point of view. The rendering of the male Chorus as a unified and undifferentiated body functions symbolically as an ironic representation of the establishment. The preservation of the ancient Greek choral conception, which is differentiated from the episodic structure, also serves comically to underline the elders' inefficiency and inability to act. By contrast, the polyphonic presentation of the female camp directs the audience's attention and sympathy towards the women. Moreover, it directly links their choral parts to the action, supporting its development. Indeed, in the Russian version unified action is primarily important, as it serves the purpose of conveying the political message of the women's mobilisation clearly and directly. Far from sacrificing the tightness of the plot, the inclusion of choral passages in the Russian version generally supports it.

The strong connection between the women's choral parts and the action becomes clearly evident when we consider their strategic placement in the Russian version. Passages instrumental to the action's progress, such as the battle of the sexes and the exchange about the defection of the women, have been left in their original position and have been incorporated into the development of the plot through the technique of individualising the chorus. All other choral parts in the Russian version are employed to mark a significant advance in the women's action towards the termination of the civil war. Significantly, most of these passages have been moved to the end of each act. With suitable modifications, they serve propagandistic purposes.

The most striking revision of a choral passage for propaganda purposes is the battle of the sexes, immediately following the exit of the Proboulos.[29] In the Russian version it takes place at the end of the second act, after the tempting of Kinesias, as the final climactic confrontation between the old men and the women before the reconciliation. Smolin imaginatively revised this choral passage into a parabasis: all speakers directly address themselves to the audience. Moreover, he transformed the original into a debate, adopting a theatrical form popular with Russian audiences in the first post-revolutionary years.[30]

The theme of the debate also had distinct contemporary resonance. The Choruses quarrel over whether women are fit to give advice on the government of the state. This is yet another confrontation between the old and conservative against the new world pressing for change. Smolin followed the same tactic of speaker assignment as in the initial battle, discussed earlier. The Chorus of old men argue against the motion, whereas women, individually and collectively, argue for it. The long choral passage has been revised into short attacks, clearly establishing points. For example, these can be as brief and succinct as 'They have squandered the wealth of their fathers / What can they bring to the temple's treasure?', which a woman puts forward against the old men. The scene thus takes the form of a modern debate, where the rival parties address themselves separately to the men and the women in the audience rallying their support. Smolin inserted contemporary references in the exchange, as is evident from the obvious anachronisms in the addresses of the women: 'dear women comrades', 'Citizens do we not render tribute / By giving sons and daughters to the State?'[31]

Smolin's revisions make the contemporary significance of the play everywhere apparent. The subject of *Lysistrata* could, of course, be directly related to recent events in the Soviet Union, as it deals with the civil war. In her final long reconciliation speech, the heroine encourages the drawing of analogies: 'I censure Spartans and Athenians both / And all of you engaged in bloody strife!'[32] However, direct references to reality are generally subtle and limited. The adaptation invites contemporary comparison mainly through its depiction of a popular uprising recast in modern terms as a political mobilisation against the status quo, which the post-revolutionary audience could intimately relate to. At the centre of the action is the conflict between the establishment and women, as the people. Through the biased glorification of the women, Smolin simultaneously glorified the people's October Revolution.

Rehearsals for *Lysistrata* lasted eight or nine months. The production opened on 16 June 1923. Nemirovich-Danchenko's rehearsal notes reveal not only his emphasis on the play's political interpretation discussed earlier, but also his willingness to experiment with new artistic forms, unfamiliar to the MAT. From the earliest period of rehearsals he appears to have explored a monumental and physical, non-psychological approach to acting, clearly and unambiguously instructing the cast, 'all must be played in an awe-inspiring scale. No rationalisations!'[33] Emphasis should fall on passion, broad gesture and feeling as opposed to painstaking refinement. Indeed, concerning the impersonation of the women, he instructs actresses 'not to present the sophisticated type of woman, but to convey the lucid voice of the heart, the luminous health, the cry of the body and the explosive force of hot temperament'.[34] Nemirovich-Danchenko's insistent description of the people in broadly corporeal terms suggests that a naturalistic approach would be inappropriate for their portrayal. Apparently, he was highly satisfied with the actors' efforts, frequently praising their work in his rehearsal notes and extolling their conscientiousness and passionate devotion to the project.[35]

Nemirovich-Danchenko's experimental spirit also prompted him to commission the set and costumes from Isaac Rabinovich, who had been strongly influenced by cubo-futurism and the work of Alexandra Exter. His designs were noted for their humour and brilliant use of colour. For *Lysistrata* he designed an abstract and functional set, which impressed Nemirovich-Danchenko highly. Lightheartedly referring to the production in retrospect, he recognised the importance of Rabinovich's influence in stimulating experimentation:

In the production of *Lysistrata* a whole series of the canons of the older productions was violated . . . While producing *Lysistrata* and working in contact with the designer Rabinovich, it was not easy for me to infringe upon my traditions as an old line realist. It all started with the decision to have all the characters make their entrance on the stage through a trap – a violation of the plausibility and the logic of realistic theatre. Having permitted myself one liberty, I proceeded to permit a second and a third. To break is to break!'[36]

In a letter to Loujsky in the spring of 1923, Nemirovich-Danchenko conveys thorough-going optimism about his project: 'You know, when I dream of *Lysistrata*'s production, I have the impression there has not been anything as beautiful in the theatre, in recent years.'[37] The opening of *Lysistrata* was a dream come true: the production was a resounding success. It held the stage of the MAT for 215 performances and was taken on tour to Leningrad as well as other major cities in the USSR. In the autumn of 1925, it was also shown in the West, in a joint bill with other Musical Studio productions. After a brief engagement in Berlin, in October 1925, *Lysistrata* opened in New York in December and was subsequently transferred to Chicago in the spring.

The production was consistent with Nemirovich-Danchenko's reading of the play, as expressed in the adaptation, as well as in his correspondence and rehearsal notes. All elements of the staging gave prominence to a popular interpretation of *Lysistrata*, immediately relevant to contemporary political reality. Moreover, the production exemplified a formal, yet realist style which, far from being idly experimental, organically served the revolutionary ideology of this interpretation.

The popular conception is immediately identifiable in the clothing of the Choruses. Rabinovich's costume sketches for

Lysistrata are inspired by a popular aesthetic, emphasising simplicity and lack of sophistication. He uses dress effectively to create a sharp contrast between the conservatism of the elders and the progressive spirit of the women. The old men's Chorus created a comical, distinctly grotesque effect, enhanced by exaggerated make-up. Exaggerated also is the emphasis on metal in the old men's costume, transparently functioning as an ironic comment on the disintegrating old world of wars. Men are heavily armed with shiny helmets and breastplates and carry shields, swords, spears, forks and sticks. The helmets are quixotic, designed in antiquated, fancy geometrical shapes, making them look like weird species of birds. The rigidity of the metal in which they are encased obstructs freedom of movement and humorously contrasts with the fragility of the elders. As a Chorus in full armour charging and being thwarted by the women, they look like pieces of garbage, thrown in a heap.

In contrast to the old men's costumes, Rabinovich's sketches for the female Chorus are not humorous. Dress is comfortable, allowing for ease of movement, and is generally not beautifying or sexually provocative. Rather, it is primarily intended to make the women wearing it look strong. Indeed, female Chorus members confront the armed old men with the strength of their bare arms and shoulders, evoking the proletariat's raised fist. Make-up boldly accentuates the eyes, contributing to a concentrated, determined look.

Rabinovich's popular costume sketches are interesting and stimulating, but his highest achievement is the set design, remarkable for its aesthetic, functionality and rich symbolism. The designer won the first 'grand prize of theatrical decoration' for the set of *Lysistrata* at the Exhibition of Decorative Arts in Paris in 1925 and is still justifiably remembered for this contribution. His design was an architectural construction extremely simple, yet synthetic and monumental. It consisted of four semi-circular colonnades of draped white pillars, one central, two on the periphery and a lower one at the back, balancing a composition of platforms on four levels, linked by stairs. The entire structure could rotate, being set on a turntable. Platforms adjusted to the circular movement of the colonnades. Certain structural elements, such as the central colonnade, could also be manually rotated by the actors. In the absence of a front curtain, all revolutions took place in full view of the audience. The gleaming whiteness of the columns contrasted with a uniform bright blue background on the cyclorama.

The set was highly functional, allowing rapid scene changes without disturbing the continuity of the action.[38] Rotation revealed new configurations, suggesting allusively a variety of distinct locales in the Acropolis. Throughout the production, the transparency of the structure allowed the audience to visualise not just a specific locale but the entire world of the drama's action, 'Hellas' or even 'the universe'. At the same time, the non-illusionist set challenged spectators to acknowledge it as a theatrical, constructed configuration of steps and platforms.

Besides defining locale and allowing for the uninterrupted use of space, rotation also comprised an integral part of the action within each scene. Movement at varying speeds was frequently used to reflect the feeling and the moods of the characters. Moreover, it even functioned as an ironic counterpoint to the action. For example, at the arrival of the old men, the set moved slowly in front of the actors, humorously emphasising their laboriousness and fragility. Rotation also heightened the excitement of the battle between the male and the female Choruses: 'Men rush around the outer stationary rim, chasing the laughing women dancing in the inner columned scene, spinning like a mocking carousel.'[39] Frantic whirling in the finale was similarly used to accentuate the exhilaration and enthusiasm of the populace. Yet another function of rotation was to highlight the heroic aspects of the struggle. At one point, the peace-signing procession, leaping and jubilant, moved in the opposite direction to the moving structure, giving the impression of a 'Parthenon frieze brought to life'.[40]

Rabinovich's set for *Lysistrata* had highly sophisticated symbolic functions, projecting popular revolutionary ideology. The design is a perfect popular interpretation of the ancient Greek Acropolis as a social institution, emblematic of the *demos* or city. The work's prominent structural elements highlight its constructed, man-made nature. The open-ended semi-circular colonnades evoke the circle, indicating this is an incomplete structure. In production, rotation in full view of the audience draws attention to the building process, especially as this is frequently undertaken by the characters themselves. Thus, the set is literally what the people make of it, the embodiment of popular aspiration. Indeed, the people are so closely identified with their construct that they magically made all entrances and exits in the production through traps in the floor, springing in the midst of the structure. The audience does not see the actors separately from the set, entering or leaving it. In the absence of the front curtain, the constant presence of the structure makes it the focal point of attention, further emphasising the symbolic significance of the Acropolis as a popular, social institution.

The incompleteness of the structure both looks back to the old men's world, as a crumbling monument of the past, and looks forward to the world of the women and the young, as a building now in the process of construction, or reconstruction. The set can be viewed both as a mock epic, parodying the solidity of the classical Acropolis and as a monument worthy of the people who achieve peace. Thus the structure is delicately balanced between irony and heroism. In capturing the Acropolis, the female Chorus set out to redefine it as an institution. Throughout the production, the set is entirely under the women's control, and they make full use of its capabilities. They move on the steps and platforms as well as on the stage floor, whereas the old men are at all times confined to the ground. The mobility of the set admirably expresses the idea that the world is in flux and that change, 'revolution' is inevitable. Significantly, it is solely the women who rotate the movable colonnade on stage, indicating that they, as opposed to the old men, are in a position to instigate and to control change.

Rabinovich's non-illusionistic set design projects a utopian conception of the Acropolis as a popular social institution, which nevertheless seemed realisable in the early post-revolutionary period. The transparency of the set invites the play's characters, as well as the audience, to know it literally inside out, as they can view it from every angle, both external and internal. Significantly, the old men on the ground have a more limited perspective. The structure is not only open to full view but also to free and unlimited use. The Acropolis as a popular institution is in the service of the people and its function is in their hands. Mobility also indicates that it is a flexible institution, capable of readily adapting to popular needs. By the end of the production, the women have achieved a redefinition of the Acropolis from an aristocratic to a democratic institution, more open to the masses than ever before.

The performance also served perfectly *Lysistrata*'s popular interpretation. In the discussion of acting, critics focused on the Chorus, emphasising collective, as opposed to individual, performance.[41] Nemirovich-Danchenko had abandoned the MAT's familiar representation of a crowd as an ensemble of varied and distinct characters. According to Pavel Markov, individual features of the Chorus members were not pronounced, so as not to divert the audience's attention from the whole. The *New York Times* critic reported that 'the action itself is mass movement as the elements of the play are mass emotions'.

Mass action is in need of interpretation. It does not refer to a stylised collective, whose members are perfectly synchronised in movement, as is clearly indicated in the production's photographs. The multiple division of choral lines to individuals, groups of speakers, as well as to the Chorus, also testifies to a non-unified polyphonic impression of vocal effects. Presumably, line assignment to the Chorus does indicate that, occasionally, prosody and movement were non-individualised. Indeed, reviewers noted the 'abundant use of line and gesture in mass formation, attuned voices and rhythmic movement'. Moreover, the Chorus occasionally formed 'an organ of voices'. However, choral uniformity was only one among the devices used in performance. According to Pavel Markov, the great achievement of the production was that, while the Chorus gave the impression of a uniform whole, its members followed both the common rhythm and their own individual distinct rhythm. This was an essentially realist – though non-naturalist – depiction of the Chorus, integrating formalist elements into a representational conception.

The cast had successfully mastered an external, non-psychological performance mode, displaying a great variety of styles from popular entertainment. The manner of performing appeared 'lusty, vigorous, forthright, rough, loud and unashamed' and there was a rowdy quality to the humour: 'the humors are elemental, mass humors, generated in the pit of the stomach rather than the mind'. The farcical spirit prevailed in the portrayal of the old men. Buffoonery, burlesque, clowning, horse-play, all boldly combined to form a grotesque, satyr-like chorus. The old men made 'creaking' motions and had 'cracked', 'squeaky' senile voices that sounded almost inarticulate. Their leader gabbled like a turkey. At other times, 'the men cavort and bellow as amusingly as clowns in a circus'. The male actors also seem to have had extraordinary miming abilities: 'Russians are vigorous, magnetic mimes. They lord it over space. They vibrate even in moments of repose. Tawny muscular masters of themselves in relation to their surroundings.'

Nemirovich-Danchenko had opted to tone down comic exaggeration in the performance of the female Chorus, so as to keep impressions sharply distinct. The advocates of peace had to be presented as heroic, while their opponents were good-naturedly reduced to ridicule. Pavel Markov noted that the men's shaky, clumsy gestures highlighted the women's graceful movements. However, the Russian critic found the choreography of the women's plastic movements ineffective. It had a fake Duncan-esque plasticity, evoking sentimentalism completely alien to Aristophanes' spirit. Reviewers unanimously praised the female Chorus when its members, forgetting plasticity, vigorously plunged into the fighting.

The popular, revolutionary *Lysistrata* appropriately emphasised the confrontation between the Choruses as the central incident in the play. Reviewers regarded performance in the choral battles as the hallmark of Nemirovich-Danchenko's production:

The battle grew monstrously comical, a milling, electrifying piece of buffa play.[42]

At one time the stage was a howling mob of the sexes. The women shrieked and the men bellowed. The women seized saucepans and household materials and pounced upon the men, belaboring them with all their might and main. They jumped into the auditorium; they pranced about the stage; they fell into the orchestra pit.[43]

[The women] pummel and shower [the men] with pretend water, they kick and tear their shirts. They chase them off the street and up the aisles with the fleetness of deer and the enthusiasm of children.[44]

The choral battle took place on the whole stage, entirely occupying the spectators' field of view. Moreover, it spread into the orchestra, openly challenging the audience's autonomy. The direct address to the auditorium in the parabasis was the culmination of a persistent effort to engage the audience. The parabasis was interpreted as a modern political rally: the men on the right and the women on the left side of the stage wildly gestured with outstretched arms, passionately attempting to secure the favour of the audience, whom they addressed as 'citizens'. Debating and quarrelling took place 'almost in the laps of the astonished spectators'.

Faithful to the interpretation's popular spirit, the production employed a variety of techniques for engaging the audience. The absence of the front curtain and the breaking of the fourth wall convention unified the spaces of the auditorium and the stage, encouraging the identification of the audience as the people. Spectators could view the non-illusionistic set from the women's all-encompassing perspective and mentally complete it, just as the women proceeded to rotate or build it on stage. Less subtle, more openly propagandistic attempts to engage the audience included the spilling of the action into the auditorium and the intervention of the parabasis.

The central features of Nemirovich-Danchenko's popular *Lysistrata* production are now clearly apparent. Simplicity, a concentration on the essential and monumentality predominantly characterised this interpretation, aiming at maximum receptivity.

The restricted palette of primary colours, the skeletonised, functional set, the physical conception of the acting represented bold formal choices, integrated, however, into a realist conception. The production's essential traits carried a distinct and easily decodable symbolism, expressing the Soviet revolutionary ideology. A central concern was the projection of a sharp antithesis between the two Choruses, highlighted by contrasting choices of costume and acting style. On stage, the antithesis was also represented spatially: the women in charge of 'revolution' occupied the mobile set, while the elders, weighed down by the metal, were hopelessly left behind by the brave new world.

Indeed, Russian critics enthusiastically received *Lysistrata* as a contemporary spectacle, directly responding to the Soviet revolution. Yury Sobolev, who had previously criticised the MAT for its failure to keep up with the times, now found that '*Lysistrata* is a spectacle engendered by the revolution, a contemporary spectacle . . . because the superb conception of the dissolution of the army is illuminated by the reflection of the great ideas of our revolutionary actuality.'[45] Clearly, the production had successfully conveyed a political message relevant to the post-revolutionary audience:

The impetus of the battle and the intense dynamism of the action are intimately related to our feelings. When the women celebrate victory, coming together in a fervent dance, it is as if the whole of humanity is celebrating with them, free to enjoy happiness; the remnants, the broken chains of the old world, the world of wars are shattered.[46]

Compliance with revolutionary politics only partly explains the production's enthusiastic reception in Russia as a contemporary spectacle. More importantly, Nemirovich-Danchenko had succeeded in expressing *Lysistrata*'s ideological content in terms of a formal conception, strongly influenced by the theatre of the avant-garde. This allowed for the identification of the spectacle as a product of the new revolutionary aesthetic. However, the director had creatively assimilated the prototype, as he diverged significantly from the avant-garde model. Meyerhold, the representative of avant-garde theatre par excellence, had originally been officially assigned the task of creating the revolutionary theatre. Though constantly attacked on political grounds, his productions had typified the features of a new style, abundantly imitated in the Soviet theatre of the early twenties.[47]

Audience engagement, boldly emphasised in *Lysistrata*, was a primary consideration in structuring a revolutionary spectacle. Since the second version of *Mystery Bouffe* (1920), Meyerhold had rejected the front curtain, letting the action spill dynamically into the auditorium. In the staging of *Dawns* (1920), he had explored techniques for drawing spectators into the action to the limit. Challenging theatre's autonomy from the real world, he attempted to re-create in the theatre an actual mass meeting. Among the devices used was the interruption of the action to deliver news from the front, followed by a meeting with the audience, skilfully engaged into participating by actors planted into the orchestra. Nemirovich-Danchenko's employment of a bold avant-garde technique such as the direct address reveals the limits of his experimentation. The exhortations to the male and female spectators to take sides in the parabasis were purely rhetorical; actual participation was neither expected nor forthcoming. Such interaction would upset the continuity of the action, whose structure had significantly been tightened in the Russian version. Moreover, it would destroy the production's chief asset, its fast tempo and dynamism. As adapted by Nemirovich-Danchenko, then, the direct address to the audience was kept within the limits of theatrical convention.

Under Meyerhold's influence, revolutionary theatre in the early twenties had discarded stage decoration as a background to action. Indeed, there was a marked preference for architectural, functional sets, dominating a bare stage. With the *Magnanimous Cuckold* (1922), Meyerhold had launched constructivism in the theatre. Rabinovich's set for *Lysistrata* has many similarities to Liubov Popova's design for F. Grommelyck's play. Both exemplify all the typical traits of a constructivist scenic conception: they are non-illusionist, highly stylised and schematic. Moreover, both define two main areas of performance, the stage floor and the raised levels of the set, reached by stairways and connected by platforms. The two structures are also comparable in function. Both are utilitarian, multipurpose scaffolds, intimately tied to the action. Performance is so tightly structured in relation to the set that the animate and the inanimate almost form a conceptually inseparable whole. Perhaps the most striking similarity between the two constructions is that they both included centrally placed rotating elements which made key contributions to the action. Moreover, certain functions of movement are analogous in the two productions. In the *Magnanimous Cuckold*, as in *Lysistrata*, the three wheels placed in the background moved quickly, slowly, separately or together, reflecting the rhythm of the acting. Also, at times, the construction itself seemed to perform, adding an ironic comment to the action.[48] Meyerhold's acknowledgement that 'much in the tone of the performance was prompted by the constructivist set' also applies to *Lysistrata*.

However, similarities should not obscure significant differences between the two constructions. Even though Rabinovich had avant-garde credentials, Meyerhold never employed him, considering his work too decorative.[49] Popova and Meyerhold insisted on the strictly utilitarian function of the set, characteristically defining it as a 'machine for acting'. Unlike Rabinovich's work, the earlier avant-garde structure was not intended to be aesthetically pleasing. Moreover, it was supposedly without symbolic meaning. Interestingly, however, as Rudnitsky has noted, turning the stage into a working place for actors immediately acquired a symbolic function: in an analogous way to *Lysistrata*, actors appeared as constructors, building the revolutionary future.[50]

The architectural organisation of theatrical space in the early twenties seemed inseparable from an external approach to acting, laying primary emphasis on physical movement. Nemirovich-Danchenko's insistence on physicality in the performance of *Lysistrata* is essentially in keeping with avant-garde practice. Meyerhold had again pioneered experimentation with non-psychological acting methods, drawing inspiration from the fairground show, as well as from the circus and the music hall. He gradually developed his own system of acting, biomechanics, which was first publicly demonstrated in the *Magnanimous Cuckold*. Performance was entirely concentrated on the actor's body conceived in mechanical terms, as a machine. Onstage movement was economical, highly stylised and responsive to the partner, giving the impression the three actors were a single triadic body.

Nemirovich-Danchenko had absorbed the avant-garde mechanised conception of acting. However, in *Lysistrata*, even though the acting is highly physical, it never ceases to be representational. Perhaps Meyerhold's earlier post-revolutionary productions can be more closely related to *Lysistrata*. The ceaseless clowning of the actors in *Tarelkin's Death* (1922) who poured water over each other, fought with sticks and bulls' bladders and struggled with the whims of the set immediately brings to mind the rich physical activity in the battle of the *Lysistrata* production. The two versions of Mayakovsky's *Mystery Bouffe* (1918 and 1921) were also an influential prototype. These productions had demonstrated that acting forms inspired from popular entertainment could be used to great effect in performance.

Mystery Bouffe is also interesting for setting the precedent of adopting sharply contrasting moods to differentiate between revolutionary and reactionary crowds, resorting to the heroic and the comic spirit, respectively. Meyerhold had characterised the play as a 'heroic, epic and satiric depiction of the times',[51] and Mayakovsky had explained that 'mystery' referred to everything that is great, while 'bouffe' to everything comic in the revolution.[52] In production, actors playing the reactionary Clean resorted to an excessively caricaturist, farcical and grotesque acting style which sharply contrasted with the lyrical pathos of the revolutionary Unclean. The latter were dressed in identical workers' overalls, as Meyerhold wanted them to merge idealistically into a single two-dimensional placard image of the victorious class. The similarities with *Lysistrata*'s contrasting conception of the two Choruses are obvious.

Clearly, Nemirovich-Danchenko then utilised forms already developed by the avant-garde to construct his production in the revolutionary spirit. The exuberant theatricality, large gestures, sharp contrasts and fast tempo of the action rendered the play's political message easily decodable as revolutionary. Inspired by left-wing theatrical practice, Nemirovich-Danchenko had also resorted to a deliberate simplification of language and imagery to augment the production's receptivity. However, agitation in *Lysistrata* is more subtle, lacking the poster-like and crudely propagandistic flavour of the early revolutionary spectacles of the avant-garde. Nemirovich-Danchenko had softened the edges of Meyerhold's style, adapting it to a representational framework.

Significantly, the conception of realism presented in *Lysistrata*, a synthesis of avant-garde and traditional features, appears faithfully to reflect in practice Lunacharsky's vision of revolutionary theatre. In the early twenties, the Narkom sharply criticised the experimentation of the avant-garde, maintaining that its non-representational character imposed on the masses incomprehensible art-forms 'vague, contradictory, terrifying'.[53] He regarded abstraction as unsuitable for expressing the revolutionary ideology and concluded in 1922 that, for all its zeal, the avant-garde 'had not provided a picture, had not been able to provide a drama'.[54]

While favouring realism, however, Lunacharsky did not subscribe to the richly detailed, naturalistic depiction of daily life. Theatre aspired to the interpretation of reality: 'to observe the manifestations of life, to represent somehow its pulse, its essence, translating life freely into theatrical forms'.[55] This interpretative task could best be served by employing the techniques and methods of the avant-garde. The schematic, enlarged drawing of character and action could render a spectacle clear, simple and immediately comprehensible to the proletarian. Moreover, the employment of popular theatrical forms such as farce and melodrama, brought to the fore by the avant-garde, added vividness to a production, further facilitating its receptivity. Formal experimentation could be valuable, provided it did not exclude representationalism.

Lunacharsky termed his conception of style 'realistic expressionism' and defined it in 1922, on the occasion of *Carmen*'s production at the Bolshoi, as 'a realism that is native and familiar to us in all its determinants, and at the same time is unusual, constructed, so to speak, entirely in the new harmony, at the pitch of modern ideas and emotions'.[56] The Narkom regarded his conception as a synthesis or compromise between the academic theatrical tradition and the avant-garde. Revolutionary theatre should preserve the former's concern for realistic representation, rejecting, however, the naturalist model. Lunacharsky advocated the development of a new aesthetic which would adapt abstract avant-garde forms to a realistic framework.

By the mid-twenties Lunacharsky ascertained that the convergent movement he had envisioned between the left and the right theatre could clearly be apprehended in theatrical production.[57] *Lysistrata* has a singular place in the development of Soviet theatre, in that Lunacharsky enthusiastically and unequivocally recognised it as an exemplary model of his conception of the new theatre. On the occasion of the MAT's twenty-fifth anniversary in the autumn of 1923, he gave a vivid description of the revolutionary theatre's aspiration, linking Nemirovich-Danchenko's work to his own vision. '*Lysistrata* magnificently exemplifies that the theatre [MAT] has found the way towards the new style of the manifesto and of monumentality, the poignant contrasts, the audacity of scenic movements, attaining whirling force, at times.' In the same article, Lunacharsky perceptively pointed out that the production's form contained borrowed elements from the leftist avant-garde. However, consistent with his views on convergence, he warmly praises the director for creatively integrating them into the MAT's artistic tradition.[58]

Following *Lysistrata*'s success, the MAT's future, for the first time since the revolution, definitely looked more prosperous. Lunacharsky's authority was a secure guarantee. The Narkom now unequivocally declared that he supported the theatre not only for its historical importance but also for its promise. Significantly, in 1923 he chose to refer to the production in the official context of the theatre's anniversary, using it as conclusive proof that the MAT had modernised its outlook, responding to the aesthetic and political needs of the revolution: 'The tendency of a studio, and of a spectacle like *Lysistrata* give us hence the certitude that the

theatre [MAT] . . . is being reorganised on a new formal conception, capable precisely of receiving the new content.'[59] Official
approval was also demonstrated by conferring on the directors of
the MAT the title of People's Artist of the Republic, in October
1923, which Meyerhold had also received a few months earlier.

Lunacharsky was not alone in regarding *Lysistrata* as evidence of
the MAT's development.[60] Impressed critics united in a loud and
clear consensus on this point. Boris Romashov in *Isvestia* found
that '*Lysistrata* is the Moscow Art Theatre's first major production
responding to contemporary requisites.' Similarly, Samuel
Margolin wrote: '*Lysistrata* is the Moscow Art Theatre's
extraordinary success, demarcating its enormous progress.' In a
more jovial mood, another reviewer commented: '*Lysistrata* has
lifted the Moscow Art Theatre out of its frame of twenty-five years
of tradition, and has whirled it off in a precipitous tempo of joy.'
E. Bieskin perhaps made the most memorable comment on
Lysistrata, significantly entitling his article, 'Burning of the Cherry
Orchard', to highlight the significance of the production. He wrote,
'The cherry trees are burning in the flames of *Lysistrata*', to which
Nemirovich-Danchenko replied, 'the orchard may burn, the soil,
never'.

The staging of *Lysistrata* seems also to have drawn attention to
the full potential of Aristophanes as a political dramatist, relevant
to the revolutionary period. Echoing Lunacharsky's famous slogan
'Back to Ostrovsky', a reviewer of *Lysistrata* urged, 'Back to
Aristophanes', referring to the 'vital need of the contemporary
audience for social satire'. Other critics similarly found that the
MAT 'had resurrected Aristophanes', 'it had brought close to us a
friend of humanity'. The ancient dramatist was viewed almost as a
modern writer, since Nemirovich-Danchenko 'had found the forms
to embody his ideas'. Yet, in spite of the critics' enthusiasm,
production of Attic comedy in the early post-revolutionary period
as well as in the Stalinist era appears to have been limited and of
marginal importance. On the celebratory occasion of the 2400
years since the birth of Aristophanes in 1954, the MAT's *Lysistrata*
was still regarded in the Soviet Union as an unsurpassed

achievement, 'the most important Aristophanic production on the Russian stage'.[61]

Lysistrata's reception in the United States in the 1925–26 season was enthusiastic, as in its home country. The production was chosen for the opening night of the MAT's Musical Studio in New York, on 14 December 1925, set up as a dazzling social event. The receiving committee included distinguished patrons and artists such as the tycoon Otto Khan and Chaliapin; 'the house was packed and the social register ransacked'.[62] The Musical Studio was brought to the USA by Morris Gest, an energetic entrepreneur who had set up an enormous publicity campaign months before the New York opening.

Prima facie, the American campaign aimed not only at impressing the public but also at edifying it. Oliver Sayler, a scholarly associate of M. Gest, had editorially supervised the English translation of all the plays and librettos of the Musical Studio's repertory on show during the American tour. Also, he had edited a luxurious souvenir programme which included Russian articles on the Studio and its productions. Moreover, Sayler wrote a book about the MAT's Musical Studio, *Inside the Moscow Art Theatre*, published in 1925. The press mainly utilised material from these sources to cover the presentation of the Studio before and after its opening.[63]

Sayler's work is important as the first and to date the only extensive Western study of the Musical Studio, devoting an entire chapter to *Lysistrata*. However, the book primarily aims to satisfy publicity purposes. *Inside the Moscow Art Theatre* may appear in the guise of scholarly impartiality, yet it is essentially manipulative in its presentation of the material. Sayler emphasises artistic concerns, divesting them entirely of their ideological context. This is a glaring fault, especially as his material is mostly derived from Russian sources. Understandably, Sayler was concerned that the Musical Studio would steer clear of problems with the American authorities, ever hostile to communist cultural imports. However, his tactic results in the distortion of facts.

There is an only too insistent concern to disassociate the MAT from the Soviet government. Sayler presents the company almost as a dissident theatre, that played the old repertory 'at the risk of prison'.[64] In renovating the lyric stage, he clarifies that 'it was not so much the good will of governmental authorities . . . as it was the naive and pliable mood of a new theatergoing public that enabled him [Nemirovich-Danchenko] to attain his goal'.[65] Indeed, Sayler over-emphasises the role of the MAT's supposedly loving, non-critical audience: 'public veneration has drawn protecting circles round the theatre and its presiding geniuses'.[66]

Discussion of *Lysistrata* entirely avoids the thorny question of its relation to the Soviet revolution. Sayler refers to the Russian interpretation's contemporary relevance, quoting Smolin on the play's 'great social and human significance'.[67] However, the passage is too general in tone to be helpful. Similarly, Sayler's gloss does not aid clarification: 'Amazing as it may be, the coin of [*Lysistrata*'s] leading motives is still current after nearly two and a half millenniums: war, peace, nature, health, men, women, sexual desire.'[68] The author mentions that in recent times the play has been related to pacifism and feminism, but he fails to specify whether and how the Russian interpretation is responsive to these concerns. As regards the adaptation, he misleadingly gives the impression it has preserved the sexual frankness of the Greek text. The 'Dionysian fervor' of the modern Russian stage allowed Nemirovich-Danchenko 'to comprehend' that 'Aristophanes . . . has infused . . . the same poetic beauty into his phallic episodes as into his scenes of moral indignation'.[69]

The American press presented the Russian interpretation as feminist, perhaps taking the cue from the solidarity and comradeship in the women's camp, emphasised in the performance.[70] Reviewers discovered the play was 'the first and most famous contribution to the drama of feminism', supplying 'conclusive evidence that the feminist movement is not modern'. Naturally, language limitations did not allow more deep-reaching analyses of the production's supposedly feminist content. However, if the Russian language was a barrier to appreciating interpretative issues, it was an asset to appreciating the production's aesthetic merit. The critic of the *New*

York Times praised *Lysistrata* as a 'technical achievement in theatrical arts' in appealing to all the senses. The numerous, profuse descriptions of the staging testify to its immediate appeal. Reports are frequently impressive in giving an extremely vivid sense of the spectacle, finely detailed, exact and inspiring:

These groupings, the flame and terracotta in which they are clothed, the white concentricity of the pillars and the stairways within which they flutter, the smiting blue of the sky which encircles everything – here are pictures so swift, so heroic, so magnificently burlesque, they seem to have been inspired by Homer on a saxophone.[71]

Overcoming cultural differences, American critics perceived the Russian *Lysistrata* almost as a product of the jazz age. Moreover, they wholeheartedly appreciated the production's guttural humour. Indeed, the spectacle was regarded as 'one of the best light comedies on view in this town [New York]', 'High entertainment, rollicking, honest to goodness fun'. Language presented no problem: 'the intensely oracular good humor of whatever they were saying or singing surged up and swept language limitations away'. The Russian *Lysistrata* then had a highly successful inter-cultural career. The obfuscation of its political content rendered the spectacle highly suitable for capitalist and proletarian popular audiences alike.

To sum up, Nemirovich-Danchenko transformed *Lysistrata* into a contemporary play, directly relevant to the Russian revolution and the civil war. He gave prominence to characteristic features of *théâtre du peuple* in his interpretation, sacrificing, in some cases, the spirit of the original. He primarily emphasised a didactic political interpretation, opting for a tighter structure and drastically limiting or eliminating the original's profound irony and the coarse sexual humour. Scenically, the production is also readily identifiable as *théâtre du peuple* in its adoption of a non-illusionist style, giving free rein to a variety of forms and devices inspired by popular entertainment. Naturally, the Chorus was the focus of the Soviet interpretation, which was partial to the women, projecting their struggle as heroic. Indeed, Lysistrata's role in this popular version is low-key. We appreciate her camaraderie to the Chorus more than her rebellious individuality.

The significance of the Soviet *Lysistrata* as an Aristophanic production cannot be over-estimated: this is the first major interpretation of Attic comedy in the twentieth century as *théâtre du peuple*. Nemirovich-Danchenko's approach is forward-looking, in that interpretations of Attic comedy as popular theatre became increasingly important after the First World War, in the work of major directors such as Charles Dullin, Joan Littlewood and Karolos Koun. The Soviet version does full justice to *Lysistrata*'s reputation as the world's foremost anti-war play and highlights the value of Aristophanes as a political playwright.

Notes

1. Maurice Donnay, *Lysistrata* (Paris: Ollendorff, 1893). The play premièred in 1892 at the Grand Théâtre in Paris. The production was directed by Paul Porel and it featured the well-known actors Gabrielle Réjane and Lucien Guitry in the lead roles.
2. Laurence Housman, *Lysistrata* (London: Woman's Press, 1911). The play premièred at the Little Theatre in London in 1910 and was directed by Gertrude Kingston, who also played the title role.
3. Oliver Sayler, *Inside the Moscow Art Theatre* (Westport, CT: Greenwood Press, 1925), p. 226.
4. V. E. Meyerhold, 'La dramaturgie et la culture du théâtre', in *Écrits sur le théâtre*, ed. and trans. Béatrice Picon-Valin (Lausanne: La Cité, L'Age d'Homme, 1975), p. 60.
5. Anatoli Vassilievitch Lounatcharsky, 'Le théâtre et la révolution (1921)', in *Théâtre et révolution*, ed. and annotated by Émile Copfermann (Paris: François Maspero, 1970), p. 93, my translation.
6. Cited in Konstantin Rudnitsky, *Russian and Soviet Theater 1905–1932*, trans. Roxane Permar, ed. Lesley Milne (New York: Harry N. Abrams, 1988), p. 52.
7. Vl. I. Nemirovich-Danchenko, letter to V. I. Kachalovu, 23 January 1922, *Izbrannye pisshchma*, vol. II (Moscow: Iskusstvo, 1979),

p. 266, my translation, prepared in collaboration with Nona Molesky. The letter to V. I. Kachalovu, dated 17 July 1921, also highlights Nemirovich-Danchenko's sensibility (ibid., pp. 230–45).

8. Ibid., letter to E. B. Vakhtangovu, 7 April 1922, p. 256, my translation, prepared in collaboration with Nona Molesky.

9. F. Crommelynck's *Magnanimous Cuckold*, directed by Meyerhold, R. S. F. S. R. Theatre I; A. Goldfaden's *The Sorceress*, directed by A. Granovsky, GOSET; Ch. Lecocq's *Giroflé-Girofla*, directed by A. Tairov, Kamerny Theatre.

10. Cited in Rudnitsky, *Russian and Soviet Theater*, p. 104.

11. Nemirovich-Danchenko, letter to F. N. Mikhalbskomu, 24 October 1922, *Izbrannye*, p. 260, my translation, prepared in collaboration with Nona Molesky.

12. J. M. Nakhov, 'E kleronomia tou Aristophane', in *Aristophanes. Meletes*, trans. into modern Greek by M. Garides (Athens: Mokhlos, 1957), p. 218, my translation.

13. Ibid., p. 217.

14. See Meyerhold, 'La dramaturgie et la culture du théâtre', in *Écrits sur le théâtre*, pp. 59–60.

15. Cited in Pavel Aleksandrovich Markov, *Rezhissura Vl. I. Nemirovicha-Danchenko v muzykalnom teatre* (Moscow: Vserossiyskoe Teatralvnoe Obshchestvo, 1960), p. 89, my translation, in collaboration with Nona Molesky.

16. Nakhov, 'E kleronomia tou Aristophane', in *Aristophanes. Meletes*, p. 225, my translation.

17. Markov, *Rezhissura Vl. I. Nemirovicha-Danchenko v muzykalnom teatre*, p. 89, my translation, in collaboration with Nona Molesky.

18. Nakhov, 'E kleronomia tou Aristophane', in *Aristophanes. Meletes*, p. 229, my translation.

19. Vl. Nemirovitch-Dantchenko and Sergei Berthensson, 'Synopses of the Repertory', in *The Moscow Art Theatre Musical Studio*, Souvenir Programme, edited by Oliver Sayler, 1925. File on *Lysistrata*, Museum of the City of New York.

20. Nakhov, 'E kleronomia tou Aristophane', in *Aristophanes. Meletes*, p. 229, my translation.

21. Nemirovich-Danchenko, letter to V. I. Kachalovu, 17 July 1921, *Izbrannye*, p. 240, my translation, prepared in collaboration with Nona Molesky.

22. Vl. I. Nemirovich-Danchenko, *Dni i Gody*, entry for 25 November

1922, pp. 360–1, my translation, prepared in collaboration with Nona Molesky.

23. Ibid., p. 224, my translation.

24. Dmitry Smolin's version was translated into English and published in the United States on the occasion of the Musical Studio's American tour: Dmitry Smolin (trans.), *Lysistrata*, trans. into English by George S. and Gilbert Seldes, in *Plays of the Moscow Art Theatre Musical Studio* (New York: Brentano's, 1925), pp. 1–78.

25. Ibid., pp 68–9.

26. Aristophanes, vol. III, Loeb Classical Library (New York: G. P. Putnam, 1931), ll. 1082–84, p. 104. Trans. into English by Douglass Parker, in *Aristophanes Four Comedies* (Ann Arbor: University of Michigan Press, 1969), p. 75.

27. Smolin, *Plays* . . ., p. 74. Loeb, ll. 1177–80, p. 112. Kinesias: 'Deliberate? Allies? / We're over-extended already! / Wouldn't every ally approve of our position – / Union Now?' Translated into English by Douglass Parker, in *Aristophanes Four Comedies*, p. 81.

28. This is clearly evident from the initial appearance of the two Choruses. Faithfully following the original, Smolin has assigned lines 254–318 to the 'chorus of Old Men', who, as indicated by the stage directions, 'march in single file', as one body (Smolin, *Plays* . . ., pp. 18–20). However, the original's lines 319–51 of the women's first choral passage have been allocated in the adaptation to several characters: small groups of women, anonymous young and old individuals, as well as Myrrhina and Lampito contribute to a polyphonic diversity (ibid., pp. 20–2). Smolin resorts to the same practice of role assignment in the ensuing battle, which in the original is taken up by the leaders of the respective Choruses (ibid., pp. 22–7). In the female camp, in addition to the speakers indicated above, we now also distinguish a 'chorus of women', which appears to be a unified defending army in direct analogy to the men's, as suggested by the provocation: 'Our numbers overawe you? . . . What you see is only a thousandth part of us!' (ibid., p. 23).

29. Ibid., pp. 61–4. Loeb, ll. 614–705, pp. 64–72.

30. The staging of reports and debates was a special genre of propagandistic theatre, which first appeared in the Red Army units during the civil war. In debates, characters in costume dramatically presented a polar clash between two views. Such features as pantomime, living placards and choruses frequently illustrated their speeches.

31. Smolin, *Plays* . . ., pp. 61–2.

32. Ibid., p. 71. Loeb, ll. 1112–35, pp. 106–8.

33. Nemirovich-Danchenko, *Dni i Gody*, entry for 30 November 1922, p. 361.

34. Markov, *Rezhissura Vl. I. Nemirovicha-Danchenko v muzykalnom teatre*, pp. 89–90, my translation, in collaboration with Nona Molesky.

35. See Nemirovich-Danchenko, *Dni i Gody*, entries for 20 January and 'Beginning of February' 1923, p. 363; Nemirovich-Danchenko, letter to V. V. Luzhskomu, 8 April 1923, *Izbrannye*, p. 268.

36. Sayler, *Inside the Moscow Art Theatre*, p. 97.

37. Nemirovich-Danchenko, letter to V. V. Luzhskomu, 8 April 1923, *Izbrannye*, p. 268, my translation, prepared in collaboration with Nona Molesky.

38. For discussion of Rabinovich's set for *Lysistrata* see Abram Efros, 'The Scenic Designers of the Musical Studio', in *Moscow Art Theatre Musical Studio*, Souvenir Programme; Sayler, *Inside the Moscow Art Theatre*; Christine Hamon-Sirégols, *Le Constructivisme au théâtre* (Paris: CNRS, 1992).

39. Efros, 'The Scenic Designers of the Musical Studio', in *Moscow Art Theatre Musical Studio*, Souvenir Programme.

40. Sayler, *Inside the Moscow Art Theatre*, p. 99.

41. Discussion of the acting in *Lysistrata* is based on the following sources: Markov, *Rezhissura Vl. I. Nemirovicha-Danchenko v muzykalnom teatre*; *New York Times*, 15 December and 17 October 1925; *American*, 15 December 1925; *Billboard*, 26 December 1925; *Journal of Commerce*, 15 December 1925; *The Sun*, 15 December 1925; *Chicago Tribune*, 24 April 1926; unidentified reviews in 'Clippings, *Lysistrata*, Moscow Art Theatre Musical Studio Production', file on *Lysistrata*, New York Public Library for the Performing Arts, New York.

42. Gilbert W. Gabriel in *The Sun*, 15 December 1925.

43. Alan Dale, *American*, 15 December 1925.

44. Unidentified review in 'Clippings, *Lysistrata*, Moscow Art Theatre Musical Studio Production', file on *Lysistrata*, New York Public Library for the Performing Arts, New York.

45. Quoted in Nakhov, 'E kleronomia tou Aristophane', in *Aristophanes. Meletes*, p. 223, my translation.

46. P. S. Kogan, quoted in ibid., p. 223, my translation.

47. I am primarily referring to the two productions of Vl. Mayakovsky's *Mystery Bouffe* (1918 and 1921), to E. Verhaeren's *Dawns* (1920), to A. Sukhovo-Kobylin's *The Death of Tarelkin* and to F. Crommelynck's *The Magnanimous Cuckold* (1922).

48. See Rudnitsky, *Russian and Soviet Theater*, p. 92.

49. Hamon-Sirégols, *Le Constructivisme au théâtre*, p. 312.

50. Rudnitsky, *Russian and Soviet Theater*, p. 92.

51. Nikolai Gorchakov, *The Theatre in Soviet Russia*, trans. E. Lehrman (New York: Columbia University Press, 1957), p. 134.

52. Rudnitsky, *Russian and Soviet Theater*, p. 42.

53. Anatoli Vassilievitch Lounatcharsky, 'Le théâtre et la révolution (1921)', in *Théâtre et révolution*, p. 101, my translation.

54. Ibid., p. 64.

55. Huntly Carter, *The New Theatre and Cinema of Soviet Russia* (London: Chapman and Dodd, 1924), pp. 141–2.

56. Ibid., p. 142.

57. Concerning the rightist theatre he wrote approvingly, 'traditional theatre has taken a step forward toward a placard quality, accelerated tempo, a certain stylisation of life'. He clarified, 'since our realism does not in the least abjure hyperbole, the caricature effect, then it is natural that the so called rightist theatre has felt it proper to assimilate some of the achievements of the very latest theatrical efforts'. Cited in Rudnitsky, *Russian and Soviet Theater*, p. 190.

58. Anatoli Vassilievitch Lounatcharsky, 'Le Théâtre d'Art de Moscou (1923)', in *Théâtre et révolution*, pp. 215–24.

59. Ibid., p. 224, my translation.

60. Discussion of *Lysistrata*'s reception in Russia is based on the following sources: Nakhov, 'E kleronomia tou Aristophane', in *Aristophanes. Meletes*; Nemirovich-Danchenko, *Dni i Gody*, entry for 16 June 1923; Sergei Berthensson, 'The Story of the Moscow Art Theatre Musical Studio', in *The Moscow Art Theatre Musical Studio*, Souvenir Programme.

61. Nakhov, 'E kleronomia tou Aristophane', in *Aristophanes. Meletes*, p. 221, my translation.

62. Alan Dale, *American*, 15 December 1925.

63. Sayler, 'Plays of the Moscow Art Theatre Musical Studio', in 'The Moscow Art Theatre Musical Studio', Souvenir Programme; Sayler, *Inside the Moscow Art Theatre*.

64. Morris Gest, in Sayler, *Inside the Moscow Art Theatre*, p. 225.

65. Ibid., p. 230.
66. Ibid., p. 224.
67. Ibid., p. 92.
68. Ibid.
69. Ibid. pp. 104–5.
70. Discussion of *Lysistrata's* reception in the USA is based on the following sources: Gilbert Gabriel, *The Sun*, 15 December 1925; Samuel Chotzinoff, *World*, 15 December 1925; *Citizen*, 15 December 1925; *New York Times*, 15 December 1925.
71. Gabriel, *The Sun*, 15 December 1925.

Irish Versions

5. Greek Myth, Irish Reality: Marina Carr's *By the Bog of Cats...*

Melissa Sihra

Echoes of classical Greek theatre permeate contemporary Irish playwriting of the last thirty years in works by Frank McGuinness, Brian Friel, Derek Mahon, Tom Paulin, Conall Morrison, Seamus Heaney, Desmond Egan, Brendan Kennelly, Aidan Carl Matthews, Tom Murphy and Marina Carr. In Brian Friel's 1980 drama *Translations*, an organic connection with Irish culture and the world of the ancient Greeks is famously naturalised into the rural hedge-school of the 1830s. Here, according to Master Hugh, the Greek and Latin languages are aligned with Gaelic as authentic forms of expression, poetry and implicit colonial resistance: 'English, I suggested, couldn't really express us . . . our own culture and the classical tongues made a happier conjugation.'[1] The tenacious exploration of classical dramaturgy by Irish playwrights has been a characteristic of theatrical production, to varying degrees, in new versions, loose adaptations and straight trans-lation, with a genesis stretching back to the works of W. B. Yeats, J. M. Synge and George Bernard Shaw and the novels of James Joyce. This tendency to revisit classical drama is due in part to the ostensible timeless quality of the ancient myths, which serve powerfully to mediate contemporary realities of transition, conflict and crisis, offering remote yet immediate spaces in which to explore and re-imagine the present day. As Declan Kiberd observes: 'The classics still provide a discourse in which the contests between the various forces contending for power in Ireland [can] be represented.'[2] The ways in which Irish playwrights incorporate the classical narratives vary according to their artistic goals, being in some cases an explicit metaphoric template for contemporary political contexts, while, in others, more of a loosely imagined aesthetic frame upon which to weave and build the story.

Within the impressive lineage of Irish playwrights who are drawn to ancient Greek drama, there is one 'rebel woman'. A visceral and poetic connection with the classical sensibility is something that emerges in the mature plays of Marina Carr, a significant proportion of which are loosely based on Sophoclean, Euripidean and Aeschylean dramatic texts. Marina Carr's retelling of the classical dramas brings the stories fully into the present day with local settings, costumes, props, idiom and colloquial dialogue while also operating on multiple layers of fantasy, imagination and poetry. The classical resonances apply not just to the form, but also to the content, of Carr's dramas, where the cultural and sexual politics of fifth-century Athenian and twentieth-century Irish society can be seen to relate closely to one another. Marina Carr's mature plays begin with *The Mai* in 1994, which is inspired by Sophocles' *Electra*. With the première of *By the Bog of Cats. . .* at the Abbey Theatre in 1998, a modern retelling of Euripides' tragedy *Medea* transposed into a contemporary rural Irish context, Carr's interest in ancient Greek drama became more apparent. In 2002, Carr's next three-act drama, *Ariel*, revealed a more explicit version of Attic tragedy in the form again of a contemporary Irish retelling of Aeschylus' trilogy *The Oresteia*.

For Marina Carr, classical Greek theatre 'is the gold that is there for the taking when looking for the archetypal story and characters. There are the clear lines in the writing, the clarity and the lack of self-consciousness. In the classical plays the Gods take over the function of consciousness.'[3] In returning to the landscapes of classical Greece, Carr's plays reveal a need in contemporary theatre for imaginative spaces of possibility, transformation and a fundamental 'search for myth' at a time which the playwright considers is plagued by a 'lack of belief' and limited by 'an existence on the rational plane'.[4] There are identifiable moments in modern history when such mythic narratives offer a necessary catharsis and existential framework. When *By the Bog of Cats. . .* opened in 2001 in San Jose, California, three days after 11 September, Carr states: 'It was a trail of pilgrimage. Forty thousand people coming up from Silicon Valley to see this dark play in a dark time.'[5]

In 'Writing in Greek', the programme note of the première of *By the Bog of Cats. . .*, Frank McGuinness asks: 'I wonder what Marina Carr believes? I think it might be the Greek Gods – Zeus and Hera, Pallas Athena. She knows what the Greeks know. Death is a big country. And hers is a big imagination, crossing the borders always between the living and the dead.'[6] *By the Bog of Cats. . .* is one of Carr's most popular plays and has had a number of award-winning professional productions, most notably in Ireland at the Abbey Theatre in 1998, where it was directed by Patrick Mason and won the *Irish Times*-ESB Awards for Best New Play and Best Actress for Olwen Fouéré, who played the lead role of Hester Swane. The play also received award-winning productions in the United States in 2001 with Chicago Irish Repertory Theater and, later that year at San Jose Repertory Theater, starring Academy Award winner Holly Hunter. *By the Bog of Cats. . .* was produced in the Netherlands in 2002 at the RO Theatre Rotterdam and was nominated for a Laurence Olivier Award for Best New Play in 2005 during its run in a new production at the Wyndham Theatre in the West End, with Holly Hunter reprising the role of Hester Swane. The play is regularly produced to acclaim on the Irish amateur dramatic circuit as well as in universities nationally and internationally.

The central character of Carr's modern version of *Medea* is forty-year-old Hester Swane, a Traveller from the Midlands of Ireland. An unmarried mother, the links with Hester Prynne and her daughter Pearl in Nathaniel Hawthorne's *The Scarlet Letter* are strong. The main characters of the play correspond to their Euripidean counterparts and the action opens on the Bog of Cats, at dawn, on the icy morning of the impending wedding of Carthage Kilbride, Hester's former lover. The classical resonances soon emerge as the audience learns how Carthage and strong-farmer Xavier Cassidy demand Hester's exile in order to clear the way for the marriage of convenience to Xavier's daughter Caroline. This strategic alliance will unite the Kilbride and Cassidy farmlands and will provide a potential for legitimate genealogical continuity. Olwen Fouéré comments: '*By the Bog of Cats*. . . is a deeply political play about the outsider. Carthage is not just marrying another woman; he's entering this land-grabbing, gombeen society. So Hester's rage is also a cultural rage, of a colonised culture which is being driven out, not allowed to exist, and where her sexuality and creativity are being suppressed.'[7] Hester and her 'bastard' daughter, Josie, are what Carr refers to as 'half-settled' as both were born of a Traveller-mother and a settled father, and, as a landless itinerant of dubious parentage, Hester radically threatens patriarchal systems of land-ownership and inheritance within the small rural community.[8]

Carr's mature plays explore the deep-rooted association of woman and motherhood in Irish culture. As Ivana Bacik states: '[T]he accepted social function for women remained firmly located within the home, expressed through Catholic Church teaching and through the law, most notably through the 1937 Constitution.'[9] The privileged position of the heterosexual nuclear family unit in both classical and Irish contexts is crucial, where the emphasis upon citizenship and legitimacy is a key characteristic of both societies. The traditional position of women in Ireland can be understood through observing the similar gender and familial roles in ancient Greek society. Oswyn Murray states:

The Athenian *polis* was essentially a male association [where] the household was an economic unit [...] The family was the source of new citizens. It became impossible for an Athenian to marry a foreigner or to obtain recognition for the children of any other type of liaison. The function of the family, intimately connected with citizenship, was the inheritance of property.[10]

The tradition of personifying the nation as woman – Mother *Éire*, Kathleen Ní Houlihan, *Roisin Dubh*, the Shan van Vocht, and in *Aisling* poetry – began in Ireland as a form of political resistance during the period of the anti-Catholic Penal Codes in the late seventeenth century, when it was forbidden to refer directly to

Ireland in ballads, poems and songs. While iconographically central, woman became subjectively disempowered, reduced to the passive, metaphoric emblem of the nation. The synonymous association of 'woman' with 'mother' also took hold in the late nineteenth and early twentieth centuries and was enshrined in Eamon de Valera's 1937 Irish Constitution, where the words are to this day used effectively interchangeably. Bacik identifies how Article 41 of the 1937 Irish Constitution promotes and enshrines a stereotypical role for women:

Paragraph 2 of the Article provides that 'the State recognises that by her life within the home, woman gives to the State a support without which the common good cannot be achieved', and further notes that the State must 'endeavour to ensure that mothers shall not be obliged by economic necessity to engage in labour to the neglect of their duties in the home.' Thus, women's 'life within the home' is afforded constitutional protection, the wording of which falls just short of making it compulsory for women to spend their lives in the home. Fathers, by contrast, are not mentioned anywhere in the Constitution.[11]

The reductive essentialist association of woman with the maternal was also a core aspect of classical Greek society. Sue Ellen Case notes:

Athenian women were confined to the house (explicitly in the laws of Solon), they were removed from the public life of the intellect and the soul and confined to the world of domestic labour, childbearing, and concomitant sexual activities. Actual women disappeared from the public life of the *polis*, lost their economic and legal powers and became objects of exchange.[12]

The relationship between space, gender and the body in *By the Bog of Cats. . .* is crucial in terms of understanding the ways in which Hester Swane threatens the dominant social order. Hester's liminal status, as woman *and* Traveller, within the community is reinforced by her relationship with the surrounding landscape. Refusing containment, and the traditionally demarcated binary spaces of the masculine public and the female private *oikos*, Hester crosses the bog by day and night and this association with the outdoors exceeds boundaries of gender, property and propriety. The radical nature of Hester's movements is reinforced when one considers, in fifth-century Athenian society, 'the regular association of women with the inside and the dangers associated with women when they go outside [and how] the requirement to keep women on the inside is so forcefully stated'.[13] Hester crosses spatial and symbolic boundaries more significantly than any other of Carr's female protagonists who either remain within, or flirt with, the threshold. In the very first scene of the play, neighbour Monica Murray asks Hester: 'Walkin' all night again, were ya? Ya'll cetch yer death in this weather.'[14] Carthage similarly recalls Hester's impulse to the outdoors when they lived together: 'I'll remember the sound of the back door closin' as ya escaped for another night roamin' the bog' (p. 74).

As a defiant, rebellious woman, the vast and unlimited quality of the bog is the only space that can adequately ontologically accommodate Hester. The radical otherness of Hester's position can be understood when we consider the relative position of women in fifth-century Greek society, where:

The family clearly served as the means of protecting and enclosing women. Women were citizens, for the purposes of marriage and procreation; but otherwise they lacked all independent status [...] At all times they had to be under the protection of a *kyrios*, a guardian; if they were unmarried, their father or closest male relative, if they were married their husband, if widowed their son or other male relative by marriage or birth. At all times the woman belonged to a family and was under the legal protection of its head.[15]

Carr observes the poetic and symbolic resonances of her *mise-en-scène*: 'landscape [is] another character in the work'.[16] She expands: 'Nature that makes a gratuitous appearance in a play does not interest me, but nature that is invested with memory or nature of character, or associations, faith, is so important.'[17] In the play, the bog is a sentient creature – porous, changeable and portentous. It is a seer, a permeable proteus of divination, which prophesies in its bog-holes, mapping on to the actual landscape the fate of the characters. In Act I, the choric-figure Catwoman reveals her knowledge of things to come when she says to Hester: 'Sure I know that too. Seen it writ in a bog hole.'[18] Embodying the sublime qualities of terror and awe, the bog of the Midlands occupies a significant place in the Irish cultural psyche and is known for its qualities of preservation, incorporating a haunting well of associations with mythic, 'bottomless' depth and subterranean rivers. Bleak and unquantifiable, the black landscape of the Midlands has long been considered a marginal, ungovernable space of subversive possibility and dissent and has been linked to insurrection, concealment and colonial resistance. In the nineteenth century, Thomas Carlyle, frustrated by the ungovernability of the bog, addressed it as though it were a sentient being: 'Abominable bog, thou shalt cease to be abominable and become subject to man!'[19] That Hester was born on the Bog of Cats and knows 'every barrow and rivulet and bog hole' further accentuates her otherness and 'ungovernability' in terms of the dominant social fabric of the community.[20]

The ghost of another rebel woman pervades the play and, though absent throughout, the 'rancorous hulk' Big Josie Swane is one of the main characters in the drama (p. 62). In By the Bog of Cats. . . Hester and her mother continually defy romantic and idealised versions of Irish womanhood and contest the iconic nationalist stereotype of the woman-mother through their ostensibly wayward behaviour. Xavier Cassidy remembers Big Josie as a *maenad*-figure – nomadic, voracious and volatile: 'Times I'd walk by that caravan and there'd be ne'er a sign of this mother of yours. She'd go off for days with anywan who'd buy her a drink. She'd be off in the bars of Pullagh and Mucklagh gettin' into fights' (p. 40). Presumably now dead, Big Josie has attained legendary status through the myriad of vivid passionate and conflicting stories about her life. Hester, the ghost of her brother Joseph, Xavier and the other choric figures in the drama, Monica Murray and Catwoman, each possess colourful and conflicting memories of the woman and reconstruct her through the partial lens of memory and imagination. Xavier, who is fixated with Big Josie, and who perhaps once had a sexual relationship with her, recalls: 'Wance she bit the nose off a woman who dared to look at her man, bit the nose clean off her face. And you, you'd be chained to the door of the caravan with maybe a dirty nappy on ya if ya were lucky' (p. 40). Big Josie's son Joseph recollects her as being: 'fierce silent – gentle I suppose in her way'. Hester remembers her otherwise: 'Gentle! She'd a vicious whiskey temper on her and a whiplash tongue and fists that'd land on ya like lightnin' (p. 62).

The quest for origins is a recurring theme of Irish theatre, where identity is frequently sought through narrative, storytelling and myth. Both of Hester's parents are absent, further compounding her position as an outsider of precarious, unquantifiable origins. Hester was abandoned by her mother at the age of seven and continually attempts to reconstruct a coherent sense of self based upon the local stories about Big Josie: 'Tell me about me mother, Catwoman, for what I remember doesn't add up' (p. 21). 'To lose one parent may be regarded as a misfortune,' says Lady Bracknell in Oscar Wilde's play of lost origins, '. . . to lose both seems like carelessness.'[21] Legitimacy is the crucial determining factor of both classical and Irish society and Hester invests in an absent, mythological father-figure who is named after an island: 'I had a father too! Ya'd swear I was dropped from the sky the way ya go on. Jack Swane of Bergit's island, I never knew him – but I had a father. I'm as settled as any of yees' (p. 43). Hester's emphasis on the settled identity of her father reveals her ambivalent wish to be a legitimate part of the society, as well as defending her Traveller genealogy: 'I was born on the Bog of Cats, same as all of yees. I'm as settled as any of yees . . . As for me tinker blood, I'm proud of it. Gives me an edge over all of yees, and allows me to see yees for the inbred, underbred, bog-brained shower yees are' (p. 35).

A tinker who is neither fully settled nor purely itinerant, Hester is aware of her dualistic status. This bifurcated subjectivity is perpetuated through Hester and Carthage's illegitimate daughter. As a result of Hester and Josie's mixed genealogy and, crucially, Josie's illegitimacy, both females can be regarded, as Julia Kristeva notes in *The Powers of Horror: An Essay on Abjection*: 'Neither Subject Nor Object'.[22] The Kristevan notion of 'neither/nor' complicates the limiting binarism of 'inner or outer'. According to this, Mother and daughter are at once excluded *and* inscribed – what Kristeva calls the 'deep well of memory that is unapproachable *and* intimate: the abject'.[23] Dominant systems of identity and authority operate as a process of expulsion, where symbolic community is defined implicitly by those it rejects. At the wedding party in Act II of *By the Bog of Cats. . .*, Hester says: 'The truth is you want to eradicate me, make out I never existed' (p. 56). In demanding her exile, the dominant economic class seeks to produce and perpetuate hierarchical hegemony through the negation and denial of the Travelling other. As in the Euripidean text, Carthage/Jason's marriage-alliance with the Cassidy/Creon household is indicative of the stability that Hester and Josie's otherness as nomads, women and illegitimates radically threatens. Hester's ambivalent paternity and her landless 'tinker's blood' disrupts Carthage Kilbride's aspirations to a stable, upward mobility and her exile is imminent. On the morning of his wedding Carthage seeks to remove Hester: '[I]t's time ya moved on to another haltin' site [. . .] just clear out of the Bog of Cats for wance and for all' (p. 302). In the final act of the play, Xavier pursues Hester with his gun, echoing Creon's sentiments in Euripides' drama: 'take this as a warning: if tomorrow's holy sun finds you or them inside my boundaries, you die'.[24] Elsie Kilbride is also willingly complicit in Hester's exile. In Act I of the play she says to her granddaughter: 'yees are tinkers [. . .]. Why don't yees head off in that auld caravan, back to wherever yees came from?' (p. 26).

Throughout Carr's play, mother of the groom Mrs Kilbride is fixated with the ostensible threat of illegitimacy and says to her granddaughter Josie: 'You're Hester Swane's little bastard. You're not a Kilbride and never will be.'[25] Mrs Kilbride is compelled to eradicate the possibility of illegitimacy at all costs: 'Don't you worry child, we'll get ya off of her yet. Me and your Daddy has plans. We'll batter ya into the semblance of legitimacy yet' (pp. 25–6). The woman's desire to manipulate the child's identity to fit within the paradigms of respectability is expressed directly to the child when the two are alone: 'Ya little coward ya, I'll break your spirit yet and then glue ya back the way I want ya.'[26] At the wedding party Mrs Kilbride is accused of being of Traveller stock herself, a fact that she is highly offended by and blatantly denies: 'My Grandfather was a wanderin' tinsmith.'[27]

Mrs Kilbride's refusal to acknowledge her itinerant genealogy reveals the deep-seated lack of place, history and identity for Travellers in Irish society. Popular anachronistic opinion holds that Travellers descend from those who became dispossessed of their land during the Great Famine of 1845. Yet the word 'tinker', first recorded in 1175, shows that there clearly was a group of travelling crafts people who played an important role in Irish society and economy and comes from the Old Irish *Tinceard* meaning 'tin craft'.[28] Marina Carr observes: 'In the play, they are all tinkers, except for the Cassidys.'[29] If what characterises Traveller identity is landlessness, then this is indeed true. Revealing a tendency towards mobility, neighbour Monica Murray looks at Hester's caravan in Act III and says, 'We'll go off in this yoke, you and me . . . Flee off from this place, flee off to Eden.'[30] The Catwoman lives alone in a hut of turf on the margins of the sinking bogland, while Elsie Kilbride and her son Carthage were 'scrubbers' of itinerant descent, possessing only a 'few lumpy ould acres' of unfarmable land before Hester came along with money and 'built Carthage Kilbride up from nothin'.[31] Monica Murray, Elsie Kilbride, Catwoman, Hester and her daughter are all marginalised women who have been abandoned, either by the society in which they live or by the men whom they have married. In a culture where 'no general legal protection is given to cohabiting heterosexual or gay couples, or to those who live alone, or to any other form of family unit that is not marriage based', these women are abject, relegated, like Travellers, to the lowest stratum of society due to their incapacity to engage with systems of legitimacy and land-ownership.[32]

In an ironic reference to J. M. Synge's 1907 play, Anthony Roche refers to *By the Bog of Cats. . .* as 'Not the Tinker's Wedding' and also 'the great bought marriage of Irish theatre'.[33] The marriage between Carthage Kilbride and Caroline Cassidy takes place in the liminal offstage symbolic playing space between Acts I and II. In

Act II, Carthage and Caroline enter with their identities transformed by legislative union. Now, too, the illegitimate young Josie will be transformed with the plans to adopt and adapt her into future legitimate barter, something of which Xavier Cassidy is only too aware. With legitimacy comes land-protection through inheritance. Sue Ellen Case identifies the identical centrality of marriage and the crucial positioning of women within the highly structured patriarchal order of ancient Greece:

While ownership became more individual and located within the family unit, it was limited to the male gender. Women were restricted to limited conditions of ownership and exchange . . . Within this new economy, women became a medium of exchange and marriage became an institution of ownership. In fact, the word for marriage, *ekdosis*, meant loan – women were loaned to their husbands by their fathers, and in the case of a divorce, they were returned to their fathers.[34]

The functional marriage in *By the Bog of Cats. . .* reveals the crucial role of legitimate, preferably virginal, female corporeality as patriarchal barter in the maintenance of land-inheritance in both Ireland and ancient Greece. Caroline Cassidy, as object of exchange between the Cassidy and the Kilbride households, is, Carr observes, 'a proper girl, respectable, with standing in the community'.[35] Elaine Aston identifies the way in which the patriarchal system of female corporeal barter operates:

[T]he female [is] a site of transaction between the old generation of patriarchy (father) and the new lover/husband to be. The female is therefore inactive, is defined only in terms of the male (as daughter, as wife-to-be), is, in short, the object of the male hero's quest, but not as a subject or initiator of action in her own right.[36]

At the beginning of Act II, with the entrance of the newly married couple, the bride and groom's fixation with material wealth and social status is apparent. Caroline's first sentiments as a married woman refer singularly to her dowry: 'This is the tablecloth me mother had for her weddin' and it's the same silver too',[37] echoing Pegeen Mike's list of requirements for her wedding to Shawn

Keogh in the opening lines of Synge's *The Playboy of the Western World* (1907):

> Six yards of stuff for to make a yellow gown.
> A pair of lace boots with lengthy heels on them and brassy eyes.
> A hat is suited for a wedding-day.
> A fine tooth comb. To be sent with three barrels of porter in Jimmy Farrell's creel cart on the evening of the coming Fair to Mister Michael James Flaherty.[38]

Talk of Pegeen's dowry also occurs in the opening moments of the play when Shawn says: 'Aren't we after making a good bargain, the way we're only waiting these days on Father Reilly's dispensation.'[39] In Carr's play, Synge's landless, nomadic, exiled and sacrificial victim Christy Mahon has now changed gender, dramatically shifting the century-old emphasis on masculine and national identity in Irish theatre. Carthage Kilbride reveals his desire for class-transition in his immediate response to Caroline's dowry comment: 'A soft-boned lady, your mother. I used to see her shoppin' with you be the hand, ya wanted to bow when she walked by, she had class. And you have too, Caroline, like no wan else around here' (p. 45). With her crucial 'class', Caroline embodies all that Carthage aspires to and is the *ideal* object of exchange between the Cassidy and Kilbride households. Like Glauce, Creon's daughter in Euripides' drama, Caroline Cassidy is a corporeal commodity that will notionally ensure the maintenance of the privileged legitimate patriarchal economy, a system which Josie will also be battered into.

The legislative implications of the marriage ceremony are crucial in terms of the politics of endogamy and exogamy. According to Kristeva, endogamy displays 'the concern with separating, with constituting strict identities without intermixture, [and], of perpetuating economic, familial and social self-reflexivity'.[40] This is a recurring theme of Brian Friel's theatre. In *Translations*, one of the 'Greek scholars'[41] Jimmy-Jack contemplates his fantasy bride *glaukopis* Athene, asking Hugh:

Do you know the Greek word *endogamein*? It means to marry within the tribe. And the word *exogamein* means to marry outside the tribe. And you don't cross those borders casually – both sides get very angry. Now, the problem is this: Is Athene sufficiently mortal or am I sufficiently godlike for the marriage to be acceptable to her people and to my people? You think about that.[42]

In *Making History* (1988), exogamy is evoked through the imagery of planting and gardening, in keeping with the historical context of the Ulster plantations. Mary Bagenal advises her sister Mabel: 'Don't plant the fennel near the dill or the two will cross-fertilise.' Mabel replies: 'Is that bad?' to which Mary responds: 'You'll end up with a seed that's neither one thing or the other.'[43] Kristeva notes how the condemnation of hybridity goes back to the Bible. In Leviticus 19:19 it is stated: 'Ye shall keep my statutes. Thou shalt not let thy cattle gender with a diverse kind: thou shalt not sow thy field with mingled seed: neither shall a garment mingled of linen and wollen come upon thee.' The extreme points of this logic are enunciated in Leviticus 18:30, as the divine Word of God: 'Therefore shall ye keep mine ordinance, that ye commit not any one of these abominable customs, which were committed before you, and that ye defile not yourselves therein: I am the Lord your God.' Thus 'abominable' becomes the term for heterogeneity, a term which has been associated with the bog and which refers to anything that deviates from singular eugenicist notions of purity and exclusivity.

The battle for land-ownership is central to *By the Bog of Cats. . .*, just as it is to most of twentieth-century Irish theatre, culture and history, from Augusta Gregory and W. B. Yeats' *Cathleen Ni Houlihan* (1902), John B. Keane's *The Field* to *Translations*. Xavier Cassidy reiterates the fundamental importance of land and legitimate genealogy when he speaks to Hester about Carthage: 'He loves the land and like me he'd rather die than part with it. With him Cassidy's farm will be safe, the name will be gone but never the farm. And who's to say but maybe your little bastard and her offspring won't be farmin' my land in years to come' (p. 69). The prevailing ideology is confirmed in Act III in Xavier's pronouncement to Carthage:

'There's nothin' besides land, boy, nothin', and a real farmer would never think otherwise' (p. 72).

The Midlands of Ireland, where Carr grew up, has a long association with Irish Travellers. Just as Medea will always be a foreigner in Corinth, Carr reveals how her central female protagonist will always be excluded from the dominant fabric of Irish society: 'I chose to make [Hester] a Traveller because Travellers are our national outsiders.'[44] As a marginalised indigenous people whose language and traditions can be traced as far back as the twelfth century, Irish Travellers are commonly associated with bigoted stereotypes of ignorance, violence and lack of cleanliness, perpetuating essentialist notions of innate impurity. In *By the Bog of Cats...*, the exile of the ostensibly 'filthy' and defiling women Hester and Catwoman is sought. Kristeva states: 'The potency of pollution is . . . not an inherent one; it is proportional to the potency of the prohibition that founds it.'[45] While references to filth are associated with Hester as Traveller, living in a 'dirty caravan', it is her excessive position *between* the two communities, her resistance to containment, her lack of conclusive paternity, her landless status and her illegitimate child that are the factors of her 'pollution', and which lead to her eventual sacrifice.

If as Kristeva asserts: 'The potency of pollution is therefore not an inherent one: it is proportional to the potency of the prohibition that founds it', Mrs Kilbride constructs and performs a fictional middle-class notion of self which is set against the necessary association of Catwoman and Hester with dirt and revulsion.[46] At the wedding party she says to Xavier:

What did ya have to invite the Catwoman for? Brings down the whole tone of the weddin. [...] She has no right to be here. Not till she washes herself. The turf-smoke stink of her. Look at her moochin' up to Father Willow and her never inside the door of a church and me at seven mass every mornin' watchin' that auld fool dribblin' into the chalice. And would he call to see me? Never. Spends all his time with the Catwoman in her dirty little hovel . . . I'd love to hose her down, fling her onto the milkin' parlour floor, turn on the water full blast and hose her down to her kidneys. (p. 50)

This prohibition of the defiling object serves to produce and maintain dominant identity. Kristeva writes that the 'filthy object . . . because it is excluded as a possible object, asserted to be a non-object of desire, abominated as ab-ject, as abjection, becomes defilement and founds on the henceforth released side of the "self and clean" the order that is this only (and therefore always) sacred'.[47] In a popular book on etiquette, *Goede Manieren*, Mrs Van Zutphen van Dedem devotes a chapter to 'the act of avoiding and excluding', in order to promote and protect the cherished middle- and upper-class categories of 'pure' and 'impure'. She notes how the more refined person was to avoid even:

the slightest contact, so far as possible, with the bodies and garments of other people, in the knowledge that, even greater than the hygienic danger of contamination, there is always the danger of contact with the spiritually inferior and the repugnant who at any moment can appear in our immediate vicinity . . . like germs in an unhealthy body.[48]

Carr's enigmatic character, Catwoman, is described in the stage-directions as: '*A woman in her late fifties, stained a streaky brown from the bog, a coat of cat fur that reaches to the ground, studded with cats' eyes and cats' paws. She is blind and carries a stick.*'[49] Inspired by Ratwife in Ibsen's *Little Eyolf*, Catwoman is Tiresias – the blind seer of the play whose lack of ocular vision is countered by her ability to divine the truth 'writ in a bog hole' and contrasts with the moral myopia of the local community (p. 23). Catwoman is a choric figure who frames the narrative, offers exposition, hovers between the landscapes of the living and the dead and is connected to the bog like no one else: 'I know everythin' that happens on this bog. I'm the Keeper of the Bog of Cats in case ya forgotten. I own this bog' (p. 74). Half-woman, half-animal, the classical and fairytale resonances of Catwoman are rich and evocative. She lives alone on the bog in a little turf hut, eats mice and sees things written in the sky, inhabiting a liminal territory between the realms of the supernatural and the everyday. Catwoman's darkened colouring, with her body '*stained a streaky brown from the bog*' further politicises her otherness and her connection to the land and the outdoors. Though she does not attend mass, Catwoman is frequently seen in the company of the local parish priest, Father Willow. Carr's first religious figure is a humorous topsy-turvy inversion of Catholicism. In Act II, the unlikely pair: 'enter *linking arms, both with their sticks. Father Willow has his snuff on hand, pyjamas showing from under his shirt and trousers, hat on, adores the* Catwoman.'[50] The priest leads Catwoman to the table and whispers: 'If ya were a bar of chocolate I'd ate ya' (p. 51). The pair engage in a carnivalesque conversation:

FR WILLOW: You'll have to cut back on the mice, they'll be the death of ya.

CATWOMAN: And you'll have to cut back on the snuff.

FR WILLOW: Try snails instead, far better for ya, the French ate them with garlic and tons of butter and Burgundy wine. I tried them wance meself and I in Avalon. Delicious. (pp. 59–50)

The hedonistic appetite for Burgundy wine, chocolate and snails in garlic-butter under a hot sun evokes an excessive sensibility more resonant of the great festivals of Dionysus than the tenets of the Catholic Church. Father Willow wears his pyjamas under his vestments, hides a gun in the tabernacle, wears earplugs during confession and cannot remember the simple prayer of grace before mealtime: 'The grace, yes, how does it go again?' (p. 52). After the wedding, Monica Murray comments to Xavier: 'Father Willow seems to have lost the run of himself entirely [. . .] The state of him with his hat on all durin' the Mass and the vestments inside out and his pyjamas peepin' out from under his trousers' (p. 48). He seems preoccupied throughout and, rather than focusing on the newly married couple, his wedding speech refers to his own loss in love:

FR WILLOW: It may or may not surprise yees all if I tould yees I was almost a groom meself wance. Her name was Elizabeth Kennedy, no that was me mother's name, her name was – it'll come to me, anyway, it wasn't meant to be, in the end we fell out over a duck egg on a walkin' holiday by the Shannon, what was her name at all? Helen? No.

MRS KILBRIDE: Would ya say the grace, Father Willow, and be –
FR WILLOW: The grace, yes, how does it go again? Rowena. That was
        it. Rowena Phelan. I should never have ate that duck egg
        – no. (pp. 53–4)

The reference to the duck egg is a fecund image of sexuality which also has erotic overtones in Synge's *Playboy of the Western World* where the local girls offer themselves sexually to Christy through the sub-text of a brace of duck eggs, to which Christy holds out his hand and comments: 'They're a great and weighty size.'[51]

Through the excessive, fantastical and supernatural figures of the Catwoman, Fr Willow, the Ghost Fancier and the ghost of Joseph Swane, Carr creates beings who organically fuse the everyday with heightened imaginative possibility and who contrast dramatically with the monological outlook of the Kilbrides and the Cassidys. The multiple layering of realities is woven into the very first moments of the play where an elegantly attired Ghost Fancier predicts Hester's death at sunset:

HESTER: Who are you? Haven't seen you around here before.
GHOST FANCIER: I'm ghoulin' for a woman be the name of Hester
                 Swane.
HESTER: I'm Hester Swane.
GHOST FANCIER: You couldn't be, you're alive. (pp. 13–14)

As a playwright who privileges landscapes of otherness and alterity, Carr's plays offer poetic spaces of ontological refuge for the female protagonists. Olwen Fouéré notes:

If imagination is a country, then Marina's maps bring me to a stretch of land and water that I recognise. The interior landscape of the bog, the colours of rage and passionate love. This place is dark, deep and conversant with a world at its most reduced and primal, a place of great anguish and great exultation: twin truths that rise and fall with parallel intensity.[52]

In *By the Bog of Cats. . .* social boundaries are tested and contested by the rebel woman Hester Swane. Outsider, exile, refugee and courageous sacrificial victim, Hester's tenacious articulation of discontent in a society which seeks to eradicate her subjectivity for not conforming to the cultural prerequisites of femininity reveals the trauma of abjection and lack of accommodation of many women in Ireland over the last number of centuries. Just as Marina Carr's female protagonists continually renegotiate boundaries of place, authority and identity in Irish culture, Carr's authorship and representation of women on the Irish stage actively forges new spaces for female subjectivity. In drawing upon the legacy of classical Greek drama, Carr's plays powerfully reinforce the reality that women were excluded from all acts of authorship and self-representation in the festivals of Dionysus in fifth-century Athens. Moreover, Marina Carr is the first woman to be considered a canonical Irish playwright and the first who has consistently represented women from the *perspective* of a woman in main-stage theatrical production and dramatic publishing in this country.[53]

Notes

1. Brian Friel, 'Translations', in J. P. Harrington (ed.), *Modern Irish Drama* (New York: Norton, 1991), p. 334.
2. Declan Kiberd, 'Introduction', in M. McDonald and M. J. Walton (eds), *Amid Our Troubles: Irish Versions of Greek Tragedy* (London: Methuen, 2002), p. ix.
3. Marina Carr, panel discussion 'Staging Greek Theatre Today', Barbican Theatre, London, 17 February 2005.
4. Ibid.
5. Lyn Gardner, 'Death Becomes Her', *Guardian,* 29 November 2004, p. 16.
6. Frank McGuinness, 'Writing in Greek', programme note for world première of *By the Bog of Cats. . .* , Abbey Theatre, Dublin, October 1998.
7. Olwen Fouéré, 'Journeys in Performance: On Playing in *The Mai* and *By the Bog of Cats. . .*', in A. McMullan and C. Leeney (eds), *The Theatre of Marina Carr: '. . . before rules was made'* (Dublin: Carysfort Press, 2003), pp. 169–70.

8. Marina Carr, play reading, Trinity College Dublin, 29 June 1999.

9. Ivana Bacik, *Kicking and Screaming: Dragging Ireland into the 21st Century* (Dublin: O'Brien Press, 2004), p. 80.

10. Oswyn Murray, 'Life and Society in Classical Greece', in O. Murray, J. Boardman and J. Griffin (eds), *Greece and the Hellenistic World* (Oxford: OUP, 1988), pp. 203–5.

11. Bacik, *Kicking and Screaming*, pp. 67–8.

12. Sue Ellen Case, 'Classic Drag: The Greek Creation of Female Parts', in W. B. Worthen (ed.), *The Harcourt Brace Anthology of Drama*, 3rd edn (Boston, MA: Thomson Heinle, 2000), p. 138.

13. Simon Goldhill, *Reading Greek Tragedy* (Cambridge: CUP, 1992), p. 15.

14. Marina Carr, *By the Bog of Cats. . .* (Loughcrew, Co. Meath: Gallery Press, 1998), p. 15. Hereafter, page references to this edition of the play appear in the text.

15. Murray, 'Life and Society in Classical Greece', in Murray et al. (eds), *Greece and the Hellenistic World*, p. 206.

16. Cliodhna Ni Anluain (ed.), *Reading the Future: Irish Writers in Conversation with Mike Murphy* (Dublin: Lilliput Press, 2000), p. 47.

17. Heidi Stephenson and Natasha Langridge (eds), *Rage and Reason: Women Playwrights on Playwrighting* (London: Methuen, 1997), p. 155.

18. Marina Carr, *Marina Carr: Plays: One* (London: Faber and Faber, 1999), p. 277.

19. Christopher Morash, 'Lever's Post-Famine Landscape', in T. Bareham (ed.), *Charles Lever: New Evaluations* (Gerrard's Cross: Colin Smyth, 1991), p. 92.

20. Carr, *Plays: One*, p. 314.

21. Oscar Wilde, *The Importance of Being Ernest*, in *Complete Works of Oscar Wilde* (London: Collins, 1971), p. 333.

22. Julia Kristeva, *The Powers of Horror: An Essay on Abjection*, trans. L. S. Roudiez (New York: Columbia Press, 1982), p. 1.

23. Ibid., p. 6.

24. Euripides, *'Medea' and Other Plays*, trans. Philip Vellacott (London: Penguin, 1963), p. 27.

25. Carr, *Plays: One*, p. 279.

26. Ibid.

27. Ibid., p. 314.

28. See Michael McDonagh, 'Who are the Travelling People?', in *Do You Know Us At All?* published by Promoting Attitudinal Change Towards Travellers (PACTT), Parish of the Travelling People, St Laurence House, Cook Street, Dublin 8, 1993, p. 11.

29. Melissa Sihra, unpublished interview with Marina Carr, Dublin, May 2001.

30. Carr, *Plays: One*, p. 322.

31. Ibid., p. 284.

32. Bacik, *Kicking and Screaming*, p. 68.

33. Anthony Roche, Synge Summer School Lecture, Rathdrum, Co. Wicklow, June 2000.

34. Case, 'Classic Drag', in W. B. Worthen (ed.), *The Harcourt Brace Anthology of Drama*, pp. 137–8.

35. Marina Carr, public reading at the Graduate Memorial Building, Trinity College, Dublin, 29 June 1999.

36. Elaine Aston, *An Introduction to Feminism and Theatre* (London: Routledge, 1995), p. 39.

37. Carr, *Plays: One*, p. 301.

38. Harrington (ed.), *Modern Irish Drama*, p. 74.

39. Ibid.

40. Kristeva, *Powers of Horror*, p. 93.

41. Harrington (ed.), *Modern Irish Drama*, p. 332.

42. Ibid., p. 374.

43. Brian Friel, *Brian Friel: Plays: Two* (London: Faber and Faber, 1999), p. 275.

44. Eileen Battersby, 'Marina of the Midlands', *Irish Times,* 4 May 2000, p. 15.

45. Kristeva, *The Powers of Horror,* p. 69.

46. Ibid.

47. Ibid., p. 65.

48. Van Zutphen van Dedem, cited in Peter Stallybrass and Allon White, *The Politics and Poetics of Transgression* (Cornell, NY: Cornell University Press, 1986), p. 136.

49. Carr, *Plays: One*, p. 271.

50. Ibid., p. 306.

51. J. M. Synge, *The Playboy of the Western World* (Cork: Mercier Press, 1974), p. 25.

52. Fouéré, 'Journeys in Performance', in McMullan and Leeney (eds), *The Theatre of Marina Carr*, p. 171.

1. Marianne McDonald.

2. Eileen Walsh as Elaine and Ingrid Craigie as Frances in the 2002 Abbey Theatre world première of *Ariel* by Marina Carr. (Photograph: Pat Redmond)

3. Two choral contingents surround Electra in Cacoyannis' *Electra*. The four women in the foreground are part of the main Chorus. The five women in the background are country maidens. (Reprinted from MacKinnon: London: Croom Helm, 1986)

4. Greek country-women in a funeral procession. (Reprinted from Danforth and Tsiaras: Princeton University Press, 1982. Photograph taken during the period 1975–6)

5. Group of Greek Orthodox nuns from the Monastery of the Protection of the Mother of God, in the Gard region of southern France, a dependency of Simonopetra on Mount Athos (the Holy Mountain). The nuns are singing a hymn for the feast day of their monastery, attended by laity. (Photograph taken on 22 July 2001. Privately held)

6. 'East Meets West'. Paquebots Poste Francais by Dellepiane, c.1930.

7. Scene from Aristophanes' *Lysistrata*, directed by Nemirovich-Danchenko (1923), for the Moscow Art Theater's Musical Studio: choral battle, act I. (By permission of the Moscow Bakhrushin State Theatre Museum)

8. Overview of the set and the cast of *Lysistrata*, directed by Nemirovich-Danchenko (1923).

9. Fiona Shaw as Medea in the Abbey Theatre 2000 production of *Medea* translated by Kenneth McLeish and Frederic Raphael, after Euripides. (Photograph: Neil Libbert)

10. Joan O'Hara as Catwoman and Olwen Fouéré as Hester Swaine in the 1998 Abbey
Theatre world première of *By the Bog of Cats...* by Marina Carr. (Photograph: Amelia Ste[

53. Carr's plays have premièred at the Abbey and Peacock Theatres, the Gate Theatre, Project and are published by Faber and Faber, London, Gallery Press in Ireland and Syracuse University Press and the Dramatists' Playwrighting Service in the United States and have been translated into nearly twenty languages.

6. Irish Medeas: Revenge or Redemption (an Irish Solution to an International Problem)

S. E. Wilmer

Irish adaptations of ancient Greek drama have recently become a boom industry. Numerous Irish poets from Seamus Heaney to Tom Paulin to Brendan Kennelly have rewritten the classics with an Irish flavour, localising the tragedies in current social and political conflicts.[1] In addition to a series of interpretations related to the war in Northern Ireland during the 1980s and early 1990s, such as Heaney's *The Cure at Troy*, Paulin's *The Riot Act* and *Seize the Fire*, and Kennelly's versions of *Antigone*, *Medea* and the *Trojan Women*, the vogue during the current peace process seems to favour the image of the rebellious or transgressive woman. In 2002 the Abbey Theatre staged Marina Carr's latest play *Ariel*, a version of *Iphigenia at Aulis* and the *Oresteia* set in modern-day Ireland with the Agamemnon figure represented by a leading Irish politician who sacrifices his daughter for his career and then is murdered by his wife, who in turn is murdered by her daughter. In February 2003, Conall Morrison set *Antigone* in a contemporary war-zone resembling the Middle East, with the eponymous heroine in quasi-Arab dress, fiercely opposing the authority of a Sharon-like demagogue. And in 2004, Seamus Heaney produced a version of *Antigone*, linked to Bush's invasion of Iraq, *Burial at Thebes*, for the Abbey centennial.

In this article I want to examine two versions of *Medea* on the main stage of the Abbey Theatre, one adapted by Marina Carr in 1998 called *By the Bog of Cats...* (directed by Patrick Mason), and the second based on Kenneth McLeish's translation of *Medea*, directed in 2000 by Deborah Warner, with Fiona Shaw as Medea. Both of these versions, which are manifestly pro-female (if not feminist) interpretations of *Medea*, experienced a prestigious afterlife. *By the Bog of Cats. . .* has been restaged in various productions in the USA including one in San Jose Rep (where Holly Hunter played the Medea character) that was adapted for London's West End in 2005. Likewise, the Deborah Warner/Fiona Shaw *Medea* took the theatrical world by storm, travelling over a three-year period via the West End, to Broadway and to Paris where it finished in April 2003. The Warner/Shaw *Medea* underwent numerous cast and costume changes, resulting in quite a different conception from the opening performance. From a beginning in Dublin where an Irish-speaking Chorus offset Fiona Shaw as an outsider, uncomfortable in a new environment, the later mani-festations for Broadway and Paris had Jason and Medea as famous heroes arriving in the provincial backwater of Corinth, where they wow the Chorus of local admirers. According to Deborah Warner's assessment of the later incarnation, Jason and Medea 'are seriously travelled, they are in hiding – they are Bonnie and Clyde'; and the Chorus are 'ordinary. Autograph hunters. The people who stand outside the Oscars.'[2]

Rather than looking at the journey that these plays took and the transformations that they underwent, I want in this essay to examine the first productions of these plays at the Abbey Theatre in Dublin, and consider what they were saying to the local audience and how the audience responded. The point that I want to make is that productions of *Medea* in Dublin at the end of the twentieth and beginning of the twenty-first centuries have raised problematic questions about the status of women in Irish society and have been viewed not as theatrical museum pieces or exercises in theatrical gimmickry and acting bravura, but as social commentaries on current events. The play deals with the power of women and their status in the domestic and the public spheres, and it has the capacity in postcolonial Ireland to subvert dominant notions of national identity.

In order to understand the reception in Dublin, one needs to understand something about Irish society and the changing position of women. Following independence from Britain in 1922, the Irish government tended to promote patriarchal values, relegating women to a subservient position. Until the 1970s, the government and the Church tried to confine women in Irish society to the domestic sphere. Women, according to Article 41 of the 1937 Constitution, were expected to be homemakers: 'mothers shall not be obliged by economic necessity to engage in labour to the neglect of their duties within the home'.[3] Men, on the other hand (as in ancient Greek society), were left to dominate the public sphere. Thus, until the 1970s, female civil servants were obliged to resign from their jobs when they married. Likewise, state legislation reflected the Catholic hierarchy's position on divorce, contraception, homosexuality and abortion. In the last twenty years, there have been rapid changes: divorce, contraception and homosexuality are now legal, and abortion has become a confused legal quagmire. Against all the odds, Mary Robinson was elected president of Ireland in 1991 and became an important role-model for young women, and provided an incentive for political parties to thrust women into prominent roles. Female politicians are now regularly appointed to cabinet level, and a woman heads one of the political parties in the current government in 2005. Meanwhile, the strength of the Catholic Church has been decimated by recurrent scandals involving child sexual abuse, the use of diocesan and third-world charity funds to suppress complaints, and the mal-treatment of young women (as seen in the television programme and film about the Magdalene laundries).[4] Thus the society has been evolving towards a secular society amid ongoing debate about gender roles and identities.

On first glance, *Medea* might seem a surprising choice for women in Ireland to adapt or direct today. The actions of Medea might prove an uncomfortable precedent for women seeking to strengthen their position in society. After all, Medea is not necessarily a likeable character and does precisely the opposite of what the Irish constitution had in mind. One of the problems, therefore, is how to persuade the audience to identify with her. The clue lies in Medea's oppressed status as an outsider and a victim: *'egô d' erêmos apolis ous' hybrizdomai pros andros . . . ou mêter', ouk adelphon, oukhi syngenê'* (I am alone, stateless, shamed by my man . . . no mother, no brother, no relative) (255–7).

Marina Carr's *By the Bog of Cats. . .* maintains sympathy for Medea by changing the story. Instead of killing Glauke and Creon as well as her own children and then flying off in a chariot drawn by dragons, Hester Swane, the Medea figure in Carr's play, is an itinerant living in a caravan whose mother left her when she was seven and for whom she pines daily. She and her lover, Carthage, have killed her brother and used his money to buy a farm where they have set up home and live with their seven-year-old daughter. When Carthage, the Jason character, marries the local big farmer's daughter and threatens to gain custody of her child, Hester takes revenge by setting fire to their farmhouse and barn and then resorts to suicide. However, through an accident of bad timing, she finds herself forced to kill her beloved daughter in the course of kill-ing herself. Thus, as Marina Carr tells the story, the marriage of Carthage to a younger woman has placed Hester in an impossible situation. Treated as an outcast as a member of the Travelling community and threatened with immediate eviction and the loss of her child, she acts in a passionate and tragic manner as a pathetic victim of the hegemonic culture.[5]

By contrast with Marina Carr's Hester Swane, Fiona Shaw's Medea is surrounded by an alien Irish-speaking female Chorus and a host of bullying men who are casting her out of her home and conniving to arrange a new marriage to exclude her.[6] She rants and raves at her treatment from inside her home (in the bowels of the stage) at the beginning of the play, and emerges to plot against her husband, transforming in costume from a middle-class cocktail dress, to a butcher's coat, wielding a carving knife and chasing her children offstage to kill them (see Figure 9). Nevertheless, after this appalling scene, one's sympathy with her returns at the end of the play as she collapses next to Jason beside a small pool, with both characters equally aghast at how events have transpired. Rather than exiting in triumph in a chariot drawn by dragons, Fiona

Shaw's Medea has been brought low by her moments of rage and rampage and she sits quietly, scarcely able to move. Thus, both productions show the capacity of women to take revenge on their philandering husbands, but both in their separate ways emphasise its tragic effect on the protagonist and thereby maintain sympathy for her despite her crimes.

The production of these two plays on the main stage of the Irish National Theatre produced very interesting responses from the critics. As mentioned above, the plays pose difficult questions about gender relations and national identity in a changing society. I want to look closely at two critical and vastly different reactions from journalists at the same newspaper, both of whom used the performances as an excuse to reflect on questions of identity. Significantly, one of the critics was female and the other male. Victoria White, enthusiastically supporting the production of *By the Bog of Cats. . .*, took the opportunity to compare Marina Carr's play to the whole canon of Irish theatre. She wrote: 'I grew to love theatre watching an Abbey stage which had no place for women. It had women on it, of course – they were in no shortage in Friel's [*Dancing at*] *Lughnasa*, for instance – but it was a symbolic space which had no place for the symbolism of women.'[7] By contrast, White said, in Marina Carr's *By the Bog of Cats. . .* , 'I saw women's rituals and psychological dynamics sketched for the first time on the national stage, on such a scale that I could see them as being significant at a national level'. Despite Irish theatre playing a major role in the social discourse of earlier decades, she argued that Ireland had no women playwrights who could reflect their position in society. She surmised that this was because women had no agency in the public sphere. 'It seemed to me at the time . . . that the theatre's obsession with great national themes played against women because they had no history of national power and they could not find the voice to make their psychological journeys symbolise those of the tribe.' White said that she had grown up seeing and reading so many plays about father–son relationships that 'I thought I had had one myself'. However, she felt that Marina Carr's play in 1998 represented the symbolism of female culture.

One could counter White's argument with examples of such figures from Irish drama as Cathleen Ni Houlihan, Pegeen Mike and Bessie Burgess as powerful characters possessing important symbolic significance, but perhaps what White had in mind specifically is the symbolic rites of passage of women and their relationships with their mothers and daughters. Although she did not discuss this particular scene, it is likely that White was partly referring to the wedding reception of the Jason and Glauke figures, during which not only the bride but a total of four females (representing three generations of women) wear competing white dresses, including bride, mother-in-law, who is obviously competing with the bride for attention (wearing not only a white dress and disingenuously commenting, 'How was I supposed to know that bride'd be wearin' white as well',[8] but also wanting to have a photograph taken of her new shoes), and the bridegroom's daughter in her white communion dress. Even Hester, in a *coup de théâtre*, turns up at the celebration wearing the white wedding dress that Carthage (Jason) had bought for her when they were first to be married, signifying through her symbolic costume that there are too many brides on stage and that the event will end in disaster (see Figure 10).

For White, the representation of women's symbology marked a new and significant statement in the theatre, by focusing on female rituals and rites of passage. White commented: 'When you see the whole symbolic system of wedding dresses and communion dresses, and mother–daughter relationships, on the Abbey stage for the first time, it is hard to understand why they took so long to get there.' Arguably they also reflected the new ability of women to claim a position of power in postcolonial Irish culture. In Foucauldian terms, one could see this as a reversal in power/knowledge. As Gayatri Spivak might argue, Carr manages to give a voice to the 'subaltern'.[9] White reckoned that not only was there now a significant female playwright putting a new dimension of society on the stage, but that the whole fabric of society had changed. In earlier times, according to White, 'Irish theatre . . . relied heavily on the fact that the audience was cohesive enough to identify *en masse* with the characters playwrights created; it . . . relied heavily, indeed, on the ability of these characters to symbolise different areas of Irish life.' However, she claimed that by the 1990s the 'audience had become so diffuse it found it hard to cod itself into being a tribe, even for a few hours'. White implied that the common identity of the Irish people had been exposed as a nationalist ploy to convince the populace of their distinctiveness from the colonising enemy. In postcolonial and increasingly post-Catholic Ireland, this essential identity was unravelling and women were now starting to play a significant role in the public sphere, and, in their transformation from a position of subservience, were subverting dominant images of national identity.

By contrast with Victoria White's enthusiastic welcome for Marina Carr's work, the male critic John Waters, on the other hand, took offence at (and seemingly felt threatened by) Fiona Shaw's version two years later. Like White, he wrote an article in the *Irish Times*, relating the play to some of the changes occurring in Irish society, especially the fall-out from the recent divorce legislation, and suggested that this production was rubbing salt into society's wounds: 'Women generally got a raw deal in Ancient Greece, being little more than chattels of their husband . . . but in modern Ireland, two-thirds of divorces are initiated by women. Ninety percent of divorces, regardless of fault, result in the wife getting the family home, custody of the children and an income for life at the husband's expense.'[10] Waters argued that Irish society had swung too far from the patriarchy of the past and was endangering the rights of men: 'This play touches down here, now, in a feminist-dominated culture, in which virtually all public discourse, including artistic discourse, is vetted for political correctness.' He felt that the Warner/Shaw production played a 'trick' on the audience by transforming the original: 'Not only are there nuanced differences in the script, but there is a set of choices made in the casting and playing, particularly of the male roles, that drives the play in a different way to the original.' John Waters presumably wanted to identify with Jason, but expressed disgust at Jason's characterisation as 'a muscle-bound himbo whose

self-justifications play as pure parody'. By contrast, Waters felt that
Fiona Shaw 'charms the harm out of Medea, winning our sympathy
by tickling our funny bones, and concealing the fact that the
production functions like a Christmas panto: the men being
pompous tyrants and the women free spirits seeking to deflate this
pomposity'. In a display of castration anxiety, Waters complained
that the play reflected the new Irish society in which women were
gaining too much control and wanted to get revenge at the expense
of male society. He expressed alarm that many women coming out
of the performance did not approve of the graphic depiction of
the deaths of Medea's children, as if these female members of the
audience wanted to witness revenge 'without being confronted by
consequences'. Waters argued that: 'Medea provides a chilling
parable of the truth about personal power in a State which daily
dispossesses fathers and children of the society of one another;
which facilitates the abuse of children by mothers (in allowing them
to be used as tools of blackmail); and routinely banishes men from
their homes on the uncorroborated word of one person.' Not
surprisingly, Waters took a sexist point of view in his column.
However, it is important to indicate that he was not simply voicing
the traditional male chauvinist position, but that of the 'new man'.
Waters, who wrote that he feared being accused of misogyny for his
views, had been involved in an unpleasant custody case with the
Irish singer Sinead O'Connor over a child that had resulted from
their brief relationship and was roughly the age of the children on
stage in *Medea*. Waters had fought hard to maintain joint custody
of his child, against the prevailing tide of public opinion that he
describes. In his reaction to the *Medea* production, clearly, Waters
was motivated by what he regarded as the dwindling rights of the
father over his children, and wanted to express his anger over not
the loss of patriarchy in society, but what he perceived as the
endangered rights of single male parents.

In addition to writing an article in the newspaper, Waters also
gave a pre-show talk in the Abbey Theatre, where he expressed
similar grievances about the production and the current state of
gender relations in Ireland. The gender debate continued as his

remarks at the Abbey were then condemned by a leading female social commentator, Terry Keane, who maintained a high profile not only as a gossip columnist but also as a highly publicised mistress of the former Taoiseach (Prime Minister) Charles Haughey. Keane labelled Waters as 'Ireland's foremost masculinist' and attacked him for mounting 'a gender-based assault' on women and for suggesting that Medea and her ilk should not go unpunished.[11] Criticising Waters' perception of the play, Keane asked: 'Having lost her husband and her own babies, are we to suppose she lived happily ever after?' Although she hadn't been present at his Abbey talk, Keane nevertheless accused him of making what she considered to be misogynist statements such as:

I don't believe in love; I don't believe in personality disorder; I don't believe in negative childhood experience; I don't believe in female biochemistry; I don't believe in postnatal depression; I don't believe in hormones; I don't believe in mood swings; I don't believe in self-pity; I don't believe in victimhood; I don't believe in heroines; I don't believe in universal motherhood; I don't believe in strong women; I don't believe in grand passion; I just believe in right and wrong.

Moreover, Keane went further and ventured from the public arena into the forbidden area of another's domestic sphere by intimating that Waters must be a poor father to his little girl: 'My sympathy goes to his toddler, Roisin. When she becomes a teenager and, I hope, believes in love, should she suffer from mood swings or any affliction of womanhood, she will be truly goosed. And better not ask dad for tea or sympathy . . . or help.'[12]

John Waters then sued Terry Keane for libel and the resultant high-profile court case gave the *Medea* production ongoing publicity in a rival theatrical performance in the law courts long after the original production had moved away from Dublin. The combative journalists emulated the principal roles of Jason and Medea, as they attacked each other over their conduct, and argued over what constituted public and private space. Asserting that Waters had given his speech at the Abbey and rushed off without allowing the right of reply, Keane proposed that, 'people like Mr. Waters did not like women to have the last word'.[13] In his defence, Waters questioned whether Keane had the right, simply because he was a public figure, 'to draw his daughter into the matter when he was on stage talking about a play that was 2,500 years old'.[14] Like a *deus ex machina*, the judge in summing up instructed the jury to consider whether Waters had strayed from the proper domain of a discussion of Greek tragedy and had 'embarked on the general "assault" on women alleged by Ms Keane'.[15] The jury, as in *The Eumenides*, were divided but eventually found for the man, and awarded Waters 84,000 euros in damages.

As one can see from these examples and as one knows from the riots at the Abbey Theatre in its early days, theatre in Ireland is taken seriously. As Victoria White observed, the national theatre is a place for asserting images of national identity. The national theatre is a symbolic space that predates the nation-state and, just as Schiller proposed of the German theatre, it helped to create the nation-state by helping to formulate notions of cultural identity. In the two productions under discussion, the patriarchal values of the nation are subverted by creating sympathy for the transgressive character of Medea. Her outsider status is neutralised as she is shown to be the victim of an exclusionary and unsympathetic patriarchal society. While Euripides maintained Medea's outsider status to the end of the play, especially by demonstrating her capacity to command dragons, the interpretations by Carr and Warner/Shaw turn the dominant culture into an alien environment and allow the audience to identify with Medea. Like the subversive work of J. M. Synge in such plays as *The Shadow of the Glen*, *The Tinkers' Wedding*, *The Well of the Saints* and *Playboy of the Western World* (which caused riots in the Abbey Theatre in the early part of the century), Marina Carr privileges the values of the transgressive figure of the Irish itinerant female over the settled inhabitants of the patriarchal Catholic community, providing a voice for a normally impotent subaltern caste in Irish society. Likewise, Warner and Shaw favoured the ostracised but attractive and cosmopolitan Medea by alienating the audience from the aggressive male patriarchy and the exclusionary world of the Irish-speaking Chorus (dressed in drab garments) that seemed like a throwback to the de Valera and Blythe government of the 1930s.[16]

Today, Irish audiences respond to plays about ancient Greece almost as if they were current events rather than classical mythology. John Waters assumed as much in his article, claiming:

It is certainly true that women seem to feel the play has the same capacity to accuse men, here and now, that it might have had in Ancient Greece. You could see women in the audience at key moments glancing meaningfully at their male partners, as if to say, 'Now, see what we have to put up with. Count yourself lucky I don't stab your children in their sleep.' The woman sitting next to me flung her hands in the air every time Jason opened his mouth.

His experience is far from unique. A similar example occurred when Fiona Shaw performed a Greek tragedy in Northern Ireland at the height of the Troubles. The journalist Mary Holland wrote:

I remember seeing [Fiona Shaw] play Electra in a sports stadium in Derry, her body hunched and distorted with grief . . . Night after night, the terrible stillness of the audience during the performance erupted into passionate debate on the subject matter of the play – violent death, filial loyalty and retribution. One evening a woman took Fiona Shaw's hands and said: 'You must not harbour these terrible feelings of bitterness and revenge. We have all of us to try and forgive, to put the past behind us. Otherwise there is no hope' – for all the world as though she was talking of an act of savagery which had happened just down the road, rather than to an actress about her performance in a Greek classical play.[17]

Judging from the critical reception of these performances, ancient Greek drama is alive and well in Ireland, continuing to engage society in current and important issues, and highlighting social change. The reviews I have examined mark *Medea* as a play of our times in Ireland, and it is an especially threatening play for a crumbling patriarchal society suffering from an acute castration complex.

Notes

An earlier version of this article appeared in *Eirene* (Prague), xxxix (2003): 254–63.

1. See Marianne McDonald and J. Michael Walton (eds), *Amid Our Troubles: Irish Versions of Greek Tragedy* (London: Methuen, 2002).
2. Karen Fricker, '"Medea" Bows out on a Parisian High', *Irish Times*, Weekend Review, 29 March 2003, p. 7. For a comparison between the London and Dublin productions, see Aoife Monks, 'Private Parts, Public Bodies: Cross-Dressing in the Work of Deborah Warner and Elizabeth Lecompte', Ph. D. dissertation, Trinity College Dublin (2002), pp. 155–9.
3. M. E. Collins, *History in the Making: Ireland 1868–1966* (Dublin: Educational Company of Ireland, 1993), p. 365.
4. A television series on the hepatitis C scandal (in which the government failed initially to support and compensate women who had contracted hepatitis C from contaminated blood) was so powerful that it arguably affected the results of the national election in 2002. The Fine Gael party lost approximately half of its seats in the election, after which Michael Noonan, who had been the Minister of Health during the hepatitis C controversy and was represented unsympathetically in the television series, resigned as head of the party.
5. Despite an economic boom in the late 1990s known familiarly as the 'Celtic Tiger', the Travelling community, which has a long tradition in Ireland, continued to be marginalised by the dominant society with repressive anti-trespass laws especially affecting them. Hester's status as part of the Travelling community clearly marks her as an outsider and foreigner even though she and her family have long associations with the place where she lives. Her victimisation by the dominant society also echoes the poor treatment of refugees and asylum-seekers in the late twentieth century both by the government and society.
6. The Irish language had declined under British imperial rule, surviving mainly in a few western regions known as the Gaeltacht. Its revival began in earnest at the end of the nineteenth century as part of the cultural nationalist movement. Aoife Monks argues that because the

audience at the Abbey would not have understood Irish very fluently, they would have had difficulty identifying with a Chorus that they could not understand (see Monks, 'Private Parts, Public Bodies', p. 156).

7. Victoria White, 'Irish Theatre Begins to Change as Audience Becomes Increasingly Diffuse: Women Writers Finally Take Centre Stage', *Irish Times*, 15 October 1998.

8. Marina Carr, *By the Bog of Cats. . .* (Loughcrew, Co. Meath: Gallery Press, 1998), p. 51.

9. Spivak argues that because the subaltern has no voice, the intellectual must represent her. See Gayatri Spivak, 'Can the Subaltern Speak?', in Patrick Williams and Laura Chrisman (eds), *Colonial Discourse and Post-Colonial Theory* (New York: Harvester Wheatsheaf, 1993), p. 104. For a discussion of the role of the intellectual giving a voice to the subaltern, see also Ania Loomba, *Colonialism/Postcolonialism* (London: Routledge, 1998), pp. 244–5.

10. John Waters, 'Problems in Excusing Medea's Murders', *Irish Times*, 19 June 2000.

11. 'Journalist Sues for Libel over Terry Keane Gossip Column', *Irish Times*, 17 April 2002.

12. Terry Keane, 'Allow Me the Last Word on John Waters' World', *Sunday Times*, 18 June 2000.

13. 'Columnist Says She Does not Consider Waters a Bad Father', *Irish Times*, 20 April 2002.

14. 'Journalist Sues for Libel . . .', *Irish Times*, 17 April 2002.

15. 'Keane Absent as Waters Wins €84,000 for Libel', *Irish Times*, 24 June 2002.

16. The Irish language was encouraged in the 1930s and Ernest Blythe, a Minister of Finance who became artistic director of the Abbey Theatre, encouraged many Irish-language plays to be performed in addition to a somewhat unimaginative Irish repertoire (e.g. by comparison with the eclectic international approach of the Gate Theatre). The Abbey Theatre, without Yeats and Gregory at the helm, tended to stagnate as a result.

17. Mary Holland, *Irish Times*, 12 October 1995.

7. Kennelly's Rebel Women

Anthony Roche

Since his emergence in the 1950s, Brendan Kennelly has been one of the most popular and prolific of Irish poets. But these have also been the very qualities which have led to his being overlooked in many accounts of contemporary Irish poetry.[1] His early poems alternate between the lyric and the satiric, but are most effective when the two modes glance off each other. With the emergence of his epic poem *Cromwell* in 1983, it became clear not only that Kennelly was developing into a major poet but that he was providing a probing of Irish history beyond the scope of most of his peers. This achievement was confirmed by his second epic, 1991's *The Book of Judas*, where he moved from anatomising Cromwell to a more global scapegoat. Though he may seem in ways a Romantic poet (celebrating the beauty of nature, addressing Ireland as subject), Kennelly in his writing has always subjected the poetic 'I' to intense investigation, deconstructing even as he gives voice to a range of attitudes. This principle is central to the achievement of his epic poems, which mobilise a series of personae and engage them in dialogue with each other – such as the exchanges between the historic figure of Oliver Cromwell and the contemporary comic Irishman Buffún. Kennelly's poetry, although it has a strong lyric vein, draws on concepts from the theatre – masks, voices, dialogue – in order to convey a psychological and cultural complexity and to express a wide tonal range, embracing satire and celebration.

The attitudes in Kennelly's poetry, for all of the deconstruction they undergo, remain those of an Irish male of his generation and for a long time the unlikeliest and most contradictory position of all seemed to be that of Brendan Kennelly and feminism. During the period he was engaged in writing the two epic poems, he produced three versions of Greek tragedies in each of which the foregrounded tragic character is female rather than male: *Antigone*, *Medea* and *The Trojan Woman*. They can be seen as part of the same epic project, extending his range and declaring a more serious ambition as a writer. But they also share in the psychic confrontation and challenge of *Cromwell* and *Judas*. Writing versions of these three classic plays enabled Kennelly to voice a female perspective and provided both a stylistic and personal challenge. I think it is no accident that all three were written in the mid- to late 1980s, when Ireland was convulsed by debates and referenda having to do with the rights of women and control of their own sexual identity in relation to abortion and divorce.[2] The 1980s were also traumatic for Brendan Kennelly and his preface to *Medea* gives the personal context in which this version emerged:

I spent the best part of the summer of 1986 in St. Patrick's Psychiatric Hospital in Dublin . . . I was trying to recover from prolonged alcoholism and I found myself listening, listening, especially to women. The women I listened to ranged in age from about seventeen to about seventy. Many of them had one thing in common. Rage. Rage mainly against men, Irishmen like myself . . . This was the rage I tried to present in *Medea*.[3]

The shared context of the psychiatric hospital, the common ground of powerlessness shared with the women, and the admission of 'prolonged alcoholism' as something which had fuelled the swaggering 'broth of a boyo' persona for many years are all relevant here.

Kennelly's version of Sophocles' *Antigone* is, in his own words, 'a straight translation'.[4] But it does not take a theory of translation as implicit invention/creation to see that Kennelly's stance of apparent objectivity, of self-effacement before the pre-existent text, cannot be long sustained. He describes his working method as follows: 'I worked from late nineteenth-century translations, six or seven of them, then put them away and wrote it out of my head.'[5] Those familiar with Kennelly's poetry will not read his version for long before encountering familiar images and realising the extent to which the themes of the *Antigone* have cross-pollinated with the most abiding concerns of the poet's imagination. Kennelly dates his version 'July 1984'. What adds to its interest, particularly as it reflects, however wittingly, on the contemporary state of Ireland, is the proximity of its writing to the long poem *Cromwell*, an interlinked sequence of 146 pages of sonnets, occasionally interrupted by longer meditations.[6] Kennelly's *Cromwell* has less to do with literal historic events than a symbolic rendering of the continuing effects of those events on the Irish psyche. What he writes in another context applies equally to his own poetic procedures in *Cromwell*: 'Many Irish poets are deeply concerned with the past, finding in Ireland's turbulent history images and personalities that, when dramatised and charged with imagination, help to shed light on current problems.'[7]

If the poem continues to reverberate in the minds of those who have read it, then it can do no less in the head of the man who generated it. In going on to write a version of Sophocles' *Antigone*, Kennelly implicitly encourages his readers to look for continuity and connection between the two endeavours. The most striking is the resemblance between Cromwell's speech and actions in the poem and those of Creon in the *Antigone*, a consonance suggested by the harsh alliteration of their names. Kennelly's Cromwell and his Creon are the source of a terrifying power in their respective domains, operating as absolute and unquestioned incarnations of political authority. Creon announces as he enters that he now occupies the throne of Thebes; Cromwell is not only the agent of English imperialism in Ireland but the Lord Protector. They derive their authority, not from orderly succession in a stable institution of civil rule, but from an act of carnage, a military exchange in which they proved their superiority by force of arms. Creon's refusal to temporise in the matter of Polyneices springs from the contradiction at the heart of his rule: the need to separate himself from the acts of blood through which he came to power. Accordingly, he speaks of Theban law as immutable and unchanging. In the case of Cromwell, the absoluteness of God's rule which he proclaims may be verbally self-evident, but it requires repeated demonstration at the end of a sword. As Creon says:

> We have a city to maintain.
> It will be maintained by rule, by law,
> By men who understand that truth. (p. 13)

When Creon asserts that this is his 'word', the Chorus is forced to admit: 'You have the power to turn your word to action' (p. 14). This same 'power' is attributed to Cromwell in Kennelly's poem. Over and over, he makes good his 'word' sheathed in the sword of action. To this, Kennelly opposes (and criticises) the Irish addiction to talk for its own sake. He undercuts 'the rhetorical man / In the pulpit who roared' (p. 126) by providing a 'welcome' for 'one who knows his own thinking, / A man for whom a word is a deed come true'. Creon and Cromwell are the most radical of poets, restoring to words their bloody immediacy. They share an avidity and ability to translate their words into deeds that speak not only to their central position within the depicted society but even more to their compelling mythic dimensions as figures for poetry and drama. In his study *Antigones*, George Steiner quotes Hölderlin's definition of the key to Greek tragic discourse, which maintains that 'the Greek-tragic word is factually deadly. It seizes upon the human body and kills it. In Greek-tragic drama there occurs . . . "real murder through words" . . . the "athletic, plastic" (Hölderlin's adjectives) immediacy of physical destruction through an act of speech'.[8]

Creon's power to translate word into deed precisely defines the nature of the threat posed by Antigone, since she herself not only makes but vindicates the same claim: 'I sought to bury my brother. / That is my word, my deed. / Word and deed are one in me' (p. 22). The single greatest shock to Creon and the Chorus up to that point is caused by the revelation that the antagonist is not male, as they have assumed, but female. The affront that Antigone offers to Creon is a challenge not only to the institutional power he claims to represent but to the inescapably patriarchal character of that power and those institutions. Creon makes it clear, when he discovers the subversive agent is female, that he is punishing her for usurping the prerogatives of his sex. Antigone's threat to patriarchy is two-fold: not only an encroachment on traditional male areas of action but also advocacy of a radically different way of being and set of values centred on the feminine. What the play, in its Greek original and Kennelly's version, does is show Antigone 'acting for and, in the perspective of prevailing conventions of society and of politics, as a man'.[9] She does so by taking over the vacated male role in the House of Laius (which leaves the traditional and marginal role of helpless, suffering femininity to Ismene). But she also takes initially uncertain but increasingly confident steps towards an advocacy and enactment of the feminist. The first issue in such a progress is that of speech versus silence. Disturbed as she is by the nature of what her sister is about to do, Ismene is even more disturbed by Antigone's lack of traditional feminine reticence, her determination publicly to articulate and take possession of her actions:

ISMENE: At least, tell no one what you plan to do.
            Be secret. So will I.
ANTIGONE: Go shout it from the roof-tops, Ismene,
            Forget your despicable silence.
            Your silence will bring contempt on you
            In the end. Be true, not silent. (p. 10)

His version is, as Kennelly himself says, a feminist 'declaration of independence'.[10] That declaration emerges fully in the key exchanges with Creon, which immediately engage the sexual dialectic. Creon addresses Antigone, not by name, but by gender, as girl, with overtones of contempt, objectification and denial of their kinship. She retaliates by addressing him in turn as man, thereby appropriating the sexist terminology and using it against him. In what she says, she stresses her obligations to her dead brother. But Antigone also makes the vitally related point that the obligations she follows, the values to which her act refers, are outside the accepted norms and conventions of established political exchange and so incomprehensible to patriarchy: 'If I seem foolish to you, this may be

/ Because you are a foolish man, a foolish judge' (p. 21). Creon's response – 'I would be no man, / She would be the man / If I let her go unpunished' (p. 22) – confirms the extent to which Antigone has rightly uncovered the double nature of the discourse, the fundamental threat she poses not so much to the status quo of stable rule (judges, kings, etc.) but to the masculine appropriation of power which its apparently disinterested objectivity scarcely veils.

Steiner points out the reciprocal logic by which, if Antigone prevails, 'a twofold inversion of the natural order will ensue. Creon will no longer be a man and, in perfect expression of the logic of reciprocal definition, Antigone will have become one . . . The masculinity of Antigone's deed, the masculinity of the risks which she has incurred . . . fundamentally impugns the manhood of Creon.'[11] But it does more than that, especially in Kennelly's skilful development of those areas of the text in which a feminist sub-text is latent. For already, by this stage in his version, the counter-assertion of non-patriarchal values by Antigone is well advanced. The Guard has described her primordial cry and maternal gestures over the corpse of her brother; but these cannot simply be interpreted as traditional womanly traits. They are coupled with an assertive and provocative deed; the effect of that conjunction is to undercut both established masculine and feminine norms through this enlarged synthesis of speech and act.

The Kennelly text goes on to assert the more threatening principle of difference which Antigone's stance embodies and which is not susceptible to Creon's attempt to address it in traditional terms:

CREON: Are you not ashamed to act
            Differently
            From all these other people?

ANTIGONE: No . . . never forget the possible difference
            Of that other world of the gods.
            Thinking of difference there
            May make us different here. (p. 24)

The difference between the living and the dead is analogous to the difference between the areas of male and female experience. Antigone's talk of 'the gods', even in the original, is never pitched consistently in terms of organised religion but serves rather as the sign for a series of personal imperatives to which only she has the key. This will also be the case in Kennelly's version of *Medea*.

The last section initiates a series of contrasting images, a cluster of associations, defining the zone in which these personal prerogatives can best be articulated. In the play's terms, these are the regions of the dead and not the living, the dark rather than the light, the hitherto unexplored regions of her own being. For Antigone is not simply put to death. Rather, she is led away to a place of confinement, a dark space where she is to sustain a liminal existence: 'When you have placed her / In that black hole among the rocks, / Leave her there, alone. / Banished from the world of men, / This girl will never see the light again' (p. 37). Not only her movement but that of the play as a whole is away from the garish light of Creon's *realpolitik*, from the discredited life and activities of the daylight world, towards the dark, physically circumscribed but in many ways open possibilities of a personal feminist space. Kennelly can go no further, both because his literary source does not and because that 'black hole' is a woman-centred space towards which the male writer can do no more than gesture. Antigone's final remarks are addressed as much to the author(s) as to the Chorus:

> . . . I am a woman
> And must go my way alone.
> You know all about men,
> You know all about power,
> You know all about money.
>
> But you know nothing of women.
>
> What man
> Knows anything of woman?

> If he did
> He would change from being a man
> As men recognise a man. (p. 35)

Brendan Kennelly writes in the Preface to his translation of *Medea* that he tried to imagine her as 'a modern woman'.[12] This approach would be in line with his giving voice to the various women he heard as a fellow patient in St Patrick's psychiatric hospital. In his version, Kennelly claims the same temporal freedom that he enjoys in *Cromwell* and *The Book of Judas*, moving between fifth-century BC Greece and late twentieth-century Ireland. When this is done by one of the characters, the effect is self-conscious and incongruous, as when the Teacher/Tutor admits:

> But come, I am leapfrogging the centuries.
> Still, that is a teacher's privilege – [. . .]
> the knowledge that all things happen at the same time,
> to the same people (though they all die)
> as the centuries flow by, smiles upon their lips
> At the spectacle of honest, helpless repetition. (p. 18)

Kennelly has opposed 'the true madness inherent in that purely chronological view of reality' (p. 7) by stressing the cyclical and circular nature of human experience. This temporal fluidity is best expressed in his version in the speeches of the Chorus, who stand at one remove from the drama, witnesses like ourselves. Their consideration of the troubled nature of the parent–child relationship is effortlessly and effectively expanded by Kennelly, not only with more lines but in terms which translate readily into the lives of contemporary parents:

> . . . those whose homes are full
> of growing children that they love
> are often eaten by anxiety and worry . . .
> How are they to rear them properly?
> What schools shall they send them to?
> How shall they speak to them?
> How show authority and not appear tyrannical? (p. 66)

In the Chorus's final speech, Kennelly adds two last lines to acknowledge explicitly that this is not the first but the latest in a long line of Medeas, that versions by contemporary writers are ways of addressing central questions which these profound dramas raise and which no one version will definitively answer or exhaust:

> And yet I wonder, and will always wonder –
> Is Medea's crime Medea's glory? (p. 75)

The cross-pollination I have already identified as operating between *Antigone* and *Cromwell* is present in Kennelly's version of *Medea* also. His writing of it came in the midst of the eight years he spent working on *The Book of Judas*: 'These women in hospital, expressing their rage at betrayal and violence and cruel indifference, entered *The Book of Judas*. And many themes and preoccupations, even obsessions, in *The Book of Judas* spilled into the rage and accusations of *Medea*' (p. 7). In the Greek plays he has chosen, Kennelly has directly taken on the voice of woman through such tragic heroines as Antigone, Medea and the Trojan Women in order to articulate a fierce, sustained protest at their treatment down through the ages. In *The Book of Judas*, the voice is usually that of a man and is split between concern at the exclusion of women and fear at their demands. One of the few individual Judas poems presented in a woman's voice is 'Night Air', an inverted modern-day Oedipus complex. It is as memorable and shocking for its breaking of taboo in its representation of the mother–son relationship as the central tragic action of *Medea*:

> My friend Rebecca returned from a party,
> Glad of the peace of home, sat in
> Her living-room listening to music.
> After a while she decided to check the children,
> Softly upstairs towards Jonathan's bedroom.
> He was twelve, her favourite. She found him
> Lying in bed, naked, asleep, his penis
> Erect in the light thrown from the landing.
> Before she knew it she was at the bedside,

Wanting the boy's penis inside her. Breathing
'Jonathan! Jonathan!', she leaned towards him, then realising
Herself, turned, closed the door, rushed downstairs, out
Into the garden, gulped the night air, her shocked mind shivering.[13]

The great theme of Kennelly's epic poem is betrayal, betrayal of others but ultimately of oneself. The betrayal occurs between and among the sexes, often in the verbal and sexual act of love; of children by parents and authority figures; and those of its members for whom society has least care. A particular concern throughout his poetry is the betrayal of trust. In the opening monologue of his *Medea*, the keynote of betrayal is sounded: 'Betrayal is the ripest crop in this land. / The more it is slashed, the stronger it grows' (p. 13). In the Notes to his 1997 Oxford World's Classics translation of *Medea*, James Morwood identifies 'the idea of the woman who is sexually slighted as a powerful one in the play' by directing attention to such lines of Medea's as the following: 'In all other respects a woman is full of fear and proves a coward at the sight of iron in the fight, but when she is wronged in her marriage bed, no creature has a mind more murderous.'[14] In this speech, claimed by Morwood as 'the most famous feminist statement in ancient literature',[15] the sexual nature of the indignities to which women are subjected is the focus. This speech is considerably amplified in Kennelly's 'translation'. The line 'We have to take a master for our body' (Morwood) explodes into

> Men, the horny despots of our bodies,
> sucking, fucking, licking, chewing, farting into our skin,
> sitting on our faces, fingering our arses,
> exploring our cunts, widening our thighs,
> drawing the milk that gave the bastards life. (p. 25)

But if the note of sexual betrayal is rendered in more physically explicit terms, the deepest concern in Kennelly's *Medea* is with the betrayal of language: 'Will the real world be destroyed / by Medea's rage? Is this her / rage – to falsify all words, so that / men and women, in their talk, / are capable of nothing but lies?' (p. 19). For

Medea what proves most wounding in Jason's betrayal of their relationship is how it strikes at the heart of the ethical covenant between word and deed, promise and fulfilment: 'I think she thinks all human words are lies, / that never again can any word be true' (p. 23).

Kennelly describes his conception of a modern Jason as 'yuppified . . . a plausible, ambitious, articulate and gifted opportunist who knows what he wants and how to get it' (p. 8). 'Articulate' here is not a term of praise, ironically commending the tone of sweet reasonableness in which Jason seeks to defend what he has done. Medea appears to submit to his demands and be reasonable. Her speech reveals (by making explicit) the logic of betrayal in everything Jason has been saying: 'Jason, I ask forgiveness for everything I said . . . But I am what I am . . . a woman, / a mere woman. I beg forgiveness, / and admit my hideous mistakes. / But now, I have turned / my mind towards sanity and hope / and sincere co-operation' (p. 58). Kathleen McCracken argues persuasively that here, as in his *Antigone*, Kennelly 'centralises the issue of language and gender'.[16] So corrupted is language by this process of lying that women can often best combat it only with their silence. Creon claims that the 'most difficult obstacle of all is a woman's silence – / it makes a man feel that his words are less / than the squeaking of mice in the sleeping dark' (p. 29). And what Medea enjoins on the Chorus of women beyond anything else is their silence, a vital component of what she will undertake:

> my sisters, I ask of you
> only one thing: your silence.
> Silence, the most powerful
> weapon of all. We
> women are known and proven
> to be gentle, warm, considerate
> creatures. But if there is
> something terrible to be
> done, a woman's
> gentleness becomes the most
> murderous weapon of all.

And it is all the more murderous
when the silence of women
surrounds the deed. (p. 27)

When the Nurse first considers what form Medea's revenge will take, she imagines that the wronged woman 'may steal into the palace / where Jason lies, drive a sword / into his heart, his belly, chop / his penis, and his testicles for the pure pleasure of revenge' (p. 14). But Medea's revenge takes a very different and less direct form. It strikes not at Jason's body but at his desire to father more children, by denying him those he already claims he has and killing the woman by whom he would father more. Antigone is forced into the position of a man in the actions she undertakes in that play; and Medea seems headed in the same direction. The world of Greek tragedy was prepared to endorse justifiable revenge between adults, usually male, even as it traced the bloody and lengthy consequences. But what Medea proposes springs not from acting as a man by wielding a sword but by not acting as a woman, in violently doing away with the very children she has created.

At the close of Morwood's translation, Jason denounces Medea as an 'artist in obscenity'.[17] This perverse compliment testifies to all of the creativity Medea has expended in devising and carrying out her plot. Kennelly develops the notion of Medea's revenge as an exercise in artistry. His Medea stresses the extent to which Jason is her creation, disclosing the ways in which she betrayed others in order to secure his victory. When she plans her revenge she reflects: 'Never before / did I feel the fullness of womanhood, / the danger emanating with every breath. / It is exhilarating, irrepressible, new, / as though I were an army in myself. / Gentleness, timidity, have buried my ferocity. /What men call "charm" has quelled my real talent' (p. 32).

The issue is the denial of female autonomy and hence of their creativity. In *The Book of Judas*, there is a poem in which Judas asks Jesus: 'How is it . . . you haven't even / A single woman among your twelve apostles?' Jesus replies with a wintry smile that he will 'bring the matter up at our next meeting'.[18] After exulting in the liberation of her suppressed talent, Medea speaks in an echo of Milton's Satan about how 'I am at home in my own evil' ('Evil, be thou my good') and expresses the possibility that a 'little poison, / properly administered, may restore the hope / of that lost justice that compelled us / to give respect to others, and dignity / to the mind of man' (pp. 32–3). The play's outcome suggests that, although her cause is worthy, Medea goes too far in its single-minded pursuit, sacrificing her own humanity in the process. The Chorus retain their sisterly sympathy for Medea's plight with regard to what Jason has done to her, even as that same source of mutual identification leads them unequivocally to condemn her action. They warn her that, though she will achieve iconic status and immortal renown, it will be achieved at the cost of being 'forever, Medea the murderess / of her own children' (p. 56). She will become a byword for lack of humanity, as Judas is for betrayal.

No matter how multifaceted a single persona may be, there is a limit to the number of possibilities it can register. And those possibilities, while they may be sounded by a character like Medea in the course of the drama, are fatally contracted when she decides on her bloody course of action. Medea becomes, for all time, identified as the woman who killed her two sons. Antigone's oppositional behaviour is consistently contrasted with and offset by Ismene's quietude. But the greatest range not just of female characters but of iconic figures with whom woman might be identified is offered by Euripides' *The Trojan Women*. Presiding over all is Hecuba, who has become a byword for grief in the lamentation she raises over the murdered members of her family and in the play's closing act of identification with the city of Troy as it is burned to the ground. But Hecuba does not have the entire stage to herself. Rather she gives way in turn to Cassandra, whose ecstatic possession leads to the description of madness; to Andromache, who has been forced out of the life of the compliant wife; and, in the most unusual turn of all, to Helen, who has to defend herself not against the charges of her deserted husband Menelaus but of Hecuba herself, who accuses Helen of wantonly causing the war and betraying her sex.

The most frequent charge against the play is that it is static, insufficiently dramatic. Philip Vellacott's view in the introduction to his 1973 translation of *The Women of Troy* is representative: 'More than one third of the tragedy is written in lyrical metres; and much of the dialogue is static. The play itself contains little that can be called either action or plot.'[19] Brendan Kennelly addresses this objection in the Preface to his own translation:

Some scholars and critics refer to *The Trojan Women* as a passive play, more a stirring spectacle than a real drama. I re-wrote this version of Euripides' play many times; and as I re-wrote it I found that it became increasingly active, although the women's situation overwhelmingly said that they were passive victims at the whimsical mercy of their male conquerors. And yet, within that apparent passivity of victims, I increasingly found a strong, active, resolute and shrewd note . . . As I re-wrote the play . . . it was this deepening sense of the reality of the various women that I found hardest to capture. A man is trapped in his own language.[20]

In a sense, Kennelly is aligning himself with the women's struggle in the play. That struggle at one level is to resist and critique the language of the male conqueror, which would reduce the Trojan women to the status of undifferentiated chattels distributed as one of the spoils of war. Kennelly's version is eloquent on this score, as when Hecuba remarks of the violation she is about to undergo: 'My body waits – for what? / A man's eyes! A man's eyes will cover me, / examine me from head to foot. / A man's eyes / can look at me in public / as if I were his private property' (p. 13). Hecuba is moved to protest but also to raise the question of how such an apparently absolute defeat can be overcome: 'Yet, may not a woman / fight, yes, fight, here and now? / May not a woman / win? / How?' (pp. 13–14). The play not only depicts an outer but an inner struggle, as each of the Trojan women struggles to realise a fuller sense of herself – a passionate dialogue of self and soul which succeeds, at least temporarily, in keeping the oppressive external circumstances at bay.

The first to do so is Cassandra. She occupies a special position in the society, as a virgin who has been reserved for the gods. The handing over of her to sexual violation thus carries a particular charge. In the dialogue between the gods with which the play opens, Pallas Athene attributes her turning against the Greeks to the lack of veneration with which both Cassandra and her temple have been treated: 'They wronged me / in my own holy place. / They have forgotten the obscenity / they committed against me' (p. 10). When Cassandra enters, she does so in full ecstatic communion with the gods, a figure feared even by her mother and not susceptible to rational discourse. What this Trojan woman gains from the access of divine madness, as Ophelia does in Shakespeare's *Hamlet*, is a much greater (albeit temporary) scope of verbal and physical freedom. As the Greek herald Talthybius who holds all the women prisoner admits, 'if I did not know that you are mad, / . . . I'd make you swallow your wild words / here and now' (p. 26). Cassandra comes on celebrating her imminent 'marriage' to Agamemnon, apparently deluded into masking the horror of what is about to happen by retreating into a fantasy. But the irony is deliberate, since she goes on to disclose that the 'marriage' she intends is the killing of Agamemnon. Kennelly adds lines showing the further onset of ecstasy, with Cassandra declaring her intention to press beyond the apparent reality of war and 'the pit / of human darkness . . . to find my special light' (pp. 23–4). That 'special light' is now shed by Cassandra on the Trojan women's plight. It reverses perspective in order to reveal the hollowness of the victors and the authentic possessions of the defeated, who have not been separated from kith and kin to die on alien soil. As long as she remains within her trance, Cassandra has a freedom even beyond that she would normally enjoy were she not a prisoner of the Greeks.

Andromache, who is next on, speaks of how little return she has had for the life she formerly enjoyed, a life where, in Kennelly's pithy translation, 'I did everything to please my man' (p. 38). Even Euripides' original expresses irony at the outcome of Andromache's social ambitions: 'I made high repute my aim, / Achieved it, and now forfeit all that I have achieved'.[21] The question of whether to stay loyal to Hector or to accommodate herself to her new man and reality is one upon which she appears to fluctuate. But the change of condition has led Andromache to question the line of social and sexual conformity she has pursued all along, to see it as artificial rather than natural. Like the other women in Kennelly's version, her mind comes forcibly into play in response to her enslavement:

> I must be
> a slave . . .
> and be the kind of woman
> that a man will say I have to be.
> And yet I clearly see
> that if my body is a slave
> an untouched portion of my mind is free. [. . .]
> My mind is crookeder and wilder
> than any dream I've ever had. (p. 40)

Andromache then learns that the son in whose future she has invested such hope is to be taken from her and killed. Although the circumstances are different, her speech has the same blend of tenderness and brutality as in Medea's farewell to her own children as they too are about to be killed. Even more evidently than with Medea, Andromache offers the spectacle of a woman brutalising herself as a mode of survival in a patriarchal society bent on war: 'Quick! I must go to a Greek's bed. / My son is dead, this is war, / there must be love somewhere. Dead' (p. 46).

When Menelaus enters looking for his wife Helen, the pattern of irony has now become clear and so it is no surprise to find he is looking for her in order to take revenge. Helen is quite ready to defend herself, but what gives a double edge to the charges she must face is that they are delivered not by Menelaus but by Hecuba: 'You know nothing of the wrongs and horrors / she unleashed in this city. / Hear her story and you'll know why / this cool, manipulating bitch must die' (p. 50). Part of Helen's defence is to point out how the other women are scapegoating her for what they have suffered. The scapegoating of Helen is enhanced in Kennelly's version when all the other Trojan women turn on her and invest her with all the negative images hurled at women over the ages. Helen is viewed in the play as negatively as the other most famous (and still living) icon of the Trojan War, Odysseus; both of them have their traditional images undercut. No one denies her beauty, whatever view they may take of her; but Helen insists on her own reality, the more necessary and difficult given how long and absolutely she has operated as a symbol: 'I use my own words / to speak my own truth. / If you choose to kill me for my truth / then kill me; but know / it is Helen's truth you kill / to your eternal shame' (pp. 54–5).

The least persuasive part of Helen's defence is when she absolves herself from all her actions by saying the goddess made her do it. This brings me to the last point I wish briefly to consider: the place of the gods in Greek drama. They are endlessly referred to and invoked throughout all three of these plays. But *The Trojan Women* is the only one in which they put in an appearance. The play begins with Poseidon preparing to take his farewell of Troy. Poseidon's departure is halted by the arrival of Pallas Athene and her request that he help her make the return of the Greeks to their home a troubled and lengthy affair. Throughout Euripides' original, an extremely wide range of views about the gods is expressed, whether they act with the best or the worst of motives or some mixture in between. Kennelly retains the onstage manifestation of the gods in his version of *The Trojan Women*, even though he has given them short verbal shrift in his two earlier versions, cutting the references to a minimum. The presence of the gods was memorably realised in director Lynne Parker's staging of Kennelly's version at Dublin's Peacock Theatre in June 1993. Poseidon was played by Birdy Sweeney, a vaudevillean who began serious acting at a time most people retire; his aged features expressed humorous compassion and wry resignation as he looked at the model ships and houses of designer Frank Conway's miniaturised Troy. The deities exuded a louche and decadent aura as they lounged and listened to one of their number improvising on a piano.

In the speeches by the women, Kennelly occasionally retains the terms 'gods' but more often replaces it with the monotheistic 'God' of Christian tradition. In one sense, the fatigued departure of Birdy Sweeney's Poseidon at the start is just that – the end of direct representation of the deities on the Greek stage, the withdrawal of the gods about which Nietzsche has so much to say. What eventually took their place was the Christian dispensation. One of the aims Kennelly's heterodoxy wants to achieve is to underline the continuity between the two religions of certain forms of worship and belief – such as the ecstatic possession of Cassandra. But for a great many people in an Irish and Western context, the Christian God has also been withdrawing in recent decades. And the questions which the Greek characters pose to their deities concerning issues of justice and how evil is allowed to prosper are precisely those that Christians agonise over. As Hecuba puts it: 'If I call on God for help / all I find is his helplessness. / Yet I must seek and I must cry / for help that seems not to exist' (p. 31). The issues throughout *The Trojan Women* have to do with power and powerlessness. In the long closing speech of Kennelly's version, considerably expanded from the Euripides, his Hecuba speaks of a 'power' she possesses that 'no man can ever touch' (p. 78). Having confronted a God whose 'hand contained nothing, / only the black seeds of our destruction' (p. 69), it is only when she listens to the music of the women's hearts that she becomes unafraid and able to locate the god within. This process enables her to 'wonder who I am / and not break apart in madness / because I don't have an answer' (p. 78).

If the classic Greek tragedies have persisted in Western consciousness, it is because they find arresting form to raise the questions for which we still have not found the answers. For Brendan Kennelly, as a male writer 'trapped in his own language', they have given him the opportunity 'to write an active drama exploring the complex reality of a few memorable women'.

Notes

1. Brendan Kennelly is afforded a mere four pages in *The Cambridge Companion to Contemporary Irish Poetry*, edited by Matthew

Campbell (Cambridge: CUP, 2003). In 'Performance and Dissent: Irish Poets in the Public Sphere', Lucy Collins has just room to register Kennelly's popularity and to suggest that there is more to his career than that in 'the engaging yet often disconcerting quality of his writing' (p. 212).

2. For more on this, see Anthony Roche, 'Ireland's *Antigones*: Tragedy North and South', in Michael Kenneally (ed.), *Cultural Contexts and Literary Idioms in Contemporary Irish Literature* (Gerrard's Cross: Colin Smythe, 1988), pp. 221–50. The material on Kennelly's version of *Antigone* in this article is drawn from this source, though it has been condensed and revised.

3. 'Preface', in *Euripides' 'Medea': A New Version by Brendan Kennelly* (Newcastle-upon-Tyne: Bloodaxe Books, 1988, 1991), pp. 6–7.

4. Brendan Kennelly's original notes to the script of his version of *Antigone* (1984). These differ from the essay 'Doing Justice to *Antigone*' appended to the published version of 1996: *Sophocles' 'Antigone': A New Version by Brendan Kennelly* (Newcastle-upon-Tyne: Bloodaxe Books, 1996), pp. 50–1. All subsequent page references to Kennelly's version of *Antigone* are to this edition and will be incorporated in the text.

5. Ibid.

6. Brendan Kennelly, *Cromwell: A Poem* (Dublin: Beaver Row Press, 1983). All page references are to this edition and will be incorporated in the text. It will be clear from the context in each case whether the page reference is to *Antigone* or *Cromwell*.

7. Brendan Kennelly, 'Louis MacNeice: An Irish Outsider', in Masaru Sekine (ed.), *Irish Writers and Society at Large* (Gerrard's Cross: Colin Smythe, 1985), p. 100.

8. George Steiner, *Antigones* (Oxford: Clarendon Press, 1984), p. 95.

9. Ibid., p. 241.

10. Kennelly, Notes to *Antigone*.

11. Steiner, *Antigones*, p. 238.

12. Kennelly, 'Preface', *Medea*, p. 8. All subsequent page references are to this edition and will be incorporated in the text.

13. Brendan Kennelly, *The Book of Judas* (Newcastle-upon-Tyne: Bloodaxe Books, 1991), p. 34.

14. Euripides, *'Medea' and Other Plays,* trans. and ed. James Morwood, introduction by Edith Hall (Oxford and New York: OUP, 1998), pp. 172, 8.

15 Ibid., p. 171.
16. Kathleen McCracken, 'Rage for a New Order: Brendan Kennelly's Plays for Women', in Richard Pine (ed.), *Dark Fathers into Light: Brendan Kennelly* (Newcastle-upon-Tyne: Bloodaxe Books, 1994), p. 135.
17. Euripides, *Medea*, p. 36.
18. Kennelly, 'The Twelve Apostlettes', in *The Book of Judas*, p. 137.
19. 'Introduction', in Euripides, *'The Bacchae' and Other Plays*, trans. Philip Vellacott (London: Penguin, 1973), p. 16.
20. 'Preface', in *Euripides' 'The Trojan Women': A New Version by Brendan Kennelly* (Newcastle-upon-Tyne: Bloodaxe Books, 1993), p. 5. All subsequent page references are to this edition and will be incorporated in the text.
21. Euripides, *'The Bacchae' and Other Plays*: 111.

8. 'Me' as in 'Metre': On Translating *Antigone*

Seamus Heaney

Verse translation is not all that different from original composition. In order to get a project under way, there has to be a note to which the lines, and especially the first lines, can be tuned. Until this register is established, your words may well constitute a satisfactory semantic equivalent but they cannot induce that blessed sensation of being on the right track, musically and rhythmically.

Readers recognise this rightness immediately. We share vicariously in the promise of openings such as 'It is an ancient mariner / And he stoppeth one of three', or 'I will arise and go now and go to Innisfree' or 'Gile na, gile do chonnaic ar slí an uaignis'. We know intuitively that when the poets wrote those lines they were feeling what D. H. Lawrence felt at the start of his 'Song of a Man who has Come Through': 'Not I, not I, but the wind that blows through me . . .' Or, to put it another way – and to quote a different poet – the gift of the right opening line helps the poet and the translator of poetry to escape from what Robert Lowell called 'the glassy bowing and scraping' of the will into a 'maze of composition' led by an 'incomparable wandering voice'.

When he wrote in those terms, Lowell was thinking of Racine, a 'man of craft' who was helped beyond craft when he found a voice for the ancient Greek heroine of his seventeenth-century tragedy, *Phèdre*. Racine may not have been translating but even so, writing lines for a character in a play still requires some displacement of the dramatist's own voice. The two jobs have at least that much in common.

I discovered this for myself recently when I was trying to get started on a translation of *Antigone*. The invitation to do this job came from Ben Barnes at the Abbey Theatre. In 2004 the Abbey was celebrating its centenary and the artistic director wanted to have at least one classical tragedy in the centennial repertoire. I was honoured to be asked, and was attracted to the commission, not least because W. B. Yeats had done versions of Sophocles' two other Theban plays for the theatre, but I still wasn't sure how to respond. How many *Antigone*s could Irish theatre put up with? Round about the time the idea was floated, Conall Morrison was touring his adaptation, setting the action in a Middle Eastern context; and a couple of years previously I had read in manuscript Marianne McDonald's unflashy and illuminating translation, where the introduction and footnotes revealed how usefully her scholar's knowledge had paid into her theatrical instincts. And if that were not enough, there was also Marianne McDonald's essay on '*Antigones*' to remind me that Brendan Kennelly, Tom Paulin and Aidan Carl Matthews had already been down the road to Thebes, so why start down it yet again?

One consideration weighed heavily in favour of a new start. Early in 2003 we were watching a leader, a Creon figure if ever there was one, a law-and-order bossman trying to boss the nations of the world into uncritical agreement with his edicts in much the same way as Creon tries to boss the Chorus of compliant Thebans into conformity with his. With the White House and the Pentagon in cahoots, determined to bring the rest of us into line over Iraq, the disposition and passion of an Antigone were all of a sudden as vital as oxygen masks, so I soon found myself doing a version of the 'wonders chorus' and publishing it as a sort of open letter to George Bush:

> let him once
> Overbear or overstep
>
> What the city allows, treat law
> As something he can decide for himself –
> Then let this wonder of the world remember:
> When he comes begging we will turn our backs.

By the time I had reached that part of the work, however, I was already at the keeping-going stage. Getting started was the problem that had to be solved first.

I was to see Ben Barnes on a Monday afternoon in January and on the Sunday night I still wasn't sure what I should say to him. Even though there was an urgent political context, there was no writerly urge. I was reading desultorily about the play in various essays and Introductions and glazing over as again and again the old familiar topics came swimming up: individual conscience versus civil power, men versus women, the domestic versus the public sphere, the relevance of the action in times of crisis, in France, in Russia, in Poland, in Northern Ireland – of course, of course, of course. But why do it again? Indeed, how do it again, if there wasn't a tuning fork?

And then I heard it, and inside seconds I had a pen in my hand and had done the three opening lines. Theme and tune coalesced. Purchase on a language, a confidence amounting almost to a carelessness, a found pitch – all arrived in a breath. 'Not I, not I,' I could have exclaimed, 'but the wind that blows through me.' What had got me going was not my study of the text of the play or the criticism surrounding it, but the words and rhythms of another work entirely. I suddenly remembered the opening lines of Eibhlín Dubh Ní Chonaill's 'Caoineadh Airt Uí Laoghaire' (Lament for Art O'Leary), lines that are both a feat of rhetoric and a spontaneous outburst of grief, the lament of an eighteenth-century woman whose husband has been cut down and left bleeding, much as Polyneices was left outside the walls of Thebes, unattended, desecrated, picked at by the crows.

> Mo ghrá go daingean thú!
> Lá dá bhfaca thú
> Ag ceann tí an mhargaidh,
> Thug mo shúil aire dhuit,
> Thug mo chroí taitneamh duit,
> D'éalaíos óm charaid leat
> I bhfad ó bhaile leat.

Is domhsa nárbh aithreach:
Chuiris parlús á ghealadh dhom,
Rúmanna á mbreacadh dhom,
Bácús á dheargadh dhom.

In Frank O' Connor's translation this goes:

My love and my delight,
The day I saw you first
Beside the markethouse
I had eyes for nothing else
And love for none but you.

I left my father's house
And ran away with you,
And that was no bad choice;
You gave me everything.
There were parlours whitened for me,
Bedrooms palmed for me,
Ovens reddened for me.

As the poem proceeds, this cadence of lamentation heightens and gathers, an indeflectible outpouring of rage and grief. It is the voice of woman as mourner and woman as avenging fury, a woman fierce in her devotion to a beloved whom she eventually finds lying beside a little furze bush, dead without the last rites, nobody close except

an old, old woman
And her cloak about you.

In a flash I saw refracted in Eibhlín Dubh the figure of the stricken Antigone, and heard in the three-beat line of her keen the note that Antigone might strike at the start of the proposed translation. There was no distinction at that moment between the excitement I felt at the discovery of the trimeter as the right metre for the opening and the analogies I could sense between the predicaments of a sister affronted by a tyrant in Thebes and a wife bereft by English soldiery in Carriganimma in County Cork. Just then, much that I had read in the commentaries was, as Wordsworth might have put it, 'felt along the blood': the contrast between the language of feeling that is spoken by Antigone and her sister Ismene and the language of power used by Creon, the furious compulsion to give the dead their due that overrides every thought of self-preservation, the imperatives of family and religion over the impositions of state authority – all of these things were momentarily palpable and in prospect because of the note I had just heard.

Inside a few minutes I had sample lines to show to the artistic director

> Ismene, quick, come here!
> What's to become of us?
> Why are we always the ones?

Nothing spectacular, admittedly, but the three-beat lines generated a desire to do more of them. And in my excitement I decided there and then that the obvious metre for the Chorus was the four-beat, Old English alliterative line, the line of the veteran Anglo-Saxons, gnomic and grim, but capable also of a certain clangour and glamour. So before I rose from the desk, I had a sample of the first stasimon to bring to the Abbey the next day as well:

> Glory be to brightness, to the gleaming sun,
> Shining guardian of our seven gates.
> Burn away the darkness, dawn on Thebes,
> Dazzle the city you have saved from destruction.

For Creon I didn't even bother with a trial run: blank verse it had to be, iambic pentameter, the obvious medium 'to honour patriots in life and death'. From then on all I had to do was to keep going, which meant getting started again and again in the course of the next three months. To help me with the sense, I kept to hand three earlier translations, those by Jebb, by Hugh Lloyd-Jones (in the Loeb edition) and E. F. Watling (in the old Penguin Classics), but without that first power surge coming through me ('me' as in 'metre') not even those authorities would have been of any use.

Rebel Women in Ancient Drama

9. Female Solidarity: Timely Resistance in Greek Tragedy

Rush Rehm

In this essay I want to extend the considerations of rebel women on the ancient stage beyond the treatment of tragic (and comic) heroines/protagonists to the broader topic of female solidarity. It seems only natural that critical discussion of women in tragedy concentrates on powerful individuals: Medea, Clytemnestra, Antigone, Phaedra, Electra, Hecuba. With such an array of 'leading ladies', who wants to talk about a chorus of suppliants or a group of mute female war captives? Knox's *Heroic Temper*, one of the seminal books on Sophocles this past century, lays out the case for powerful, inflexible, immutably heroic individuals in Sophoclean tragedy, who stand up on their own against all that society and the cosmos can hurl at them.[1] I daresay Knox's notion of the heroic, coupled with the star system that sells theatre tickets, has influenced the way we think about rebel women not only in Sophocles, but in Aeschylus, Euripides and Aristophanes as well.

The paradigm of the solitary hero/heroine *über – oder unter – alles*, does, however, carry its own concealed ideology, one that fits handsomely into our dominant mode of thinking today. To be drastically reductive, I'd call this contemporary ideology 'individualist, libertarian, and capitalist', where the individual – understood as a free and independent consumer – can soar above an otherwise lock-step world, with the full confidence that his or her self-fulfilment represents the be-all and end-all of human achievement. Paradoxically, of course, this same ideology dovetails perfectly with the falsely advertised 'free market', where one's individuality can be enhanced or burnished by the right combination of mass-produced and marketed products. Two epigraphs from my recent book *Radical Theatre* (in the chapters entitled 'The Fate of Agency, the Agency of Fate' and 'Tragedy and Ideology') summarise the paradox. A television commercial for a soft drink exhorts us to 'Be original, an individual, / like Dr. Pepper', and on the next channel (both – in fact, all – owned by a small group of multinational media giants) a bright, energetic voice intones: 'Be all that you can be / in the U.S. Army.'[2]

Fortunately, no Greek tragedy stoops to this level of marketing the fulfilled individual, no matter how rebellious. When we think about ancient Greek culture, we recognise the strength of the opposite norm: namely, the value placed on collective action and group solidarity. We see this reflected in various Athenian social institutions: in the military, from rowing triremes to fighting in a hoplite phalanx; in various levels of democratic participation; in religious cult; and so on. At the broadest level of generality, a collective ideology underlies the twinned unifying strands of Greek society, the *oikos* and the *polis*. As social historian Cynthia Patterson has persuasively argued, these two institutions proved far more complementary and mutually informing than nineteenth- and twentieth-century scholars committed to the model of binary oppositions would have us believe.[3]

Given the focus on rebel women, the following question arises: How does the collective spirit basic to Athenian democracy manifest itself in the portrayal of tragic female characters? Or, in a somewhat different guise, how does female solidarity affect the way we understand 'rebel women' on the ancient stage? I propose a quick and dirty taxonomy of four categories, aimed less at exhausting the possibilities than at opening up the subject for discussion: (1) solidarity within a Chorus of women, who already share a situation in common; (2) solidarity between a tragic female character and a female Chorus; (3) solidarity between two female characters; (4) female solidarity that extends to males. In each case, I hope to show that a significant aspect of rebellious female characters on the ancient Greek stage involves a form of collective rebellion, or at least 'timely resistance' of a collective sort.

The clearest example of the first category (resistance by a group of females trapped by common circumstance) is the Chorus in Aeschylus' *Suppliant Women*. Fleeing forced marriage with their Egyptian uncles, they supplicate Pelasgus, the king of Argos, eventually gaining his promise of protection. Following Garvie's reconstruction of the Danaid trilogy, the Egyptians defeat the Argives in battle and force the women to marry, but the unwilling brides unite in slaying their husbands on their wedding night, all save Hypermnestra, who spares Lynkeus.[4] We cannot be sure how the women came to their collective conclusion regarding the murders. However, we see an image of their desperate solidarity earlier, when the suppliants inform Pelasgus of their 'beautiful contrivance' (*mêchanê kalê*, A. *Supp.* 459), namely that with their 'breast bands and girdles' they will hang themselves in the sanctuary of the gods if the Argive king fails to answer their request for help. As they do later on their wedding night, the women make use of what they have – in this case their potentially fatal lingerie.

As well as collective thinking and action within a female Chorus, Greek tragedy frequently dramatises solidarity between a single female figure and the group. In Euripides' *Trojan Women* and *Hecuba*, the surviving women of Troy and the Trojan queen Hecuba face slavery at the hands of the Greeks. In the latter play, the women's collective action involves blinding the brutal Polymnestor with knitting needles and murdering his infant sons. In Euripides' *Electra*, the wretched heroine – married but chaste – finds support from her nubile girl friends who visit her lonely cottage to invite her to the festival of Hera. Electra declines their invitation, but the maidens stay with their friend, even when events take a bloody turn. In Euripides' *Medea*, the Chorus of Corinthian women appear in response to the cries of the rejected protagonist,[5] who bares her soul to them and requests that they keep quiet about the revenge plot she is hatching: 'I ask you to do this for me – / if I find some means or method / to pay my husband back for all his injustice, / keep quiet' (Eur. *Med.* 259–63). They do. Significantly they speak out against Medea's plan only to her, and only after she decides that it will include the murder of her own children. In their famous Ode to Athens, the Corinthian women portray Medea as a war-like presence that is about to invade Athens, the city where the play was first performed. As I have argued elsewhere, their song alludes to the Peloponnesian War, which had already broken out in the naval battles between the Athenian and Corinthian fleets around the island of Corcyra not long before the play's première in 431 BC.[6] We will return to the theme of females resisting war.

Let us look more closely at four other examples of solidarity between an important female character and a Chorus of women: Electra and the household slaves in *Choephori*; Creusa and her handmaids in Euripides' *Ion*; Aethra and the chorus of Argive suppliants in Euripides' *Suppliant Women*; and Helen and the Chorus of captured Spartan women in Euripides' *Helen*. In Aeschylus' *Choephori*, the slave women from Asia who serve in the palace of Clytemnestra and Aegisthus give the lie to the claim that Greek tragic Choruses never directly affect the action. Following the *parodos*, they persuade Electra to change the prayer that accompanies the offering at Agamemnon's tomb, an offering commanded by Clytemnestra in response to her nightmare. Instead of placating the murdered king's spirit, they exhort Electra to include Orestes in her prayer, and to invoke Agamemnon's help in taking revenge on Clytemnestra and Aegisthus for the blood they have spilled (A. *Cho.* 84–123). Later, the women persuade the Nurse Cilissa – also a palace slave from Asia Minor – to alter the message she is meant to take to Aegisthus, so that he comes to the palace alone, without bodyguards, allowing the disguised Orestes to kill the murderers and restore the house (766–82). In *Choephori*, female solidarity takes the form of staunch loyalty to the *oikos* (Agamemnon's, not Aegisthus'), with resistance to illegitimate political power that has been achieved by assassination and usurpation. It serves a notion of retributive justice (*Cho.* 123, 400–4, 639–51, 804–6, 935–52), which will be transformed later in the trilogy by an act of quasi-female solidarity between Athena and the Furies in *Eumenides* (*Eum.* 406–14, 476–81, 794–1047).

In the case of Euripides' *Ion*, the childless Creusa, queen of Athens, has come to Delphi with her Euboean husband Xuthus to inquire about the prospect of future offspring. There Creusa meets the temple slave Ion, unbeknown to her the very child she had borne in shame, and abandoned, as a result of her rape by the god Apollo. When it appears (wrongly) that Ion is his own illegitimate son, Xuthus plans to foist him on Creusa and insinuate Ion into the royal line of Athens. He swears the Chorus to secrecy, under penalty of death: 'And you, handmaids, keep quiet; I command it, / or you will die, if you say anything to my wife' (Eur. *Ion* 666–7). When Creusa later asks her servants what the oracle has proclaimed, they respond with cries of woe (*iô daimon, iô tlamon,* 752, 754), before confronting the issue: 'What shall we do, when death lies in our path?' / [. . .] / 'Shall we speak or stay silent? What should we do?' (756–8). The 'what shall/should we do?' question, *ti drasô* or, in this case, *ti drômen, ti drasomen,* represents *the* tragic question (as Vernant puts it), emphasising the dilemma of human agency, of the need to act even in the face of doom.[7] Here the Chorus defy male authority and risk death, telling Creusa what they know of the oracle and of Xuthus' plans regarding Ion: 'It will be told, even if we die twice for speaking' (760). Scholars have shown great interest in (and exercised great ingenuity over) the issues the play raises about Athenian autochthony, Apollonian patriarchy, and the sexism in Euripides' representation of reproduction.[8] However, to my knowledge few critics of *Ion* have lingered over the remarkable fact that a Chorus of slave women are ready to risk their lives for their mistress. Their solidarity in a time of crisis sets the stage – admittedly, in tortuous Euripidean fashion – for the eventual turning of the tables on Xuthus. At the play's end, Xuthus still operates under the blissful assumption that Ion is *his* son, when in fact Ion is revealed as Creusa's child by Apollo, a divinely legitimised heir to the Erechtheid line of Athenian rulers, and founder of the Ionian race.[9]

In Euripides' *Suppliant Women,* Aethra finds herself moved by the appeals of foreign women from Argos, who supplicate her to help them recover the bodies of their slain sons for burial. When her own son Theseus rejects the Argives' plea, Aethra weeps with compassion at their plight, prompting Theseus to ask why these non-Athenian women should affect her so deeply (Eur. *Supp.* 286–96). Encouraging her to speak, he opens the political discourse to a female voice, and Aethra delivers the first of the play's overtly political speeches. She challenges her son to uphold the Panhellenic norm regarding the burial of the dead, and he reverses his earlier decision, choosing to go to war to recover the corpses (297–331). The female solidarity between Aethra and the Argive women, prominent at the outset, re-emerges later in the actions of Theseus, who washes the corpses he has recovered in battle. A highly uncharacteristic action for a male in Greek society, Theseus' care for the dead shocks the Argive king Adrastus, when he learns about it from the Messenger:

ADRASTUS: He himself washed the poor men's wounds?
MESSENGER: Exactly. He laid out the bodies and covered their limbs.
ADRASTUS: What a terrible burden and shame to take on himself!
MESSENGER: Why should we think of our common grief as shame?

(766–9)

In the opening scene of the play, the poignancy of mourning and the simple eloquence of supplication yield to political discourse with a strong fifth-century accent, albeit delivered by a female character. After the recovery of the corpses, that situation temporarily reverses, as Theseus, general and king, undertakes the ritual actions for the dead normally reserved for women. In Euripides' *Suppliant Women*, fellow-feeling among women yields to acts of solidarity between cities, across gender and generations.

In *Helen*, Euripides emphasises the 'phantom' causes of the campaign on which the play – and much Greek mythology – depends, namely the Trojan War. Adopting Stesichorus' version of the story, Euripides has the Greeks wage war over an ersatz Helen, an effigy sent to Troy by Zeus, who has whisked the real Helen off to Egypt. The transported Helen sympathises with the women of Troy, who have lost their loved ones in a senseless war:

> Ah, Troy, the unhappy,
> for things done that were never done

you died, suffering terribly. The gifts
that Aphrodite gave to me have brought on you
a flood of tears, showers of blood, pain
on pain, tears of lamentation and grief.
Mothers saw their children die,
maidens cut their long hair, all
for their loved ones who fell by the waters
of river Scamander.
Greece too has wept, wept
aloud in lamentation, beaten her head
with her hands, torn her soft cheeks
her nails leaving trails of blood. (Eur. *Hel.* 362–74)

Helen not only laments the suffering of the Trojan women, but metaphorically converts Greece into a mourning female, bewailing her collective loss. A similar sensibility governs the Chorus of Spartan maidens, apparently spirited off to Egypt along with their mistress. It is in the context of female solidarity that we might best understand their outcry against the madness of war:

Fools, who would win glory
by war and the spear's cutting edge,
senselessly you try to end
the burdens of humanity by killing.
As long as contests of blood settle
human conflict, then hateful strife
will never leave the cities of men. (*Hel.* 1151–7)

Consisting of maidens from Sparta, Athens's enemy in the Peloponnesian War, the Chorus (played by Athenian males) claim that war perpetuates violence rather than resolving it. Their observation had special resonance for the original audience, given the coincidence of the play's première with the disastrous Athenian expedition against Sicily in 414–13. In *Helen*, solidarity extends from the Spartan heroine to the women of Troy, from the Chorus of Spartan maidens to the contemporary victims of war, both Lacedaimonian and Athenian, and – by virtue of the male performers behind their masks – from males to females and back again, both in and out of the play. *Helen* is a drama of mirrors, doubles, and *doppelgänger*, but its shimmering surface forces the audience to confront the casualties of war, with sympathy that originates in solidarity among women.

The third category in our rough-and-ready taxonomy involves solidarity between individual female characters in tragedy. Sophocles' *Antigone* opens with the archetypal rebellious woman seeking her sister's help in burying their brother Polyneices. Initially Ismene rejects Antigone's request to join her in breaking Creon's new decree (S. *Ant.* 39–79). However, after Antigone's arrest, Creon recalls having just seen Ismene 'raving and beside herself' (492), and he summons her from the palace (526–30). He accuses Ismene of 'lurking in the house like a snake', of 'having a share in this burial' along with Antigone (531–5), a charge Ismene chooses not to deny: 'In your time of trouble I am not ashamed / to make myself a fellow voyager in your suffering [*xumploun emautên tou pathous poioumenê*]' (*Ant.* 540–1). Although Antigone rejects her sister's belated change of heart – their exchange (536–60) resembles the prologue in reverse – Ismene's willingness to accept responsibility for the act indicates the spreading influence of Antigone's resistance. Indeed, Creon sees them as two crazy peas in a pod: 'I say of these two girls [using the dual] – one of them just now has revealed herself as mad, but the other has been so from birth' (561–2). He has his guards lead them both back inside, where women should be confined (577–9), and he condemns them both to Hades (580–1, 769). Only when the Chorus question his judgment does he spare Ismene, who did not 'touch the body' (771). But Ismene's solidarity with her sister indicates that Creon cannot control the spatial dislocations he has tried to decree, keeping the dead from burial and interring the living beneath the earth. From Antigone to Ismene to Haimon to Teiresias to Eurydice and eventually to the Chorus, reaction against the injustice of Creon's decree spreads like the pollution emanating from Polyneices' corpse. Significantly, that reaction begins with Ismene's change of heart, when she chooses to stand with her sister and is willing to share her fate.

In Sophocles' *Women of Trachis*, we find an even more surprising example of female solidarity. On seeing the captured women brought to her *oikos* as Heracles' war booty, Deianeira responds with compassion verging on the subversive:

How can I fail to rejoice, hearing of my husband's
triumphant success and seeing it manifest here?
It is right for my joy to match his.
Nevertheless, those who think things through
fear for the man who succeeds, lest fortune
trip him up.
Friends, a strange pity comes over me
when I see these wretched women, homeless,
fatherless, adrift in a foreign land.
Once, perhaps, they were daughters of free men,
but now they live the lives of slaves.
[.../ .../ ...]
[*to Iole*] Unhappy one, of all the maidens captured here who are you?
Have you no husband? Are you a mother? You seem
out of place, unprepared for this, a princess perhaps.
[.../] [*to Lichas*] Who is her mother? What man fathered her?
Tell me, for I pitied her most as soon as I saw her,
in so far as a woman alone can feel and understand. (S. *Trach.* 293–313)

Observing Greek proprieties, Deianeira puts her husband's victory first, but her speech reveals her conflicted feelings. She moves from fearing the reversal of fortune that the enslaved women embody to expressing outright pity for them in their captive state. Deianeira then focuses on a single individual, Iole, for whom she feels particular solidarity, as a woman alone herself. A speech that began with male triumph ends with an expression of sympathy for its female victims, and with one victim in particular.

Deianeira and Iole are both casualties of Heracles' erotic passion. When she learns that her husband sacked Oechalia in order to seize Iole as his concubine, Deianeira does not humiliate her rival, as one might expect (compare Clytemnestra's treatment of Cassandra in *Agamemnon*, or Hermione's of Andromache in *Andromache*). Rather, Deianeira tries to regain Heracles' affection by using a love-potion that (unknown to her) is a poison, which leads to her husband's death and her own suicide. Reversals abound in *Women of Trachis*, but – as Deianeira fears when she sees the captive women – they operate within a context of female solidarity. In doing so, they serve to question the patriarchal order and its assumptions about women.

Sophocles plants the seed for Deianeira's sympathetic response to Iole in an early exchange with her Nurse, a domestic slave:

NURSE: My mistress, Deianeira, how often before
                 have I seen you bewail Heracles' absence,
                 weeping your heart out in grief.
                 But now, if a slave may give advice
                 to those who are free, then I must speak...

DEINEIRA: ... words even from the low-born
                 can hit the mark. This woman here is a slave,
                 but all she says is spoken by a free mind. (*Trach.* 49–53,
                 61–3)

Deianeira recognises that advice depends on the quality of what is said, not on the class or status of the speaker. In *Women of Trachis*, the female characters' intimate relationships are quite different from those of the dominant male world, which has driven them together.

Even Heracles undergoes a womanly transformation, suffering like a female when he is forced to endure events over which he has no control. Sophocles presents Heracles as a victim of destructive *eros*, a typically female affliction in Greek myth. Screaming in agony when he appears onstage, Heracles cries out just like a woman, condemned to weakness and pain rarely associated with a male hero:

... Pity me,
pitiable for so many reasons, for now I weep and cry
like a girl. Never before could anyone say
he saw me, a man, behave in such a fashion.
Without tears I always endured what evil befell me.
But now torment has shown me as a wretched woman. (*Trach.* 1070–5)

We find many examples in tragedy of the feminisation of male heroes, suggesting an underlying similarity that Greek sexual stereotypes tend to occlude – among them, Admetus in *Alcestis*,

Heracles in *Heracles*, Jason near the end of *Medea*, Talthybius in *Trojan Women*, Philoctetes in *Philoctetes*, Pentheus in *Bacchae*, and, as hinted at earlier, Haimon in *Antigone*. In that play, as in *Women of Trachis*, Sophocles sets the stage for the revelation of female-like males by first presenting scenes of solidarity between women.

With this transformative potential in mind, let us turn to our fourth and final category: female solidarity with a male figure, signalling timely resistance to fate, despotism, or a combination of both. In *Oedipus at Colonus*, Ismene and Antigone care for their blind, mendicant father, sacrificing whatever life they might have led, in contrast to the male members of Oedipus' family, his sons and brother-in-law Creon. As well as tending to her father, Antigone demonstrates a deep sympathy for her brother Polyneices, who comes to Colonus as an exile and suppliant, much like Oedipus. Initially, the father refuses even to meet his son, but, under pressure from both Theseus and Antigone, Oedipus relents. Antigone appeals to him in his role as a parent (S. OC 1189–94), maintaining (as Winnington-Ingram puts it) 'that a father, of all people, should not retaliate upon a son for whose *phusis* ["nature," "being,"] he is responsible, not even if that son commits the most impious of crimes, which is neglect of duty towards a father'.[10] In his commentary on the play, Jebb offers the relevant gloss: 'The relationship between parent and child is indelibly sacred. No wickedness on your son's part can alter the fact that he is your son.'[11] Indeed, Antigone implores her father to think of what he suffered from his parents, reminding him 'how evil is the end that waits on evil wrath' (1197–8), with Oedipus' own mad act of self-blinding providing the evidence (1195–200). But Oedipus ignores Antigone's plea not to return evil for evil on his own flesh and blood. Instead, he delivers a horrific execration on both his sons, a curse 'the effects of which he can neither limit nor, for all his prophetic power, foresee . . . destroying the daughter he loves along with the sons he hates'.[12]

Following Oedipus' strange disappearance reported by the messenger, the emotionally wrought closing scene makes two things clear: Antigone and Ismene are distraught at not being able to perform the death ritual for their father; and disaster lies ahead for Thebes, including the violent deaths of Oedipus' accursed sons and of Antigone as well. She has bid a tearful farewell to her brother only 300 lines earlier, during which he entreats his sisters to provide for his burial at Thebes (1405–13). We can be sure the original audience had Antigone's fate in mind – a fate dramatised in Sophocles' earlier play – when she asks Theseus to send her back to Thebes to stop the impending bloodshed at the end of the play.

As Gellie points out, the word *charis*, 'a gift or grace offered', occurs twenty-two times in *Oedipus at Colonus*, associated primarily with Antigone's service to her father.[13] It is precisely this quality that Oedipus lacks when he rejects her plea on behalf of Polyneices, for Oedipus' curse takes down more than his hateful sons; it sweeps away his beloved Antigone as well. In his recent book *Das Ende des Ödipus bei Sophokles*, Bernard reminds us that the escalation of destructive violence – represented in Sophocles' play by the male members of Oedipus' family – has been a defining fact of the twentieth century, one that shows little signs of stopping in the twenty-first.[14] He provides compelling evidence of the disasters that result when a female *charis* is ignored in *Oedipus at Colonus* in favour of retaliatory violence that has no time for wisdom and no place for compassion.

In tragedy, female solidarity with male figures also extends beyond immediate blood relations. Alcestis' willingness to die for her husband in Euripides' *Alcestis* proves that an 'outsider' – as an exogamous, non-incestuous wife is by definition – can be much closer than a blood-relative such as Admetus' father Pheres. Tecmessa in Sophocles' *Ajax* – like Iole in *Women of Trachis* – is a war-prize, slave and concubine. However, she lives with her captor as his wife and the mother of his son. Recovering from his humiliating madness, Ajax thinks of ending his life, prompting Tecmessa to deliver one of the great speeches in tragedy, echoing Andromache's plea to Hector in *Iliad* Book 6 (407–39). Tecmessa reminds her husband of all *she* has suffered, urging him to follow her example and endure his present misfortune:

My lord Ajax, there is no greater evil for humans
than fate [*tuchê*] imposed by necessity.
I was born of a free father,
the wealthiest man in all of Phrygia,
but now I am a slave. Thus it was settled by the gods,
and – above all – by your strength. As a result
I share your bed and think well of you.
I beg you, by Zeus who protects the hearth,
and by your own bed where you and I have joined,
do not let me suffer hurtful words from
your enemies, abandoning me to their uses.
If you die, and by dying abandon me,
know that on that day I will be taken
violently by the Greeks and live out
a slave's life along with your son. [/.../]
There is no one else for me to look to
other than you. You annihilated my country in war,
and another fate dragged my mother and father
down to Hades, to dwell among the dead.
What country, what means of support are
open to me? My only safety lies in you.
Hold me in your thoughts, for surely a man
should remember the pleasure that has come his way.
A grace given [*charis*] should beget another, always.
But if a man lets the memory of those gifts
slip away, then his good name goes with them. (S. *Aj.* 485–99, 514–24)

Tecmessa has suffered humiliation, powerlessness and violation far
worse than Ajax, and she faces an even bleaker future (along with her
son) if Ajax fails to ward off impending disaster. Forced into
marriage, with no choice in the matter and no means of escape,
Tecmessa learns to make the best of things, to embrace her
circumstances, to love the man and their child, and to struggle against
a desperate future. Her instinct for survival is both realistic and noble,
and her solidarity with her husband in his time of desperation is a call
for courageous endurance. Ajax's refusal to meet his own *peripeteia*
with comparable resilience looks like failure. In Sophocles' play, a

slave woman emerges as wiser and more admirable than her heroic husband, whose shame and self-pity all but blind him to those who serve, love and depend on him, as manifest in his rejection of the *charis* so movingly offered by Tecmessa.

Finally, let us turn to Aeschylus' *Prometheus Bound*. In his pity for the human race, Prometheus gives humans the gift of fire, and with it language, science, number and the ability to learn from the past as they/we confront the future. His solidarity with benighted mortals incurs the wrath of Olympus, and only his combination of stubbornness, pride, foresight and courage keeps Prometheus from succumbing to Zeus' torture. No less remarkable, however, is the stance of the normally timid Oceanids, the daughters of Ocean who comprise the Chorus. Through most of the play, fear (*phobos*, a word that runs through the text) rules their reactions to the beleaguered Prometheus, and also to Io, Zeus' human victim. But at the crucial, climactic moment, when Hermes warns the Chorus to leave or suffer Prometheus' fate, the Oceanids choose to stand their ground. They conquer both terror and cowardice (*kakotêta*, 1066) in an act of fellow-feeling, as the earth opens and swallows them along with the tortured protagonist. Their pity – the other-directed correlative to self-regarding terror, as Aristotle reminds us – proves sufficient to overcome their fear of imminent destruction.

The otherwise docile Oceanids offer an example we might wish to emulate today, confronted as we are with arrogant and deadly power, disguised as concern for 'security' and 'democracy', which only causes more pain and destruction on innocent Iraqi civilians who have suffered enough already. They, and others – the Palestinians in occupied East Jerusalem and the West Bank, the peasant and labour organisers in Colombia, the indigenous population in Chiapas – cry out for the kind of solidarity that money cannot buy, timely resistance to illegitimate power and authority, which presents itself as fate, or as a *fait accompli*, only to discourage us from struggling against it. As I have suggested in this essay, there is classic inspiration and example available to those of us who need it in the various acts of female solidarity in Greek tragedy.

Notes

1. B. M. W. Knox, *Heroic Temper* (Berkeley: University of California Press, 1964). All translations are my own.
2. Rush Rehm, *Radical Theatre: Greek Tragedy and the Modern World* (London: Duckworth, 2003), pp. 65 and 87.
3. Cynthia Patterson, *The Family in Greek History* (Cambridge, MA: Harvard University Press, 1998).
4. A. F. Garvie, *Aeschylus'* 'Supplices': *Play and Trilogy* (Cambridge: CUP, 1969).
5. For the 'extra-rational' manner in which the women of Corinth hear (apparently from some distance) Medea's cries from within her own house, see Rush Rehm, *The Play of Space: Spatial Transformation in Greek Tragedy* (Princeton, NJ, and Oxford: Princeton University Press, 2002), p. 253.
6. Rush Rehm, '*Medea* and the *logos* of the Heroic', *Eranos*, 87 (1989): 97–115.
7. Jean-Pierre Vernant, 'Greek Tragedy: Problems of Interpretation', R. Macksey and E. Donato (eds), in *The Structuralist Controversy* (Baltimore, MD: Johns Hopkins University Press, 1972), pp. 273–95, at p. 285; for further discussion, see Rehm, *Radical Theatre*, pp. 65–86.
8. See, among others, Arlene Saxenhouse, 'Reflections on Autochthony in Euripides' *Ion*'; P. Euben (ed.), *Greek Tragedy and Political Theory* (Berkeley: University of California Press, 1986), pp. 252–73; Page duBois, *Sowing the Body: Psychoanalysis and Ancient Representations of Women* (Chicago, IL: University of Chicago Press, 1988), pp. 42–5, 57–64, 169; Nicole Loraux, *The Children of Athena: Athenian Ideas about Citizenship and the Division between the Sexes*, trans. C. Levine (Princeton, NJ: Princeton University Press, 1993; Paris 1984); and Froma I. Zeitlin, *Playing the Other: Gender and Society in Classical Greek Literature* (Chicago, IL: University of Chicago Press, 1996), pp. 285–338.
9. For the troubling ironies that operate during the play and cast their shadow over the end, see Rush Rehm, *Greek Tragic Theatre* (London and New York: Routledge, 1994), pp. 133–47.

10. R. P. Winnington-Ingram, *Sophocles: An Interpretation* (Cambridge: CUP, 1980), p. 263.

11. R. C. Jebb, *Sophocles: Plays,* 'Oedipus Colonus', ed. P. E. Easterling, intro. R. Rehm (London: Bristol Classical Press and Duckworth, 2004; orig. 1900), on *OC*, pp. 1189ff.

12. Winnington-Ingram, *Sophocles*, p. 275.

13. G. H. Gellie, *Sophocles: A Reading* (Melbourne: University of Melbourne Press, 1972), p. 182.

14. Wolfgang Bernard, *Das Ende des Ödipus bei Sophokles: Untersuchung zur Interpretation des* 'Ödipus auf Kolonos', *Zetemata* v. 107 (Munich: Beck, 2001), pp. 252–5.

10. Outside Looking in: Subversive Choruses in Greek Tragedy

J. Michael Walton

Goddesses, Whores, Wives, and Slaves: that is the title of Sarah Pomeroy's 1975 book on women in classical antiquity.[1] How are we to read this? Is it a hierarchy? A catalogue of job opportunities? A list of necessary qualifications for what men expected in a wife? Or do expect in a wife?

Pomeroy sums up the aim of her book in an introduction which begins: 'This book was conceived when I asked myself what women were doing while men were active in all the areas traditionally emphasized by classical scholars.'[2] The uncovering of what women were getting up to while men were involved with their commercial, military and social lives, which traditionally formed the substance of 'proper' history, now receives its due attention, and is among the most vital areas of historical research. The delving of Pomeroy, and many other notable scholars, into the less obviously documented areas of the classical world has revealed not only the detail of the lives led by women in a variety of circumstances, but also the concern, suspicion and naked fear exhibited by men who, however apparently dominant in their political and domestic lives, demonstrated a lack of security about what they might be *unaware* of in the lives of their women.

The public lives of women in Athens were circumscribed. Marriages were arranged; the rules over dissolution of a marriage were hugely loaded in favour of men; political rights were non-existent. There were women-only festivals but the sexual assaults that occurred to furnish the plots of Middle and New Comedy with foundlings, mostly took place when a woman was attending such, and was consequently out-of-doors and by herself: this, from a male point of view, apparently made her fair game for the marauding rapist. As to what women got up to in private, men were suspicious. Scandal, drink and sex were about the limit, according to Aristophanes, whose plays like *Thesmophoriazusae*, *Lysistrata* and *Ecclêsiazusae*, cheerfully fed their prejudices.

Later comedy, Menander's *The Woman from Samos* in particular, offers a different picture, the behind-the-scenes world of domestic life, revealed via a series of onstage descriptions. There is a mine of information in this single play about the Adonis festival; the conduct and preparation of a wedding; the geography of the kitchen; social niceties and not so niceties; attitudes to adoption and illegitimacy; the influence of women who do appear in the play and those who don't. Chrysis, the title character, is the one female speaking character in the cast but the audience is made aware too of the importance offstage of Niceratus' wife, without whose approval Niceratus dare not sanction the marriage of his daughter; and Moschion's old nurse and a younger domestic who are overheard compounding a deception about the baby. The plot revolves around this deception in which the entire female household is complicit. It is also quite clear that Chrysis, though she has no legal status and is harshly treated onstage, is the accepted mistress of the household off it.

These offstage characters form the equivalent of an onstage chorus, the chorus being otherwise in Menander a virtually unknown quantity with no influence on the plot. It is through the reported actions about what is happening offstage that we become aware of the seething and subversive behind-the-scenes world of gossip and intrigue, the 'downstairs' of backstage, compared with the 'upstairs' of onstage, as juxtaposed in all manner of dramatic traditions up to and including Robert Altman's film *Gosford Park*.

In a fascinating book entitled *News and Society in the Greek Polis*, Sian Lewis investigated the thirst in ancient Greece for the dissemination of information, and the need for it.[3] Men had their public fora in Athens, in barber-shop or assembly, but women had parallel networks. Some of these were, in part, behind closed doors, but plenty of citizen women did find legitimate occasion to leave the house, while many more were wage-earners in their own right:

Emphasis on women's exclusion from this domain [news travelling by word of mouth] is based on ideas of female exclusion in general. The initial reliance on evidence suggesting that most women were kept in seclusion has been superseded in recent years, by a recognition that not only did many women leave their houses to play public roles, but that for some it was a necessity.[4]

This may throw a different light on the dramatic choruses. The world of constant bystanders that the tragic chorus implies may distort the reality of life in Athens but was not a wholly alien concept. It is the subversiveness, or potential subversiveness, of such groups in tragedy that I want to look at further. Examples from the tragedians of the fifth century can then be matched to the inclinations of a number of modern playwrights to investigate the world of women and their influence in contemporary versions of myth, especially those where the dramatic impetus is driven by a powerful political agenda.

There are two principal ways in which subversive attitudes or behaviour may manifest themselves. The first is by acts of defiance against the temporal authority. For characters such as Antigone, Electra or even Medea, such acts are likely to be overt and their results of major consequence. Sometimes they amount to the main dramatic focus for the play. For most choruses, though, the path is less prescribed, if only because overt opposition is unlikely to prove effective. Choruses of Furies or Bacchants are few and far between. For the others, whether suppliants, slaves or simply citizens, their social position would appear to deprive them of any significant influence on the outcome of events. The resistance is often there, nevertheless, a covert resistance, a special kind of subversiveness that recognises the limit of its range but may be fully exercised within what is possible. Such may well have been, Lewis suggests, the real world in Athens. The tragedies – comedies, too, though in different ways – with that curious intersection of myth and social politics, offer insights into the art of the possible for those whose power seems at first sight to be severely restricted.

There is a further dimension to this sense of the subversive. Many female choruses justify their presence by offering themselves as a sympathetic ear to the troubles faced by the leading characters. It can be no accident in the light of their situations that, in Sophocles, Deianira and Electra have a female Chorus to talk to, Antigone faces a group of men. In Euripides, Hecuba (twice), Iphigenia (twice), Electra (twice), Andromache, Phaedra, Helen, Creusa, Jocasta and Medea all have women in whom they confide. Agave does too, but *Bacchae* is a special case (see below). Alcestis and Megara play in front of a male Chorus. The composition of the chorus reflects in a number of ways the balance of sympathy. What may be more interesting, but something that can only be touched upon here, is the extent to which such female choruses may be critical of the heroines, frequently telling them they are wrong-headed, over-reacting or simply stubborn. If this is a different sense of the word 'subversive' there are occasions where resistance to authority *per se* correlates to resistance to the stance of the leading character.

The extent to which this may reflect life in the Athens of the first productions is open to debate. Greek tragedy exists in a world of the playwright's imagination, a world that never was, a world that never is. Authority functions through kings and queens. Cruel, insane and murderous behaviour is requited through personal justice, for the most part, with only the occasional challenge. And yet, from the earliest tragedies about which anything is known, these plays, through parable, had a dimension of immediacy for an Athenian audience which permitted – more, endorsed – inquiry into any aspect of, or attitude to, contemporary life. This becomes more blatant as tragedy develops in the latter part of the fifth century BC. The more domestic tragedies of Euripides are full of examples of how the spreading of information is shown to be part of the fabric of society. The Tutor in the opening scene of *Medea* enters saying to the Nurse, who is, as it happens, talking to the audience:

What do you think you are doing out here,
Telling the world your troubles? (50–1)[5]

And, a few minutes later:

I was pretending not to listen,
But I did hear someone say – down by the fountain
Where the old gaffers play dominoes – (67–9)

In *Andromache*, Hermione offers as an excuse for trying to kill Andromache:

Evil-minded women came visiting and filled my head with nonsense:
'You really want to share your bed with a sluttish prisoner-of-war? [. . .]
she'd get no pleasure in my bed and live to tell the tale.' [. . .] never should
a man of sense let his wife entertain gossips. Women who go visiting are
up to no good. (930–5, 943–6)[6]

This sub-world of rumour and chatter sometimes belongs to the
principal characters; more often it is the province of the socially
inferior, or of those who, in dramatic terms, are the socially inferior,
the choruses who appear to shrink from direct involvement in the
action and disown the life of commitment, but find the need, at least
as the playwrights created them, to serve as witnesses to the activities
of their 'betters'. Beyond this, it is difficult to resist the notion that,
alongside the forceful and active heroines who offer an upfront
rebellion in Greek tragedy, there are frequently choruses of women,
who, by acting collectively, do move beyond the passive: who,
corporately, within their limited powers, offer a form of subversion
that has its own vitality.

Of the choruses in the surviving thirty-two tragedies, women make
up five out of seven in Aeschylus, two out of seven in Sophocles and
no fewer than fourteen out of eighteen in Euripides. As implied
above, the Euripides choruses offer comfort to, and solidarity with,
such forceful 'rebels' as Hecuba, Andromache, Creusa, Helen,
Medea and Phaedra. Of these fourteen female Euripidean choruses,

most are free women; the slaves, for the most part, as in *Hecuba* or *Iphigenia in Tauris*, are victims of what might be called 'relevant circumstance'. What do these choruses do? They ponder out loud; they engage and disengage; they sympathise; they offer advice, generally of a fairly bland kind; they gossip; they are *there*. True. But they are sometimes rather more than that.

A close examination of what the Chorus actually say in almost any tragedy shows that, far from being inert non-participants with vaguely engaged sympathies, most choruses are quite capable of independent thought that is neither led by the need to offer the playwright's viewpoint, nor by a requirement to assume a passive role in the plot, even when they have a special sympathy with one of the characters.

The daughters of Danaus in Aeschylus' *Suppliants* are very much at the forefront of their drama. Though accompanied by Danaus, who serves as their public spokesman before the people of Argos, the initial case to King Pelasgus is argued by them with enough force of persuasion to put the king into a real quandary about what to do for the best. Danaus accompanies his fifty daughters who are fleeing from the threat of forced marriage to the fifty sons of Aegyptus, Danaus' brother. Their *parodos* lasts for a hundred and seventy-five lines but it is their father who suggests how they must present their case to the Argives. 'Children be cunning' (176),[7] he says (a slightly free translation of *paides, phronein chrê*), then:

> Speak when you're spoken to:
> Respectful, tearful, as strangers should be –
> These people must understand:
> You're exiles, yet guilty of no crime.
> Quiet voices, downcast looks [. . .]
> Be submissive. (194–200)

When they face Pelasgus, they are a deal more forceful than Danaus had anticipated. They repudiate this forced marriage as incest:

KING: Because you hate them, or because it is wrong?
CHORUS LEADER: Of course, it's wrong! To be your own kinsman's
                  slave! (336–7)

They argue against subjugation to men:

> No *man* our master! God grant it,
> Law or no law. (392–3)

They then demand the rights of sanctuary and finally threaten suicide. It is these last two protestations, more emotional blackmail than any such demure representation as their father has recommended, that have the strongest effect on the king and ultimately lead to the unanimous support of the people of Argos in assembly.

The Egyptian Herald is soon dispatched and the play ends with the daughters' apparent victory: not the trilogy, though. The marriage subsequently does take place, we must assume in the absence of the remaining plays, followed by the mass murder of the bridegrooms by the brides, with the solitary exception. Without the rest of the trilogy it is difficult to take this argument any further. As it is, though, the forcefulness of the Chorus in this play must have created a shudder or two in Aeschylus' audience who realise that these women are quite capable of the mass murder to come. Here is evidence of this creeping anxiety about women that neither Sophocles nor Euripides does much to alleviate.

The obvious point of linkage between Aeschylus, Sophocles and Euripides comes with the Electra story, about which all three wrote. Here again the choruses offer an uncomfortable perspective on a story that by rights concerns only the royal family.

The choruses of all three Electra plays are basically sympathetic to Electra. In other words, they are all subversive – they condone plotting against the temporal authority. In Aeschylus' *Libation-Bearers* their given identity is as *choros aichmalôtidôn*, 'a chorus of female slaves'. As such, their enthusiasm for Electra in her revolt against her treatment in her own house goes beyond any generalised

sympathy. It is an act of rebellion in its own right. Clytemnestra
might have only the haziest knowledge of, or interest in, what her
slaves think of her, but the point is strongly made elsewhere in Greek
drama that, for most slaves, the prosperity of the house is in their
own interests. It is the maintenance of a *status quo* that allows them
to get on with their own lives in relative peace and quiet. The
question frequently asked at dramatic moments when conspiracies
or secrets are about to be publicly revealed is, 'Can we trust the
Chorus?' The answer has to be 'Yes'; otherwise their presence will
paralyse any further action. But the question needs to be asked
because in stage life, as much as in real life, civil disobedience is
seldom in the interests of the underdog.

The Chorus of *Libation-Bearers* are the friends and *confidantes*
of Electra. They also happen to be palace slaves who scratch their
cheeks, beat their breasts and tear their clothes, sharing the grief of
Electra even though she is a princess. They hate the queen; they
hate what has happened to the royal household; they lament that
once upon a time there was a proper kingdom here, 'irresistible,
beyond challenge'. All this is described during their *parodos*.

Well-disposed to Agamemnon they may be, but it is by no means
clear quite why. At the end of their entry ode they identify who they
really are:

> From our native land,
> To be exiles, slaves,
> To suffer just and unjust alike.
> Our fate is to submit,
> To choke our hatred down
> And smile on the queen.
> But in secret, behind the veil
> Tears badge our eyes,
> Ice chokes our hearts
> With grief for the fates of kings. (75–83)[8]

The text is corrupt and the sense in some dispute. There is at least
a slight inference that these are slaves brought to Argos from Troy –
some translations identify them as such – by Agamemnon, the man

who sacked their city, who probably slaughtered their fathers, husbands and brothers, and certainly brought back their sacred princess as his concubine. Even if they are merely victims of some previous or subsequent military escapade, their loyalty to Agamemnon's memory is surprising. They have either become extremely fond of Electra or extremely unfond of Clytemnestra and Aegisthus.

Robert Fagles expresses it neatly when he suggests that for these Libation-Bearers 'their mourning is a form of resistance'.[9] The word 'resistance' is especially worth noting in the present context. From here on in, the loyalty of the Chorus to the cause is not in question. They join in the *kommos* without reservation, and without further reference to their own background. They are simply on the side of Orestes. Of course, they have to be, but, as the other two Electra plays show, their identity as palace slaves was not a *sine qua non* of the plot.

It is later in the play that their real contribution is made. In contrast to the ineffective protests of the old men in *Agamemnon* to the slaughter of their king, these slaves *do* actually change the course of the plot. When Cilissa, the Nurse, emerges from the palace, sent to bring a message to Aegisthus, they tell her to change it:

> Give him a different message. Tell him
> To come alone. Smile, say there's nothing to fear –
> Your lips can give the facts a twist. (771–3)

This, without telling the Nurse *why*. When Aegisthus does turn up, they are careful not to lie to him, merely confirming that they heard what he has heard. They may know whose side they are on but there's no point, if you are a slave, in condemning yourself should things fail to pan out the way you hope. Slaves cover their backs. And when the cries of Aegisthus are heard from indoors their reaction is appropriate for non-combatants who are interested, but primarily as bystanders:

> Shh!
> What's happened?

Who's won?
Stay back till it's settled.
Stay innocent of blood. (870–3)

After the final departure indoors of Orestes and his mother, the Chorus, for the only other time in the play, refer to Troy, paralleling the *barudikos poina*, the 'heavyweight justice' that fell upon the sons of Priam with what has happened here in Argos.

In Sophocles' *Electra*, the Chorus are not slaves, but local women whose support for Electra offers an intriguing contrast to the Aeschylus approach. Because the structure of the play delays contact between brother and sister until a mere 400 lines before the end, the dramatic emphasis falls upon the stricken Electra. The Chorus are in the position of knowing no more than she does about what is happening with Orestes. The audience, on the other hand, do know that the plot is proceeding very nicely without her involvement so that her behaviour is that of an emotional loose cannon. The attitude of the Chorus is ambivalent: such sympathy as they have for Electra is offset by their belief that Chrysothemis is right and that Electra should be more submissive. They may hope for the death of Clytemnestra:

May the one that did this die
If I may pray for such a thing. (126–7)[10]

But their tolerance of Electra's behaviour is wearing thin:

Your weeping is not going to bring back
Your father from the dead [. . .]
You are destroying yourself
With your immoderate and impossible grief. (137–41)

You are not the only person to suffer, child,
There are those indoors,
Who share your blood and ancestry. (153–6)

. . . if you have any sense
You will do just what she [Chrysothemis] says. (464–5)

I see how furious she [Clytemnestra] makes you, but whether
She is justified is something you don't consider. (610–11)

There are, of course, as many supportive lines from the Chorus, though only a single and decorous expression of grief over Orestes in the presence of Clytemnestra. Nor are they ever put in the position of having to do anything positive in the presence of Clytemnestra or Aegisthus, at least until Clytemnestra is dead and Aegisthus about to meet his come-uppance. What is unusual, perhaps, is the extent of their challenge to the legitimacy of Electra's behaviour; how critical they are of her extended grief. Choruses in Greek tragedy almost always accuse the rebellious of over-reacting. Their privileged position in Aeschylus of being in on the plot will inevitably turn them into accomplices. Sophocles leaves them in the same position as Electra, not knowing for almost three-quarters of the play what is really happening. Their inclination to passivity aligns them instinctively with Chrysothemis, but it also amounts to an invitation to the audience similarly to question any emotional alignment with such a troubled heroine. If, as is still an unresolved issue, the Euripides *Electra* did follow that of Sophocles, the younger playwright was simply extending the challenge to the audience to treat the vengeance of brother and sister as natural and appropriate.

In the Euripides *Electra*, the Chorus have more reason to feel uncomfortable with Electra's behaviour, though not quite so far as to reveal anything to Clytemnestra. Here they are simply local country-women who offer friendship, as they would to any other farmer's wife. Her attitude towards them is dictated by the emotional flagellation which seems to dictate her every word and action. They, on the other hand, seem happy enough to applaud the murder of Aegisthus, despite its dubious circumstances. The murder of a mother is something else. At the moment of the killing they offer only grief and dismay:

> I sing sorrow because your children slay you. (1168)[11]

> A bitter fate, a fate that made you suffer,
> Mother of sorrows!
> Unrelenting pain and more,
> All at the hands of your children. (1185–8)

Both the above sentiments are offset by a briefer qualification about how Clytemnestra deserved what she got for killing Agamemnon, but to Electra, returning from indoors with the body, they now offer nothing but condemnation :

> Your mind is as light as the breeze,
> Blowing here and blowing there.
> You fear god now, but not earlier
> When you persuaded Orestes
> To do these terrible things
> He never wanted to. (1201–5)

A quick word of consolation for Orestes is followed by further repudiation:

> The poor woman! How could you bear to look
> At your dying mother,
> As she breathed away her life? (1218–20)

That is the closest they can get to echoing the Sophoclean chorus with their concluding lines:

> Children of Atreus,
> How much suffering you had to endure
> In your struggle for freedom
> Before you won your victory. (1508–10)

The extraordinary *volte-face* of the Chorus in Euripides, rendering the matricide an act that is wholly shocking – an attitude matched in Euripides' subsequent *Orestes* – is compounded by the Chorus asking the Dioscuri why they didn't turn up a little earlier and prevent what has happened. A typical Euripidean question gets a suitably lame answer and the Chorus speak again only to wrap up the play. Their act of subversion here is to rule out the act of matricide as in any way acceptable, something which Aeschylus debates as a legal and moral issue, Sophocles effectively as neither. Euripides kills off any possibility of justification.

The acts of rebellion of these choruses, then, vary from active opposition to the ruling authority of Aeschylus' *Libation-Bearers*, through the reservations over the excesses of Electra's obsession in Sophocles, to the downright rejection of what Electra has done in Euripides. They are all choruses with attitude.

At this point it seems appropriate to return to *Medea*. The feature of this play which stands out in the present context is the way in which Medea manipulates the Chorus of local women of Corinth, not merely to become complicit in her act of infanticide, but to question the whole process of motherhood. The opening prologue from the Nurse gives way to a short scene between the Nurse and the cynical male Tutor. They are interrupted by Medea's passionate cries offstage and the arrival of the Chorus. This Chorus consists of Corinthian women, locals whose initial response is equivocal. Jason has behaved badly but:

> Your husband's deserted you
> For someone else's bed.
> That's not the end of the world.
> The god will work it out
> You mustn't take so hard the loss of a husband. (155–9)[12]

By a process of manipulation which encompasses everyone from Creon to Aegeus, Medea achieves her aim of making the murder of the children possible. Most significantly, she whittles away at the Chorus's resistance. But they are already primed for resistance. Before Jason makes his first entrance they sing an ode of defiance:

> Rivers flow backwards,
> What's right is wrong,
> Corrupt counsel prevails:
> There's no faith in god,
> Because of men.
> But times are changing:
> Our deeds will be glorified.
> An end to those slanders,
> Celebration of women. (420–30)

It takes time to gain their acquiescence to the violence she is planning but she wins them round, first to stand by while she contrives to kill her rival (and Creon, an unexpected bonus); then to permit the murder of the children. She transforms them into women who betray nature to such an extent that, while the princess and the king are dying horribly offstage, the Chorus onstage are offering the following sentiment:

> And I say this. Those who miss out,
> On experience,
> Who never have children,
> They're the lucky ones.
> They never know, the childless –
> They never have the chance –
> What a child may bring,
> Joy or grief, grief or joy.
> The childless never see
> That first sweet enchantment
> Shrivel, with time, into despair. (1090–100)

This is a Chorus who not only subvert their own royal family, but come passively to accept the subverting of nature itself. They change their world and their way of viewing the world.

If the supernatural Furies of Aeschylus' *Eumenides* are the most immediately alarming of choruses, the Bacchants in Euripides' *Bacchae* invoke a terror of their own. They arrive at Pentheus' front door as fanatical disciples and consistently call attention to themselves through their vocal and musical accompaniment to the play. This draws no more than a mild reproof from Pentheus:

> As for this pack of followers he brought with him
> I'll sell them or set them to work sewing,
> Instead of making all this din. (511–14)[13]

This is a threat he makes no attempt to carry out. As converts to, and representatives of, the Dionysiac religion, the allegiance of these women to Dionysus is absolute. Their corporate nature is both a protection and a challenge to the authorities, whether criticising

Pentheus to his face or applauding his death, ripped to pieces by his own mother. Theirs is a comprehensive act of defiance against temporal power in the name of the divine. What is so remarkable about them as a theatrical device is the way they function as a living embodiment of the religion itself without ever needing to do more than pose a threat by their presence. But, at one moment, even they seem to waver, allowing a human compassion to reveal a chink in their armour, 'Cadmus, I feel pain for you' (1327). Inconveniently, this comes just before the break in the manuscript and the epiphany of Dionysus so there is no means of knowing the extent of their pity. By the resumption of the full text, Dionysus has returned and reeled them back in. Any spark of humanity has been snuffed out; their tiny act of rebellion against the god has returned to the blanket rebellion against human authority.

In the circumstances of the Greek theatre, the use of the mask clearly helps the Chorus, offering, as it does, both a solidarity with the group – assuming that choruses originally wore identical masks – and the possibility for the personal statement, rendered safe by its anonymity. For a female chorus encroaching on male space outside the house, this is especially important. The mask is a means of being present while also being invisible, offering the anonymity of the group who are all dressed, and who all look, exactly alike.

The implication is that the questioning of authority or of the conventional view may be found more in the world of women, or through the eyes of female characters rather than male. Their means of demonstrating it are also much subtler. If this is true, then it may reinforce the idea that what appeared to be repressive in the social practice of the fifth and fourth centuries BC proved less so at the time than it does in retrospect. What is familiar in one period, however unacceptable in another, will have seemed the norm to those who knew nothing else. There is something protective about invisibility, about the mask. The sense that the restriction on women's lives in Athens was merely coercive may be as misguided as Augusto Boal's mistaken view of all Greek tragedy as coercive. Athenian women had a culture of their own which was productive, complex and every bit as necessary to the functioning of the state as was that of the men. Greek history records that when you sacked a city you killed the men and sold the women into slavery. The women became slaves, but they learnt the techniques of survival.

Rather than follow this line further, I want now to carry the argument forward from the original plays and into the realm of modern interpretations or reinventions of the classical themes. Writers since classical times, using the Greeks as their model, have come up with various solutions as to how to handle the Chorus, some more successful than others in finding integration between Chorus and main characters, and an equivalent link between reflection and narrative. The range of possible examples is so huge as to provide evidence for almost any proposition, but frequently the Chorus is reduced in number to what is manageable or explicable in literal terms. The single male figure who functions as a Narrator, as in, for example, Brian Friel's *Living Quarters: after Hippolytus*, or Jean Anouilh's *Antigone* and *Oedipe ou le roi boiteux*, provides a sense of privileging authority. This is a perfectly reasonable dramatic device but fails to address the sense identified above of the Chorus as representatives of an underclass, with an alternative culture in a liminal or parallel world.

Such a world, most often revealed by the Greeks as a female world, impinges upon the main action, imposing a quiet influence upon it, while declining to move centrestage. Particularly effective is the infrequently used Narrator in Rita Dove's reworking of the Oedipus story set in antebellum South Carolina, *The Darker Face of the Earth*. The relevant character here is identified as both Chorus and Narrator, and as Woman, and Black, and Slave. Her solution to the dangerous world in which she finds herself is very Greek: 'Don't sass, don't fight!', she tells her fellow-slaves, 'Lay low, grin bright' (61).[14] But she senses too the power she and they may have, limited though it is:

> A sniff of freedom is all it takes
> to feel history's sting;
> there's danger by and by
> when the slaves won't sing. (76)

Wole Soyinka's *The Bacchae of Euripides: A Communion Rite*, originally commissioned by the UK's National Theatre, offers a note below the castlist in the printed text to the effect that 'The Slaves and the Bacchantes should be as mixed a cast as is possible, testifying to their varied origins.'[15] This identification of the women with the oppressed class, irrespective of gender, seems at first sight to substitute issues of class for those of gender. This is only partly true. Dionysus, in his opening speech, still talks of 'my wild-haired women, long companions on this journey home'. The entrance of the Bacchantes is delayed until after a male-dominated ritual for Dionysus but when the Bacchantes do appear, the Slave Leader attempts to dominate them, so exciting the women that they engulf him. His followers barely save him from *sparagmos*. This occurs barely a fifth of the way through the play, but sets the agenda. The power of destruction in what Dionysus stands for is never in doubt. The Chorus give the play a permanent sense of threat.

The Bacchantes leave the scene – their physical presence is much less dominant than in Euripides – but some of them to return as fellow-captives with Dionysus. Such is the actual power of these Bacchantes, demonstrated in a way that Euripides only hints at, that it is they who conjure up the earthquake. And when Agave finally returns with Pentheus' head there is no moment of pity or concern from them. They can only applaud, one of them running up a ladder to display Agave's *thyrsos* while Kadmos and Tiresias bring in the rest of Pentheus. The rule of law has succumbed to the lynch-mob and even when the streams of blood that burst from the impaled head turn out to be not blood but wine, the final stage direction reads: '*The light contracts to a final glow around the heads of Pentheus and Agave.*'

Elsewhere, and in another context, the Chorus point to despair. In an article for the *Guardian* in January 2003, Michael Kustow recalled going to a production of *The Oresteia* in Israel only three hours after a suicide bomber had killed himself and twenty-two others in the bus station in Tel Aviv.[16] The play was an adaptation by Rina Yerushalmi which, in Kustow's words 'sums up the bloody cycle of violence and revenge which is tearing Israelis and Palestinians apart'. Updated productions of Greek tragedy in Israel are inevitably more immediate and more telling than in many another country but, Kustow tells us, this production was also 'more female'. This *Oresteia* was, in fact, an adaptation, based on Aeschylus, but also using material from Hugo von Hofmannsthal and Sartre.

In this Israeli production the Furies took Orestes and Electra back to Troy to confront Hecuba and the Trojan Women, and force them to watch while the effects of all the dead soldiers were heaped and bundled into a mass grave in an action, as Kustow put it, 'shockingly reminiscent of skeletal corpses tipped into the pits of Belsen'. The Furies of Aeschylus are fearsome but Athena subdues them, thus suggesting a possible way forward from the endless cycle of murder and recrimination. No such hope in Israel in this production. The message was as bleak as it could be: no reconciliation; no absolution.

In Ireland, though, glimmers of hope have been invested in the sharper female choruses of the Greeks. By a nice paradox, one is in an adaptation of the only Greek tragedy without a female character, Sophocles' *Philoctetes*. Seamus Heaney's *The Cure at Troy: A Version of Sophocles' Philoctetes*, substitutes a chorus of women for the Greek sailors prescribed by the original. Heaney's reasons for this are interesting as spelled out in his Production Notes:

I suggested three women for the Chorus, in order to give a sense that the action was being invigilated by the three Fates, the Weird Sisters or whoever – this was the mythical dimension to the decision. There was also a gender-politics aspect, insofar as the militaristic, male-bonding world of the Greek army is challenged by the anima (shall we call it?) impulse in Neoptolemus.[17]

They introduce a female dimension into a play that originally has none and seem almost to mellow it. It is one of this Chorus of three who turns into the *deus ex machina*, Hercules (the Sophoclean Heracles) through whom the irreconcilable is reconciled. About the lines he gives to the Chorus, Heaney talks too of contextualising the action both within, and beyond, Northern Ireland politics. All this, plus Heaney's later insistence on the clarity of what the Chorus say, help this Chorus to a broad and positive series of statements. Their gender draws attention to a significance way beyond Odysseus' shipmates in Sophocles, who have come along for little better reason than to offer muscle if it is needed.

Tom Paulin discovers the extra dimension of reproof and truculence in the Chorus of his *Seize the Fire*, a reworking of Aeschylus' *Prometheus Bound*, which drives the most mythical of all Greek tragedies directly into the path of contemporary politics.[18] As in Aeschylus, Prometheus is pegged out against his cliff-face for defying Zeus and bringing 'fire' to mortals. The Chorus, winged daughters of Oceanos, arrive to sympathise:

> I'm crying,
> everyone is crying
> the whole wide world
> is crying
> crying for Prometheus
> the whole wide world
> is crying.[19]

At the same time, they are critical of him:

> Prometheus,
> you're too free with your tongue,
> you lash out and shout.
> The dull, the corrupt,
> those dogged thickos and their lackeys –
> you'd strip them naked.
> Reach some bloody compromise
> and you're the one that shouts
> 'I must protest
> it's all just crap!'
> Freebooting, maverick,
> fickle as the fire you nicked,
> dissenting from the state –
> the state you helped set up – [20]

At one moment they will offer the party line:

> I revere Zeus
> he holds the entire universe
> between his palm and thumb.[21]

The next, reveal the true situation in the state:

> Now every speech that's made,
> it's vetted by a censor first.
> Zeus is the eye and centre of this state.[22]

So, what is their ultimate position? That of most people who cling on to what freedom they can; most oppressed people; most pragmatists; most choruses:

> I'm sorry for you.
> But new rulers mean new laws.
> I ride the wind,
> I let it take me.[23]

But, when the chips are down, and Prometheus demands a choice from them about whose side they are on, they take sides against Hermes, the 'flunky':

> It's simple then –
> we stick by you.
> Out on a limb
> and stubborn –
> that's us all over.[24]

Here they echo the Aeschylean Chorus, in a moment whose political implications in an Irish setting are blatant. The Chorus of Aeschylus' *Prometheus Bound*, too, turn against Hermes and the gods, with their final line, albeit not the final lines of the play, elliptically, but forcefully translated as: 'We spit on those who betray their friends' (1068–70).[25]

What these modern re-readings succeed in doing, I believe, and there could be plenty of other examples, is extending the ways in which the female choruses of the Greek tragedians could show their capacity for survival through acts of sometimes noisy, but usually quiet assertiveness: by making decisions which matter in a way that takes issue with the rules of class and gender that dominated their lives. The Athenian theatre was a public forum for the examination of all manner of issues to do with conflict between gods and men, family and state, morality and expediency. What these choruses show, however much filtered through primarily male writing and, in classical times, exclusively male portrayal, is that the playwrights may also have reflected something of the realities of female influence in this largely male world. The reality of subversion, at private or public level, proves rather more subtle than the oppression that makes it necessary.

Notes

1. Sarah B. Pomeroy, *Goddesses, Whores, Wives, and Slaves: Women in Classical Antiquity* (New York: Schocken Books, 1975).
2. Ibid., p. ix.
3. Sian Lewis, *News and Society in the Greek Polis* (London: Duckworth, 1996).
4. Ibid., p. 22.
5. Euripides' *Medea*, trans. J. Michael Walton, in *Euripides Plays: One* (London: Methuen, 2000).
6. Euripides' *Andromache*, trans. Marianne McDonald and J. Michael Walton (London: Nick Hern Books, 2001), p. 34.
7. Aeschylus' *Suppliants*, trans. Frederic Raphael and Kenneth McLeish, in *Aeschylus Plays: One* (London: Methuen, 1991).
8. Aeschylus' *Libation-Bearers*, trans. Frederic Raphael and Kenneth McLeish, in *Aeschylus Plays: Two* (London: Methuen, 1991). Numberings recorded are to fit the Oxford Text in Greek. The number of lines in English translations often vary from the original.
9. *The Oresteia*, trans. Robert Fagles (London: Wildwood House, 1966), Introduction, p. 43.

10. Sophocles' *Electra*, trans. Marianne McDonald and J. Michael Walton (London: Nick Hern Books, 2004).

11. Euripides' *Electra*, trans. Marianne McDonald and J. Michael Walton (London: Nick Hern Books, 2004).

12. My translation.

13. Euripides' *Bacchae*, trans. Walton in *Euripides Plays: One* (London: Methuen, 1988).

14. Rita Dove, *The Darker Face of the Earth*, rev. edn (Ashland: Story Line Press, 1996).

15. *The Bacchae of Euripides: A Communion Rite*, in Wole Soyinka, *Collected Plays 1* (Oxford: OUP, 1973), p. 234.

16. Michael Kustow, *Guardian*, 7 January 2003.

17. Seamus Heaney, 'The Cure at Troy: Production Notes in No Particular Order', in Marianne McDonald and J. Michael Walton (eds), *Amid Our Troubles: Irish Versions of Greek Tragedy* (London: Methuen, 2002), pp. 172–4 and 179–80.

18. Tom Paulin, *Seize the Fire: A Version of Aeschylus' Prometheus Bound* (London: Faber and Faber, 1990).

19. Ibid., p. 29.

20. Ibid., p. 17.

21. Ibid., p. 33.

22. Ibid., p. 13.

23. Ibid., p. 11.

24. Ibid., p. 59.

25. Aeschylus' *Prometheus Bound*, trans. Frederic Raphael and Kenneth McLeish, in *Aeschylus Plays: One*.

11 The Violence of Clytemnestra

James Diggle

You cannot show murder on the Greek tragic stage. Indeed, you cannot show physical violence. On the stage you can only threaten to commit murder or an act of violence. At the end of the *Agamemnon*, Aegisthus threatens that his attendants will use their swords against the Chorus of old men, and the old men, in their turn, threaten that they will defend themselves with their staffs. This is the closest we come, in tragedy, to a full-scale fight on the stage. But we ourselves know that no such fight will be shown on stage, because the conventions of tragedy forbid it to be shown. Tragedy has many murders; but they are all committed offstage. Sometimes we hear the death-cries of the victims, but we cannot see their deaths. In Sophocles' *Electra* we hear the death-cry of Clytemnestra, when Orestes kills her inside the house; and at the end of the play, when Orestes tells Aegisthus that he too must die, he does not kill him onstage but commands him to enter the house so that he may be killed behind the scenes. Messenger-speeches abound in narratives of murder and violence. The tragic messenger sees what the audience is not allowed to see, and he narrates, often at great length, scenes of violence, murder and mutilation. And so the conventions of tragedy allow two possible representations of murder: either we may hear the sounds of murder at the moment that it is being committed, or we may hear the details of a murder after it has been committed; but the conventions do not allow us to see a murder with our own eyes.

This, then, is a convention, a law, of Greek tragic drama. Murder may be heard but not seen. That law is observed by Sophocles and

Euripides, and by Aeschylus too. And yet Aeschylus found a way to show murder on the stage without breaking the law. He did this in the *Agamemnon*. Clytemnestra murders her husband Agamemnon onstage, before the eyes of the spectators. But how, you ask, can she do that without breaking the dramatic law which forbids murder to be shown on the stage?

The death-cry of Agamemnon rings forth from inside the palace at line 1343: ὤμοι πέπληγμαι καιρίαν πληγὴν ἔσω (Oh! I am smitten deep with a mortal blow!). A few moments later the central door of the *skene* is opened, and through it is wheeled the *ekkuklema*, the platform which enables the dramatist to display an interior tableau. On the *ekkuklema* stands Clytemnestra. At her feet lie the corpses of Agamemnon and Cassandra, whom she has just killed – or rather, Agamemnon lies in his bath, where he fell, and the bath, too, we must suppose, was shown as part of this tableau. Clytemnestra holds in her hands the murder-weapon. What is this weapon? Scholars have long disputed whether it is a sword or an axe. Most probably it is an axe. Look at the representation of the murder scene on a Krater which is nearly contemporary in date with our play.[1] Aegisthus, holding a sword, grasps Agamemnon by the hair. Behind Aegisthus stands Clytemnestra, holding a double-headed axe. This scene does not reflect Aeschylus, because in Aeschylus Aegisthus has no part in the murder. It probably reflects Aeschylus's predecessor, the lyric poet Stesichorus. If Stesichorus gave Clytemnestra an axe, it would be natural for Aeschylus to give her the same weapon. The identity of the murder-weapon is important. You use a sword to strike the body. With an axe you strike the head. If, then, Clytemnestra used an axe, she delivered the blows to Agamemnon's head, and his slaughter was all the more brutal and horrifying.

So there she stands, with the axe in her hands, and the corpse of Agamemnon before her, lying in his bath, shrouded in the robe, the fishing net, as she calls it, with which she entwined him. And as she speaks she re-enacts the murder. She murders him again in mime. We cannot see the murder as it happens, because the conventions forbid that, but we can see it re-enacted after it has happened. This is the earliest example of a technique with which we are familiar from televised sport: the action replay. And as she goes through the violent and horrifying motions of murdering her husband in mime, the violence and horror of her actions are matched by the violence and horror of her language.

Here is her speech, with a translation:

> ἕστηκα δ' ἔνθ' ἔπαισ' ἐπ' ἐξειργασμένοις.
> οὕτω δ' ἔπραξα, καὶ τάδ' οὐκ ἀρνήσομαι,   1380
> ὡς μήτε φεύγειν μήτ' ἀμύνεσθαι μόρον·
> ἄπειρον ἀμφίβληστρον, ὥσπερ ἰχθύων,
> περιστιχίζω, πλοῦτον εἵματος κακόν·
> παίω δέ νιν δίς, κἀν δυοῖν οἰμώγμασιν
> μεθῆκεν αὐτοῦ κῶλα, καὶ πεπτωκότι   1385
> τρίτην ἐπενδίδωμι, τοῦ κατὰ χθονὸς
> Διὸς νεκρῶν σωτῆρος εὐκταίαν χάριν.
> οὕτω τὸν αὐτοῦ θυμὸν ὁρμαίνει πεσὼν
> κἀκφυσιῶν ὀξεῖαν αἵματος σφαγὴν
> βάλλει μ' ἐρεμνῆι ψακάδι φοινίας δρόσου,   1390
> χαίρουσαν οὐδὲν ἧσσον ἢ διοσδότωι
> γάνει σπορητὸς κάλυκος ἐν λοχεύμασιν.

I stand where I struck, with the deed done. And I so performed it – I will not deny it – that he could neither escape nor ward off his doom. An endless wrapping, like a fish-net, I throw around him, an evil wealth of dress. And I strike him twice; and with two groans, here on the spot, he let his limbs go slack; and then, when he has fallen, I add a third stroke, a thanksgiving for answered prayers to the Zeus beneath the earth, the saviour of the dead. So he pours forth his own life as he lies there. And blowing forth a swiftly flowing bloody slaughter, he strikes me with a dark shower of gory dew. And I rejoice in it no less than the crop rejoices in the rich blessing of the rain of Zeus, during the birth-pangs of the corn.

Clytemnestra still stands at the place of murder ('I stand where I struck'). She has not moved from the time she struck the blows. The scene has been, so to speak, frozen in time; and time itself has stood still. Then she begins to re-enact the murder. First she renders Agamemnon a helpless victim, by swathing him in a bath-robe, which will encumber his limbs, so that he cannot escape her blows. She calls the robe an ἀμφίβληστρον, literally, 'that which is thrown around, a wrapping'. And this 'wrapping' is 'endless': it is a huge robe, which will smother its wearer in its voluminous folds. But then the 'wrapping' takes on a more sinister colouring. It is 'like the wrapping which envelops fish'. It is like a fishing-net. The victim will be reduced to the status of a fish, caught in a net, squirming helplessly, helplessly gasping for breath. But after the world of simile, when the robe is transformed into a net, we return to the literal world, and the robe becomes a robe again, but a sinister robe, 'an evil wealth of clothing'. The wrapping is, in reality, no cheap net such as the humblest fisherman might own, but a valuable object, such as only the wealthy would possess. It is just such an object as we know that the palace of Clytemnestra possesses. For we have recently seen the stage strewn with such objects, the rich fabrics with which Clytemnestra paved the path of Agamemnon from his chariot to the palace.

And so Agamemnon is entrapped. He cannot move. He is a helpless victim, who cannot defend himself. Such is to be the fate of a soldier, commander-in-chief of all the Greeks. He will not die in battle, in full armour, transfixed by the sword, glorious in death. He will die ingloriously, struck down by the axe, weaponless, immobile, wrapped in a bath-robe.

And now she strikes. And the verb which she uses is in the present tense. She does not say, 'I struck him'; she says, 'I strike him'. She uses the present tense because she strikes again in mime. And she strikes not one blow but two ('I strike him twice'). And as she speaks these words, we may infer that she wields the axe again, so that we witness the blows. And the blows which she strikes are aimed at the head. At each blow Agamemnon utters a groan of agony. And his limbs go slack. And they go slack αὐτοῦ, 'on the spot'. This word reminds us, once again, that the place where Clytemnestra stands and the corpse of Agamemnon lies is the actual place where the murder was committed. But two blows are not enough. She adds a third, and blasphemy accompanies this blow. The third blow is described as 'a thanksgiving for answered prayers to the Zeus beneath the earth, the saviour of the dead'. This is Hades, in his role as the Zeus of the underworld. Zeus receives her thanks for answering her prayers. She rewards him with a thanks-offering, a sacrificial victim, not an animal victim but a human life.

And Agamemnon dies. He is now like the fish in the net, gasping for breath. As he breathes his last, the blood pours from his mouth. He breathes forth 'a swiftly flowing bloody slaughter'. This is horrifying enough; but the worst horror is yet to come. The blood splashes Clytemnestra. And what is her reaction? Is it terror? Is it revulsion? Does she flinch from the cascade of gore? No, she exults in it. She bathes herself in it. She sees not blood but dew, δρόσος. She compares this bloody dew to the rain sent by Zeus. The drops of bloody dew are black, ἐρεμνῆι ψακάδι, but she likens them to the bright sheen of glistening rain, γάνος. Furthermore, this is the rain which brings to birth the ear of corn.

This final image is her culminating act of violence. The physical violence which she has performed against her husband is now matched by a metaphorical violence which she performs against the world of nature. She usurps and perverts the language of the natural world.

Let us consider a famous Homeric simile, in which the violent death of a man is illuminated by an image from the world of nature. In the 8th book of the *Iliad* the son of Priam, Gorgythion, is struck by an arrow in the chest. His head sinks to one side, like a poppy: μήκων δ' ὡς ἑτέρωσε κάρη βάλεν, ἥ τ' ἐνὶ κήπωι, / καρπῶι βριθομένη νοτίηισί τε εἰαρινῆισιν (306–7) (He dropped his head to one side like a poppy in the garden, bent by the weight of its seed and the spring showers). This image caught the imagination of Homer's successors. It was imitated first by Stesichorus in the *Geryoneis* (Page, S15. 14–17): ἀπέκλινε δ' ἄρ' αὐχένα Γαρ[υόνας / ἐπικάρσιον, ὡς ὅκα μ[ά]κω[ν / ἅτε καταισχύνοισ' ἁπαλὸν [δέμας / αἶψ' ἀπὸ φύλλα βαλοῖσα] (He bent his neck aside, as when a poppy, which, spoiling its delicate shape, quickly shedding its petals . . .). And it was imitated also by Virgil (*Aen.* 9. 433–7): 'uoluitur Euryalus leto, pulchrosque per artus / it cruor inque umeros cervix conlapsa recumbit: / purpureus ueluti cum flos succisus aratro / languescit moriens, lassoue papauera collo / demisere caput pluuia cum forte grauantur' (Euryalus rolls to the ground in death, and the blood flows over his beautiful limbs, and his neck grows limp and droops onto his shoulders: like a purple flower which languishes and dies when it has been cut by the plough, or like poppies which hang their heads when they are burdened by rain and their necks grow weary). In each of these passages a dying man is likened to a poppy: his head droops, just as the head of a poppy droops. In Homer and Virgil the poppy droops because its petals are heavy with rainfall. In Stesichorus it droops perhaps because it too is dying, and as it sheds its petals it spoils its delicate shape. In all three passages the image is entirely visual: the heads of man and poppy droop. We may, if we wish, find pathos in the comparison of heroic man with a humble flower of the field, which blooms for only a season. Or we may think that the poppy is not such a humble flower, and may remember its glorious red colour, and find pathos in the notion that a thing of such beauty is at the mercy of the elements of nature or the passing plough. So we may say that the fate of the poppy illustrates graphically the pathos of a human death. But, if we find pathos in these passages, we do not find in them the horror which we find in Aeschylus. That Clytemnestra should use an image from the natural world is *un*natural, and that is why her imagery horrifies us. She uses the language of innocent nature for her own unnatural purposes.

We can appreciate the unnatural horror all the more clearly if we remember another Homeric simile, which is the direct inspiration for Clytemnestra's words. In the 23rd book of the *Iliad*, the heart of Menelaos was warmed with joy: τοῖο δὲ θυμὸς / ἰάνθη ὡς εἴ τε περὶ σταχύεσσιν ἐέρση / ληΐου ἀλδήσκοντος, ὅτε φρίσσουσιν ἄρουραι (597–9) (His heart was warmed with joy, just like the dew upon the ears of corn of a ripening crop, when the ploughlands are bristling). In both the Homeric and the Aeschylean passages we have the same image, the ripening of the ear of corn. In the *Iliad*, the warming of the heart of man is likened to the warming of the dew on the corn. Here man and nature are in harmony. But, when Clytemnestra likens the blood of Agamemnon to the rain which helps the corn to grow, she transfers an image of life into a context of death, and, most importantly, she introduces into the image a new dimension, the notion of birth.

In all of Greek tragedy, there is no image more horrifying than this. Here stands Clytemnestra, bathing herself in her husband's blood. She compares that blood to the rain from heaven. The rain is a precious blessing from Zeus: it gives life to man and nature alike. She compares her joy in the blood in which she bathes to the joy of the crop when it bathes in heavenly rain. The crop rejoices because the rain brings life, because the rain assists in the birth of new corn. Clytemnestra evokes an image from orderly nature – she who has violated the natural order; at the moment she brings death she evokes an image of birth.

Note

1. E. Vermeule, 'The Boston Oresteia Krater', *American Journal of Archaeology*, 70 (1966): 1–22; cf. M. Davies, 'Aeschylus' Clytemnestra: Sword or Axe?', *Classical Quarterly*, 37 (1987): 65–71.

12. An Archetypal Bluestocking: Melanippe the Wise

John Dillon

We have been hearing much in this collection of essays about Euripides' outrageous heroines, and the influence they have had on later European, and indeed non-European, drama, but inevitably the primary focus has been on the heroines of surviving plays, such as Medea in the *Medea*, Hecuba in the *The Trojan Women*, or even Iphigeneia in the two plays devoted to her. I would like, however, to direct our attention to a rather different type of Euripidean heroine, who outraged Athenian male sensibilities not by her violent actions, or even passions, but rather by the quality of her intellect.[1] As such, she seems eminently suited to treatment in a collection of essays devoted to our present honorand.

The heroine to whom I refer is Melanippe, accorded the sobriquet of *sophê*, 'the wise' or 'the intellectual'. Melanippe was the daughter of Aeolus by Hippo,[2] the daughter of the Centaur Chiron, whom Aeolus had waylaid on Mt Pelion, and had his way with. Hippo had inherited much of her father's wisdom, which she in turn passed on to her daughter, who in consequence emerges, in the works of Euripides, as the archetypal bluestocking, replete with the latest philosophical theories of Anaxagoras and his followers, as well as sophistic theories about the equal intellectual capabilities of women and men (cf. Fr. 487 N^2).[3] This did not save her, however, from being raped, in due course, by a thoroughly anthropomorphic Poseidon, and in due course producing twins, named – at least later – Aeolus and Boeotus.[4] These twins, in fear of her father's wrath, she exposed in the royal cow-byre. Here they were suckled by a cow, and guarded by the bull, in consequence of which, when found thus by some of the royal cowherds, they were thought to be monstrous births (*terata*) from the cow, and were brought to King Aeolus by the cowherds, to ask him what to do with them. He proposes to immolate them, as such, and hands them over to Melanippe (whom he recognises as an authority on matters of religion, among other things) to prepare them for sacrifice.

This puts Melanippe in an interesting situation. In her effort to save her children, she makes a long speech to her father, in which she presents various rationalistic arguments as to why they could not possibly be monsters. In the course of this comes the famous utterance – possibly at the beginning of it, if we may judge from Plato's use of it in the *Symposium* (177A):

Not mine the tale – I heard it from my mother –
that once heaven and earth showed one same form,
but when they then were parted from each other,
gave birth to all and brought them to the light,
trees, birds, beasts and what the brine produces,
and the race of mortals. (Fr. 488 N^2)

How exactly this suited her argument we do not know, but it is a good account of Anaxagoras' doctrine of cosmogony, though with a suitable mythological, 'Hesiodic' colouring to it.

Her reported argument against the possibility, or at least the portentous significance, of accidents of nature may well involve a reminiscence of a famous story about Anaxagoras, told by Plutarch, in his *Life of Pericles* (ch. 6). A country-man once brought to Pericles the head of a ram which had a single horn growing from the middle of its forehead. The soothsayer Lampon accepted this as an omen, and interpreted this as meaning that, of the two rivals at that time for supreme power in Athens, Pericles and Thucydides, son of Melesias, that one would prevail to whom the head had been brought. Anaxagoras, however, had the skull split open, and in a brief anatomical lecture explained the natural reasons for the anomaly. The people, says Plutarch, were full of admiration for his knowledge, but transferred their admiration to

Lampon when, a short time afterwards (in about 443 BC), Thucydides was ostracised, and Pericles took over the sole political control of Athens.

Similarly, in Melanippe's case, the fact (or at least the *dramatic fact*) is actually more remarkable than the notion of the children's being the offspring of a cow; they are the offspring of a mortal maiden and a *god*. Alas, Melanippe's rational arguments fail, and she has finally to admit that the children are her own; whereat, in the original myth (as relayed to us by Hyginus, *Fab.* 186), her father, in a rage, blinds her and locks her up in a dungeon. In Euripides' version, though, it seems, our heroine is saved by the intervention of Poseidon, or possibly of her mother Hippo, appearing as a *deus/dea ex machina*. The divine parentage of the twins is revealed, and, in a typical Euripidean conclusion, their future role as eponymous heroes of Boeotia and the Aeolid respectively is prefigured.

This play incurs the disapproval of Aristotle (*Poetics* ch. 15, 1454 a 31), as an example of unsuitable language being put into the mouth of a character – in this case avant-garde philosophy into the mouth of a supposedly well brought-up young lady. This unsuitability would seem to have begun even in the opening scene, where Melanippe, at the outset of a typically Euripidean genealogical prologue, speaks the shocking first lines of the play:[5] 'Zeus, whoever Zeus may be – for I know of him only by report –[6] engendered Hellen' – that is to say, the father of Aeolus, and Melanippe's grandfather. By this opening line there actually hangs a tale, though it is hard to know quite what to make of it. It is told by Plutarch, in the *Erotikos* (756 BC):[7]

You have no doubt heard what an uproar burst upon Euripides when he began his *Melanippe* with this verse: '*Zeus, whoever Zeus may be – for I know him only by report . . .*'

Well, he got another chorus[8] (for he had confidence in the play, it seems, since he had composed it in an elevated and elaborate style), and changed the verse to the present text: '*Zeus, as the voice of truth declares . . .*'[9]

The scenario presented by Plutarch is by no means an impossible one, though it is slightly troublesome that the second version of the opening line also seems to have been used at the beginning of another play, the *Pirithous*.[10] On the other hand, the surviving papyrus version of the prologue[11] contains the revised opening line, and Aristophanes' satirical use of it in the *Frogs* (1244) probably refers to the opening of this play;[12] so we may accept Plutarch's story, I think. At all events, we can see Euripides, in this fascinating and provocative play, probing the permissible limits of propriety for his own characteristic purposes – even if he then had to back off somewhat.

It is not only Plutarch who transmits a memory of this scandalous detail. Lucian also, in his skit *Zeus Tragôidos* (s. 41) – a title which might be rendered 'Zeus Gives Out' – quotes the line, as one of Euripides' notorious atheistical utterances, as if that were the accepted beginning of the play – linking it, interestingly, with another scandalous utterance from an unidentified play (Fr. 941 N):

> Ὁρᾶς τὸν ὑψοῦ τόνδ' ἄπειρον αἰθέρα
> καὶ γῆν πέριξ ἔχονθ' ὑγραῖς ἐν ἀγκάλαις;
> τοῦτον νόμιζε Ζῆνα, τόνδ' ἡγοῦ θεόν.

> You see on high this boundless sweep of air
> that laps the earth about in yielding arms?
> Deem this to be Zeus, this hold as God!

There is actually quite good evidence, based on the probable filling of a lacuna in Probus' commentary on Virgil (ad *Ecl.* 6. 31), that this comes from Euripides' *Antiope*, in which case it would be spoken dismissively by the intellectual Amphion, in response to his mother Antiope's claim that he and his brother Zethus were sons of Zeus (who had raped her, even as Poseidon had raped Melanippe). Plainly, Euripides enjoyed ironic situations of this sort: he makes use of the motif in the *Ion*, with Creusa and Ion, and also in the other play that he composed on the story of Melanippe, to which I shall return presently, the *Melanippe Desmotis*, or 'Melanippe in Chains'.[13]

This, however, is by no means the only scandalous passage in the play of which we have evidence. The statement by Melanippe that I have alluded to above as being used by Aristophanes in the *Lysistrata* plainly also impressed itself (unfavourably) on the Athenian consciousness:

ἐγὼ γυνὴ μέν εἰμι, νοῦς δ' ἔνεστί μοι·
αὐτὴ δ' ἐμαυτῆς οὐ κακῶς γνώμης ἔχω·
τοὺς δ' ἐκ πατρός τε καὶ γεραιτέρων λόγους
πολλοὺς ἀκούσασ' οὐ μεμούσωμαι κακῶς.

Woman I may be, but yet I possess intellect.
I am not ill-equipped with good judgement;
And having listened to many words of wisdom
Both from my father and from other ancestors,
I am in no way deficient in culture.

If Aristophanes can put this into the mouth of Lysistrata – with some expectation, presumably, that the allusion would be picked up[14] – that is a good indication of how he reckoned that the ordinary male Athenian would have reacted to Melanippe. At this point in the play, Lysistrata is actually making excellent sense, in reminding the Spartans and the Athenians of how much they owe each other, by way of urging them to make peace, but she is nevertheless a distinctly uppity female, much too smart for her own good, and it is not her place to be talking like this.

The image of the Euripidean Melanippe is thus already plainly fixed and notorious in 411, and her speech beginning 'Not mine the tale . . .' was still embedded in Plato's mind a full generation later, when he was composing the *Symposium* in the later 380s. A generation later again, as I have mentioned above, the speech beginning with this line constituted for Aristotle a paradigm of 'unsuitability' (*aprepeia*), and we find the line used repeatedly in writers of the Roman imperial period, such as Dionysius of Halicarnassus, Aristides, Plutarch and even the Emperor Julian, though merely as a tag. It even turns up in Horace, in Latin translation (*Satires* II 2, 2): *nec meus hic sermo est . . .*

One other line from the play seems to have jarred on the sensibilities of Athenians. At some point or other, Melanippe swears an oath – perhaps to buttress her claim that her children are not *terata*: Ὄμνυμι δ' αἰθέρ, οἴκησιν Διός . . . (I swear by the aether, dwelling-place of Zeus).

This might seem harmless enough – *aithêr*, one might think, like 'Olympus', could be taken as a poetical characterisation of whatever transcendent realm Zeus might be deemed to inhabit – but in the mouth of Melanippe, and in conjunction with all this avant-garde Anaxagorean philosophising, it plainly rankled. Aristophanes uses the phrase thrice, first in the mouth of Euripides himself, at *Thesmophoriazusae* 272, where it is reacted to sceptically by his relation Mnesilochus, whom he is sending in to spy upon the women ('Why not just swear by the lodging-house of Hippocrates?');[15] and twice in *Frogs* (100 and 311), first in the mouth of the Euripides-loving Dionysus, and then (mockingly) in the mouth of his personal servant Xanthias. The implication is, presumably, that, as for 'Socrates' in the *Clouds*, Zeus is really nothing but the aether (as he was, certainly, for Anaxagoras' follower, Diogenes of Apollonia), and that is what the audience is meant to pick up on.

That is unfortunately all that can be recovered of the specifically outrageous aspects of Euripides' portrayal of Melanippe. However, there is one other phase, this time a lyric passage, and so presumably uttered by the Chorus, that stuck in people's memories. This is a praise of Justice (Fr. 490 N²):

> Δικαιοσύνας τὸ χρύσεον πρόσωπον·
> οὔθ ἕσπερος οὐθ' ἑῷος οὕτω
> θαυμαστός.

> The golden face of Justice:
> neither the evening nor the morning star
> is so wondrous.

The latter part of this is quoted by Aristotle, with every sign of approval, at *Nicomachean Ethics* V 2, 1129b28f., as a fine description of the virtue of Justice.[16] Plotinus also picks up on this, in two places (*Enneads* I 6, 4, 11 and VI 6, 6, 39), but he makes reference also to the 'face of Justice', which Aristotle does not, so he must have independent (though not necessarily first-hand) knowledge of the passage.

On the face of it, then, there is nothing at all subversive about this passage. However, if we were to allow ourselves to speculate for a moment, we could see this as the joyous reaction of the Chorus to the appearance of Poseidon (or Hippo) at the end of the play, where Melanippe is saved from the miserable fate of being blinded and imprisoned by her father (as seems to have been her fate in the original myth), and all is put right. In that case, especially if the Chorus were a chorus of women, as is not improbable, we may discern a subversive Euripidean twist to this utterance: well and good, justice is done, but not a moment too soon, and only in the wake of a great deal of injustice, both from gods and men, both of whom ought to have known better!

All in all, then, it is easy to see why *Melanippe the Wise* was regarded as one of Euripides' more iconoclastic productions.[17] By way of an appendix to this, however, I would like to give brief attention to the other play that Euripides devoted to Melanippe, the *Melanippe Desmotis*, or *Melanippe in Chains*. We do not know in which order these plays were written, but it would seem that Melanippe's character and fate attracted Euripides enough for him to have two cracks at her, and, as in the case of Iphigenia, utilising two different versions of her story.[18] In this version (which develops elaborations worthy of a Greek novel – of which it may be regarded as one of the Euripidean antecedents), Aeolus, after discovering that Melanippe is pregnant, and dismissing her story of having been raped by a god, gives her over to the charge of the king of Metapontum in southern Italy, who happens to be visiting. This king (whose name is not preserved, unless it be in fact Metapontius) takes her home with him, and in his palace she gives birth to twins.[19]

These the king, according to Diodorus of Sicily, in obedience to an oracle, adopts as his sons, but also married a wife, Autolyte – Melanippe remaining, it seems, in some menial role in the palace, but not allowed contact with her sons, who seem to grow up with no idea who their real mother (or father) is. But all does not go smoothly.[20] Autolyte in due course herself gives birth to sons, and in consequence begins to plot against the lives of her stepsons, Aeolus and Boeotus.

The plot comes to a head during a hunting expedition on which the pair have set out, during which their stepmother has arranged that they be assassinated by her two brothers, their uncles. We have, preserved in a papyrus fragment,[21] a large portion of the messenger speech which relates what happened. An ambush takes place, the two lads are taken by surprise, but none the less manage to slay their would-be murderers, who, before dying, let the cat out of the bag by abusing them as 'sons of some slave-girl, who have no right to assume the royal sceptre and throne'.

After killing their uncles and scattering their followers (one of whom returns to the palace as the Messenger), the twins come back, execute their stepmother, and then free Melanippe (who seems to have been imprisoned at the instigation of Autolyte) – presumably to the accompaniment of some kind of recognition scene. The killing of the queen, however, provokes a crisis, which was probably resolved by the appearance (once again) of Poseidon *ex machina*, who decrees that the young men depart the kingdom, and sail away to found, respectively, Aeolis and Boeotia. Melanippe herself, meanwhile, probably married the king.

Melanippe in this play may not be quite as disconcertingly *sophê* as she was in the other, but she seems to have some good lines none the less. One section of the papyrus strings together some formerly scattered fragments, to produce the following feminist manifesto:[22]

> Vain is the abuse that men direct against women
> and their ill talk – the twanging of an idle bowstring!
> For they are better than men, and I will prove it.
> Women's covenants need no witness [. . .][23]
> They manage the home, and guard within the house
> The sea-borne wares. Absent a wife
> No house is clean or blessed with wealth.
> And in religion – highest I judge this claim –

We play the greatest part. In the oracles of Phoebus,
Women expound Apollo's will. And at the holy seat
Of Dodona, beside the sacred oak,
A woman conveys the will of Zeus
To all Greeks who may desire it. And as for the rites
Performed for the Fates and for the Nameless Ones,
They are not holy in the hands of men –
It is among women that they flourish all.
So righteous is women's part in holy service.
How then is it fair for the race of women to be abused?
Shall they not cease, the vain reproaches of men,
And those who deem too soon that all women
Must be blamed alike, if one be found a sinner?
Let me speak on, and make this due distinction;
Nothing is worse than the base woman, but than the good
Nothing is much superior; their natures differ.

What brought on this mighty tirade we do not know – possibly
an unjust accusation levelled at Melanippe by the queen, and
believed by the king (thus providing an analogue to Melanippe's
apologia before her father in the other play); but it is plain that
Euripides is using her, as he uses Medea and Phaedra, to utter
unsettling truths about Athenian male chauvinism.

There are various other snippets preserved from this play, many
uttering home truths that may well have come from Melanippe's
mouth,[24] but this is enough, I should say, to give an idea of how
Euripides is making use of Melanippe here. As Euripidean heroines
go, over both of the plays devoted to her, she is someone more
sinned against than sinning, but she is still a formidable figure, and
thus fully worthy of inclusion in the present collection.

Notes

1. There are of course other heroines in lost plays just as outrageous (for
   the usual reasons) as Medea or Phaedra, such as Stheneboea, Ino, or
   indeed the Phaedra of the first *Hippolytus*.

2. Euripides in the play (*Prologue* l. 21) has Melanippe give her name as Hippo. Her name comes out as Hippe in the (very late) version of the myth by Gregory of Corinth, but that is probably just an error.

3. Fr. 487 Nauck[2]. This passage, which I will discuss below, is actually preserved by Aristophanes, who allows Lysistrata to borrow it, for his own satirical reasons, in his play of that name (1124–7).

4. The theme of an honest and intelligent maiden being raped by a god, and undergoing prolonged sufferings as result, is one which plainly attracted Euripides, for his own ironic purposes: Antiope, and Ion's mother Creusa, are cases in point. In Melanippe's case, presumably, the indignity is compounded by the fact that she, as a 'modern' intellectual, did not believe in Poseidon as a personal divinity, no doubt allegorising him as 'the wet element', or something such.

5. Most conveniently available in the Loeb volume, *Select Papyri*, vol. III, ed. D. L. Page (Cambridge, MA, 1970), p. 118.

6. Ζεὺς ὅστις ὁ Ζεύς, οὐ γαρ οἶδα πλὴν λόγῳ.

7. I borrow the Loeb translation of W. C. Helmbold, with minor variations.

8. That is, he was given another chance to present the play. This is unusual, but not unparalleled; it also seems to have happened in the case of the *Hippolytus*, which proved too shocking in its first form, and which Euripides redrafted successfully (we have the second version). Another possibility, perhaps, is that Euripides had this version of the line in the play at its preliminary reading before the archon, the *proagôn*, and the reaction to it was so strong that he hastily changed it; but if so, Plutarch has slightly garbled the story.

9. Ζεύς, ὡς λέλεκται τῆς ἀληθείας ὕπο . . .

10. The *Pirithous*, admittedly, is alleged by some ancient authorities to have been composed not by Euripides, but by the reactionary politician and sophist Critias, which complicates the scenario even further, if true.

11. *Select Papyri*, vol. III, ed. D. L. Page, pp. 118–19.

12. In the *Pirithous*, after all, it occurs, not as the first line, but as the fourth, and Aristophanes seems to be parodying *first* lines, unless he indicates otherwise.

13. Antiope, we may note, is not a 'rebel' in the sense being focused on in the present collection of essays, but rather one of Euripides' 'victims', as is Creusa – and Melanippe herself, so far as we can see, in the *Desmotis*.

14. The *Lysistrata* was produced in 411. We do not know how long before that the *Melanippe* was produced, but even to have the lines remembered from one year to the next is an indication of their notoriety.

15. Τί μᾶλλον ἢ τὴν Ἱπποκράτους ξυνοικίαν. The exact reference of this is not clear. It could be an allusion to the famous doctor of that name, and *synoikia* could refer to his community; or it could simply, as I prefer to believe, refer to some well-known sleazy boarding-house in Athens run by some other Hippocrates. Either way, the point is clear: this so-called oath ain't worth a damn!

16. It is only the scholiast ad loc. in the *codex Parisinus* who tells us that this is a reference to the *Melanippe*, and who supplies the first line.

17. We have no didascalic record, unfortunately, as to when it was produced (except that it was probably not too many years earlier than 411), or with what other plays, or how well it did; but we may assume, I think, that it did not win first prize.

18. It is, I suppose, conceivable that, even after being straightened out by Poseidon, Aeolus decided to exile his daughter, but that is surely most unlikely. We may reflect that Euripides is perfectly prepared to use two different versions of a myth; apart from the case of Iphigenia, consider the case of Helen, in the *Trojan Women* and in the *Helen*.

19. It is most peculiar, by the way, that Diodorus of Sicily (*Histories,* Book IV 67, 3–5), in telling what is manifestly the same story, identifies the heroine as a certain Arne, daughter of Aeolus, Melanippe being listed as wife of Mimas, and Aeolus' *mother*. Diodorus is, of course, more than capable of confusion in the use of his sources, but it is not impossible also that Euripides has conflated traditions, in order to obtain a more interesting character.

20. There is actually an intriguing fragment (494 N²), preserved in Stobaeus, criticising childless persons who adopt sons, thus twisting fate in an untoward direction. This has obvious reference to the king, and could have been spoken by Melanippe. This does not of itself make clear whether he was married or not at the time, but he probably was, since there is no point in panicking about childlessness if one is not yet married!

21. See *Select Papyri*, ed. D. L. Page, vol. III, pp. 108–16.

22. I borrow Denys Page's translation, with some modifications.

23. Just ends of the next four lines survive, in which Melanippe plainly continued her litany of types of female superiority.

24. There is one about slavery (Fr. 515 N^2) which is vintage Euripides, and may well have come from the enslaved Melanippe: 'The name (sc. of slave) will not destroy the good slave; many slaves are better than free men.' This is reminiscent of various other utterances of Euripides' in similar vein, as that concerning the Farmer in the *Electra* (ll. 40–54, from the Farmer's prologue speech), and Alexander in the *Alexandros* (Fr. 53 N^2).

Appendix: Scene from a new play about Hildegard of Bingen

Athol Fugard

For Marianne

Note:

In the last year of her life, at the age of eighty-two, Hildegard of Bingen faced the severest of all her challenges. She had permitted the burial in her convent grounds of a nobleman who had at one point in his life been excommunicated, but whom she believed had repented and been accepted back into the Church. However, her superiors, prelates of Mainz, believed that this was not the case and that the sentence had never been lifted. They ordered her therefore to dig up the body and have it thrown outside her convent grounds. Hildegard refused to do this, so they placed her and her community under interdict. In the following scene she has travelled to Mainz to defend herself before the prelates. Her secretary, the monk Guibert of Gembloux, has accompanied her.

SCENE V

(The hushed and solemn silence of the Cathedral in Mainz. The **Abbess,** *weary and exhausted by a long journey on foot and supporting herself with her crozier, comes forward humbly to address the* **Prelates of Mainz. Guibert** *is at her side. The* **Messenger** *is also present. In the course of her address she will grow from a figure of abject humility into one of prophetic power and authority.)*

The Abbess

My Lords and Masters, I thank you most humbly for allowing me to come before you and for your willingness to hear and consider my petition. As you all know, I have travelled the road between Bingen and Mainz many times in my life, but never before with a heart as heavy with sorrow and confusion as the one I carried within me this time. You have it in your power to relieve that heart of its burden and I pray to Almighty God that when you have heard me out you will find mercy and compassion in yours to do so. I must start with a confession. You ordered me and my daughters to dig up and cast away the body of Frederick of Hordt. I lower my head now in shame and confess that we have disobeyed you. He still lies buried in our cemetery. Now please, my Lords, before your anger seals off your ears to my words, I beg you to believe me when I say that our disobedience is not because we take lightly the advice of honourable men or the orders of our Superiors. It is because we trembled with fear that in obeying you it would appear as if our foolish female natures had led us to violate the sacraments of Christ! . . . because, if you give it just a moment's thought, that is surely what we would have been guilty of if we were right in maintaining that the dead man has been reconciled to the Almighty and received back into the bosom of the Church just before his death. I say to you yet again, my Lord and Masters, that that is in fact the truth of this matter. Before his death he had made his confession and received absolution from the priest at his bedside. I can bring that priest and other witnesses to stand here before you and swear to it. Why will you not believe me? What have I done to deserve your distrust? Would I have carried this decrepit body all the way from Bingen to stand here in a temple of the Almighty and brazenly perjure myself?

My days are numbered now. It won't be long before I stand in front of a greater judge than you and I will have to answer to Him for this moment.

But let me hasten to add that my sisters and I have not been totally disobedient. We have strictly obeyed your punishing injunction and have stopped singing the Divine Office and no longer celebrate the Mass. Burdened as I am by all this, I then had a vision in which The Voice said to me:

'You have done wrong in obeying orders to abandon the Holy Sacraments of God. He is your only salvation. Go to the prelates who ordered you to do that, and ask them for permission to return to celebrating the Mass.'

And so, I stand here before you, my Lords and Masters, imploring you to lift this heavy burden from the sorrowing souls of me and my sisters. But now I beg you again be patient with me, for that is not yet all. In that same vision I saw that in ceasing to sing the Divine Office, and now only whispering it as you ordered, we were guilty of yet another violation. The voice in my vision reminded me of the words of David:

> Praise ye the LORD. Praise God in his sanctuary: praise
>   him in the firmament of his power.
> Praise him for his mighty acts: praise him according to
>   his excellent greatness.
> Praise him with the sound of the trumpet: praise him with
>   the psaltery and harp.
> Praise him with the timbrel and dance: praise him with
>   stringed instruments and organs.
> Praise him upon the loud cymbals: praise him upon the high
>   sounding cymbals.
> Let every thing that hath breath praise the LORD. Praise
>   ye the LORD.

Consider those words carefully, because they remind us that outward, visible things can guide us to and teach us about inward spiritual realities. And they can most powerfully do this if they give shape and substance to our praise of the Almighty. For this reason those ancient prophets, inspired as they were by the Holy Spirit and knowing that the soul of man is symphonic, composed psalms and canticles and devised various kinds of musical instruments to accompany their songs of praise. Learning from them, wise and clever men of later ages invented still other musical instruments so that they might also express the joy that rose up in their souls when they looked inward to their creator.

This is a divinely inspired industry in which I also have laboured long and happily. There will be no end to it, my Lords. For as long as men live and draw breath, voices will be raised in old and new praises of the Lord. Yes, others will come with new sounds and instruments, strange languages, building through the ages a cathedral of sound in which all of mankind will celebrate creation and worship the Almighty. The sounds we make now in our churches are truly but a whispered hint of the Alleluias that will thunder out in ages to come.

But that Dark Angel, man's great deceiver, seeing that man had begun to sing through God's inspiration and knowing that this could lead him out of his exile from paradise, is greatly tormented. He applies himself with great cunning and without pause to devising ways of confounding these praises of the Lord. He will stop at nothing in his evil desire to gag the mouths of the faithful.

Therefore, those who carelessly or spitefully silence a Church and so prevent the singing of God's praises, or cut it off from the Divine Sacraments, will lose their place among the chorus of angels. Those who have been entrusted with the Keys of the Kingdom must beware that they do not open that which must be kept closed, or close that which must be kept open.

Now a figure of threatening power and authority.

I have heard a voice asking: 'Who created Heaven?' – and the answer came thundering back: 'God!'

'Who opens Heaven to the faithful?' – and the answer came: 'God!'

'Who is like Him?' – 'There Is None Like Unto Him!'

So you men of faith, do not resist or oppose Him. You will not escape punishment if you do. He will fall upon you with all his power and destroy you utterly.

She collects herself, and after a pause is once again the old woman who first shuffled in.

Knowing that you will want to consider carefully all that I have said to you, as indeed I did with the message you sent to me, I have written it all down.

A gesture to **Guibert,** *who hands over a letter to the* **Messenger.**

My lords and masters, I most humbly ask you to remember that in taxing your patience with her clumsy words, this miserable figure of an old woman has only been acting as God's messenger. I myself am as void of original thought and inspiration as a blank sheet of parchment.

She turns and walks slowly away, **Guibert** *coming forward to take her arm once again.*

Marianne McDonald:
A Bio-bibliography

Marianne McDonald is Professor of Theater and Classics in the Department of Theater at the University of California, San Diego, and a member of the Royal Irish Academy. A recipient of many national and international awards, including a Patté award from KPBS, and a Billie for Artist of the Year from *San Diego Playbill* (2004), she has also written many articles and books about modern versions of the classics, a field in which she was a pioneer, including: *Euripides in Cinema: The Heart Made Visible* (1983), *Ancient Sun, Modern Light: Greek Drama on the Modern Stage* (1992), *Sing Sorrow: Classics, History and Heroines in Opera* (2001), *Amid Our Troubles: Irish Versions of Greek Tragedies* (2002), and *The Living Art of Greek Tragedy* (2003).

She has translated and written versions of many Greek tragedies: her Sophocles' *Antigone* was directed by Athol Fugard in Ireland (1999); her version of Euripides' *The Trojan Women* was directed by Seret Scott at the Old Globe Theater (2000); her translation of Euripides' *Children of Heracles* (dir. Delicia Turner Sonnenberg) was performed at 6th at Penn (2003); *Medea, Queen of Colchester* (dir. Kirsten Brandt) at Sledgehammer Theatre (2003); translations of Sophocles' *Oedipus Tyrannus* and *Oedipus at Colonus* (dir. George Ye, 2003–04); *The Ally Way* (dir. Robert Salerno, 2004) and *Hecuba* (dir. Esther Emery, 2004) at 6th at Penn.

List of Contributors

James Diggle is Professor of Greek and Latin at the University of Cambridge and a Fellow of Queens' College, and was University Orator from 1982 to 1993. He is the editor of the Oxford Classical Text of Euripides. Among his other books are *Studies on the Text of Euripides* (1981), *Euripidea: Collected Essays* (1994), *Cambridge Orations* (1994), *Theophrastus, Characters* (2004) and an edition of *The Classical Papers of A. E. Housman* (1972). He is also a Fellow of the British Academy and a Corresponding Member of the Academy of Athens.

John Dillon is Regius Professor of Greek at Trinity College, Dublin. His publications include *The Middle Platonists* (1977; 2nd edn 1996), *Alcinous, The Handbook of Platonism* (1993), *The Heirs of Plato* (2003), *Salt and Olives: Custom and Morality in Ancient Greece* (2004). His articles have been published in two collections, *The Golden Chain* (1991) and *The Great Tradition* (1997).

Athol Fugard is South Africa's leading playwright. His best-known works include *The Blood Knot, Hello and Goodbye, Boesman and Lena, Sizwe Banzi is Dead, The Island* (devised with John Kani and Winston Ntshona and including a play within a play based on *Antigone*), *Statements after an Arrest under the Immorality Act, Master Harold and the Boys, The Road to Mecca, My Children My Africa, Valley Song* and *Sorrows and Rejoicings*. He is currently writing a new play based on the life of Hildegard of Bingen. Long persecuted by the apartheid regime, he divides his time now between the new South Africa and California.

Edith Hall, after holding posts at the universities of Cambridge, Reading and Oxford, was appointed to the Leverhulme Chair of Greek Cultural History at the University of Durham in 2001. She is also co-founder and co-director of the Archive of Performances of Greek and Roman Drama at the University of Oxford. Her books include *Inventing the Barbarian: Greek Self-Definition through Tragedy* (1989), an edition, with translation and commentary, of Aeschylus' *Persians* (1996), *Greek and Roman Actors* (co-edited with Pat Easterling, 2002), and (co-authored with Fiona Macintosh), *Greek Tragedy and the British Theatre 1660–1914* (2005).

Seamus Heaney, Ireland's most distinguished living poet, won the Nobel Prize for Literature in 1995. He has been Boylston Professor of Rhetoric and Oratory at Harvard University (1992–96), and Professor of Poetry at Oxford (1989–94), and currently holds the position of Emerson Poet in Residence at Harvard. His best known works include *Death of a Naturalist* (1966), *North* (1975), *Station Island* (1984), *The Haw Lantern* (1987), *The Government of the Tongue* (1988), *The Spirit Level* (1996), his two dramatic adaptations *The Cure at Troy* (1991) and *The Burial at Thebes* (2004) based on *Philoctetes* and *Antigone* respectively, and a version of *Beowulf* (1999).

George Huxley is Honorary Professor of Greek in the School of Classics, Trinity College, Dublin, and formerly Professor of Classics at Queen's University, Belfast. He is a member of Academia Europaea and of the Royal Irish Academy. His writings include *The Early Ionians, Early Sparta, Greek Epic Poetry from Eumelos to Panyassis* and *On Aristotle and Greek Society*. He was joint editor of *Kythera: Excavations and Studies*.

Marina Kotzamani is an Assistant Professor in Theatre History at the Theatre Department, University of the Peloponnese, Greece. She has published articles on twentieth-century production of classical Greek drama, as well as on modern Greek theatre and film in journals such as *Western European Stages*, *Theater Journal* and the *Journal of Modern Greek Studies*. Dr Kotzamani is currently the guest editor of a special project of PAJ entitled, *Aristophanes'*

Lysistrata on the Arabic Stage. She has also collaborated as a dramaturg and translator with professional companies in New York City, including CSC and LaMama. She was a participant in the *Lysistrata Project*, an international effort to protest the war against Iraq through theatre.

Fiona Macintosh is Senior Research Fellow at the Archive of Performances of Greek and Roman Drama at the University of Oxford. Her publications include *Dying Acts: Death in Ancient Greek and Modern Irish Tragic Drama* (1994) and *Greek Tragedy and the British Stage 1660–1914* (2005), co-authored with Edith Hall. She is currently working on a production history of *Oedipus Tyrannus*. With Edith Hall and Oliver Taplin, she has edited *Medea in Performance: 1500–2000* (2000); and *Dionysus Since 69: Greek Tragedy at the Dawn of the Third Millennium*, co-edited with Edith Hall and Amanda Wrigley (2004).

Rush Rehm, Professor of Drama and Classics at Stanford University, is the author of *The Play of Space, Marriage to Death, Greek Tragic Theatre* and, most recently, *Radical Theater: Greek Tragedy and the Modern World.* He is also a freelance actor and director.

Anthony Roche is Senior Lecturer in Anglo-Irish Literature and Drama in the School of English at University College, Dublin, and Director of the Synge Summer School. He is the author of *Contemporary Irish Drama: From Beckett to McGuinness* (1994) and of many articles on Irish theatre. He was editor of the *Irish University Review* from 1997 to 2002, including special issues on Brian Friel and Thomas Kilroy. Work in progress includes a monograph on 'Synge and the Making of a Modern Irish Drama' and *The Cambridge Companion to Brian Friel.*

Melissa Sihra is Lecturer in Drama at Queen's University Belfast. She has published a number of articles on Irish theatre and has worked as a dramaturg on productions of Friel, Shaw and Carr in the United States and in Ireland at the Abbey Theatre. She is co-editor of the forthcoming volume *Contemporary Irish Theatre* and is currently writing a monograph on the theatre of Marina Carr.

Isabelle Torrance completed her Ph. D. in Classics at Trinity College, Dublin, in 2004. She is now a post-doctoral research fellow at the University of Nottingham, working on Alan Sommerstein's Leverhulme-funded project 'The Oath in Archaic and Classical Greece'. Her research interests are primarily in Greek tragedy and its reception. Forthcoming publications include *Aeschylus: Seven Against Thebes* (London: Duckworth), 'Religion and Gender in Goethe's *Iphigenie auf Tauris*' in *Helios* (edited by Barbara Goff), and 'Andromache *Aichmalōtos:* Concubine or Wife?' in *Hermathena*.

J. Michael Walton was Professor of Drama and Founder/Director of the Performance Translation Centre at the University of Hull until retiring in October 2003. He has written four books on Greek theatre, and was joint editor with Marianne McDonald of *Amid Our Troubles: Irish Versions of Greek Tragedy* (2002). He is series editor of Methuen Classical Drama, the forty-six surviving plays of Greek tragedy and comedy in thirteen volumes. He has edited and contributed translations to three anthologies, *Six Greek Comedies*, *Six Greek Tragedies* and *Four Roman Comedies*; published a series of co-translations with Marianne McDonald with whom he is joint editor of the forthcoming *Cambridge Companion to Greek and Roman Theatre*; and was editor of *Craig on Theatre*.

S. E. Wilmer is a Senior Lecturer in Drama and Fellow of Trinity College, Dublin. He is the author of *Theatre, Society and the Nation: Staging American Identities* (2002), and has edited *Beckett in Dublin* (1992), *Portraits of Courage: Plays by Finnish Women* (1997), *Writing and Rewriting National Theatre Histories* (2004), and co-edited *Theatre Worlds in Motion: Structures, Politics and Developments in the Countries of Western Europe* (1998), *Theatre, History and National Identities* (2001) and *Stages of Chaos: Post-war Finnish Drama* (2005).

Select Bibliography

Adams, William D., 'Iphigeneia's Truth: Revisiting Classical Themes as War Looms', *Colby Magazine* (Winter 2003)

Aeschylus, *The Oresteia*, trans. Robert Fagles (London: Wildwood House, 1976)

Alexiou, M., *The Ritual Lament in Greek Tradition* (Cambridge: CUP, 1974)

Amiard-Chevrel, C., *Le Théâtre Artistique de Moscou 1898–1917* (Paris: CNRS, 1979)

Aretz, Susanne, *Die Opferung der Iphigeneia in Aulis. Die Rezeption des Mythos in antiken und modernen Drama* (Stuttgart and Leipzig: B. G. Teubner, 1979)

Aristophanes, *Meletes*, trans. from Russian into Greek by M. Garides (Athens: Mokhlos, 1957)

—— *Lysistrata*, trans. Gilbert Seldes, illus. Pablo Picasso (New York: Limited Editions Club, 1934)

—— *The Poet and the Women*, trans. David Barrett (London: Penguin, 1964)

Aristotle, *On the Art of Poetry*, trans. Ingram Bywater (Oxford: Clarendon Press, 1920)

Arrowsmith, William (ed.), *Four Comedies*, trans. Douglass Parker and Richmond Lattimore (Ann Arbor: University of Michigan Press, 1969)

—— (ed.), *Three Comedies*, trans. Douglass Parker and Richmond Lattimore (Ann Arbor: University of Michigan Press, 1969)

Art in Revolution: Soviet Art and Design since 1917, Exhibition Catalogue (London: Hayward Gallery, 1971)

Aston, Elaine, *An Introduction to Feminism and Theatre* (London: Routledge, 1995)

Azama, Michel, *Iphigénie ou le péché des dieux* (Paris: Ed. Theatrales, 1991)

Bablet, Denis, *The Revolutions of Stage Design in the 20th Century* (New York: Leon Amiel, 1977)

Bacik, Ivana, *Kicking and Screaming: Dragging Ireland into the 21st Century* (Dublin: O'Brien Press, 2004)

Bain, David, 'The Prologues of Euripides', *Iphigenia in Aulis*, *Classical Quarterly*, 27 (1977): 10–26

Bareham, Anthony (ed.), *Charles Lever: New Perspectives* (Gerrard's Cross: Colin Smythe, 1991)

Barton, John and Kenneth Cavander, *The Greeks: Ten Plays Given as a Trilogy* (London: Heinemann, 1981)

Belli, Angela, 'Lenormand's *Asie* and Anderson's *The Wingless Victory*', *Comparative Literature*, 19 (1967): 226–39

Benedetti, Jean, *Stanislavski: A Biography* (London: Methuen, 1988)

Bierl, Anton, *Die Orestie des Aischylos auf der modernen Bühne* (Stuttgart: M & P Verlag, 1997)

Billington, Michael, 'Ariel', *Guardian*, 5 October 2002

Blanchart, Paul, *Le Théâtre de H.-R. Lenormand: Apocalypse d'une société* (Paris: Masques-Revue Internationale d'Art Dramatique, 1947)

Blundell, Sue, *Women in Classical Athens* (Bristol: Classical Press, 1998)

Bogard, Travis and Jackson R. Bryer (eds), *Selected Letters of Eugene O'Neill* (New Haven, CT: Yale University Press, 1988)

Bradley, Anthony and Maryann Giulanella Valiulis (eds), *Gender and Sexuality in Modern Ireland* (Amherst: University of Massachusetts Press, 1997)

Braun, Edward, *The Director and the Stage. From Naturalism to Grotowski* (London: Methuen, 1982)

Brodman, Barbara, 'The Cult of Death in Irish (and Mexican) Myth and Literature: From Fatalism to Fire of the Mind', in Bruce Stewart (ed.), *That Other World: The Supernatural and Fantastic in Irish Literature and its Contexts* (Gerrard's Cross: Colin Smythe, 1998)

Brown, John Mason, *The Modern Theatre in Revolt* (New York: W. W. Norton, 1929)

Burkert, Walter, 'Die Absurdität der Gewalt und das Ende der Tragödie: Euripides' *Orestes*', *Antike und Abendland*, 20 (1974): 97–109

Burnet-Vigniel, Marie Claude, *Femmes Russes dans le combat révolutionnaire* (Paris: Institut d'Etudes Slaves, 1990)

Buxton, R. G. A., *Persuasion in Greek Tragedy* (Cambridge: CUP, 1982)

Cacoyannis M., '*Iphigenia*: A Visual Essay', in M. Winkler (ed.), *Classical Myth and Culture in the Cinema*, rev. edn (Oxford: OUP, 2001), pp. 102–17

Cameron, Averil and Amélie Kuhrt (eds), *Images of Women in Antiquity* (London: Routledge, 1993)

Carlisle, Carol Jones, *Helen Faucit: Fire and Ice on the Victorian Stage* (London: Society for Theatre Research, 2000)

Carr, E. H., *History of Soviet Russia* (New York and London: Macmillan, 1950)

Carr, Marina, *By the Bog of Cats. . .* (Loughcrew, Co. Meath: Gallery Press, 1998)

—— *Marina Carr: Plays One* (London: Faber and Faber, 1999)

—— *Ariel* (Loughcrew, Co. Meath: Gallery Press, 2002)

Carson, Anne, 'Euripides to the Audience', *London Review of Books*, 5 September 2004, p. 24

Carter, Huntly, *The New Theatre and Cinema of Soviet Russia* (London: Chapman and Dodd, 1924)

—— *The New Spirit in the Russian Theatre 1917–1928* [1929] (New York: Arno Press and the *New York Times*, 1970)

Case, Sue Ellen, 'Classic Drag: The Greek Creation of Female Parts', *Theatre Journal*, 37 (3) (October 1985)

Chang, Dale, 1986, 'Role Inversion and Its Function in the *Iphigenia at Aulis*', *Ramus*, 15 (1986): 83–92

Cheney, Sheldon, *The New Movement in the Theatre* (Westport, CT: Greenwood Press, 1914)

Chioles, John, 'The *Oresteia* and the Avant-garde: Three Decades of Discourse', *Performing Arts Journal*, 45 (1993): 1–28

Collins, M. E., *History in the Making: Ireland 1868–1966* (Dublin:

Educational Company of Ireland, 1993)

Corti, Lillian, *The Myth of Medea and the Murder of Children* (Westport, CT: Greenwood Press, 1998)

Coster, Samuel, *Samuel Coster's Iphigenia. Treur-spel* (Amsterdam: Nicolaas Biestkins, 1617)

Csapo, Eric and William J. Slater, *The Context of Ancient Drama* (Ann Arbor: University of Michigan Press, 1995)

Danforth, L. M. and A. Tsiaras, *The Death Rituals of Rural Greece* (Princeton, NJ: Princeton University Press, 1982)

Davies, M., 'Aeschylus' Clytemnestra: Sword or Axe?', *Classical Quarterly*, 37 (1987): 65–71

de Quincey, Thomas, 'The *Antigone* of Sophocles as Represented on the Edinburgh Stage', in *The Art of Conversation and Other Papers*, vol. xiii (Edinburgh: Adam and Charles Black, 1863), pp. 199–233

Diderot, Denis, *Entretiens sur 'le Fils naturel'*, with *Paradoxe sur le comédien*, intro. Raymond Laubreaux (Paris: Garnier-Flammarion, 1967)

Dixon, Michael Bigelow and M. Christopher Boyer (eds), *Moscow Art Theatre: Past, Present and Future* (Louisville: Actors' Theatre of Louisville, 1989)

Dolce, L., *Ifigenia, tragedia* (Venice: Domenico Farri, 1551)

Dove, Rita, *The Dark Face of the Earth* (Ashland: Storyline Press, 1996)

Duncan, William and Paula Scully, *Marriage Breakdown in Ireland: Law and Practice* (Dublin: Butterworths, 1990)

Eagleton, Terry, *Sweet Violence: An Essay on the Tragic* (Malden, MA and Oxford: Blackwell, 2003)

Edmonson, Linda Harriet, *Feminism in Russia, 1900–1917* (Stanford, CA: Stanford University Press, 1984)

Eisner, Robert, 'Euripides' Use of Myth', *Arethusa*, 12 (1979): 153–74

Erasmus, Desiderius, *Euripidis tragici poet[a]e nobilissimi Hecuba et Iphigenia: Latin[a]e fact[a]e Erasmo Roterodamo interprete*

(Paris: J. Badius, 1506)

Ertel, Evelyne (ed.), *La Tragédie grecque: les Atrides au théâtre du Soleil, Théâtre aujourd'hui*, no. 1 (Paris: Centre National de Documentation Pédagogique, 1992)

Euripides, *'Medea' and Other Plays,* trans. Philip Vellacott (London: Penguin, 1939)

Ewen, Stuart, 1996, 'Changing Rhetorics of Persuasion', in his *PR! A Social History of Spin*, Part III (New York: Basic Books, 1996)

Fanon, Frantz, *Black Skin, White Masks,* trans. Charles Lam Markmann (London: Pluto Press, 1986) [*Peau noire, masques blancs* (Paris: Éditions du Seuil, 1952)]

Fischer-Lichte, Erika, 'Thinking about the Origins of Theatre in the 1970s' [2004], in E. Hall and F. Macintosh (eds), *Dionysus Since 69: Greek Tragedy at the Dawn of the Third Millennium* (Oxford: OUP, 2004), pp. 329–60

Foley, Helene, 'Marriage and Sacrifice in Euripides' *Iphigenia in Aulis', Arethusa,* 15 (1982): 159–80; rev. version in Helene Foley, *Ritual Irony: Poetry and Sacrifice in Euripides* (Ithaca, NY and London: Cornell University Press, 1985), pp. 65–105

—— 'The Female Intruder Reconsidered: Women in Aristophanes' *Lysistrata and Ecclesiazusae', Classical Philology,* 77 (1982): 1–21

—— *Female Acts in Greek Tragedy* (Princeton, NJ: Princeton University Press, 2001)

—— 'Bad Women: Gender Politics in Late Twentieth-century Performance and Revision of Greek Tragedy', in E. Hall, F. Macintosh and A. Wrigley (eds), *Dionysus since 69: Greek Tragedy at the Dawn of the Third Millennium* (Oxford: OUP, 2004), pp. 77–111

—— (forthcoming), *The Theatrical Cast of Athens: Interactions between Ancient Greek Drama and Society*

—— (forthcoming), 'The Mother of All Sea-battles: the Reception of Aeschylus' *Persians* from Xerxes to Saddam Hussein', in E. Bridges, E. Hall and P. J. Rhodes (eds), *Cultural Responses to the Persian Wars* (Oxford: OUP)

Frazee, C. A., 'Greece', in W. M. Johnston (ed.), *Encyclopedia of Monasticism* (Chicago: Fitzroy Dearborn, 2000), pp. 543–50

Freeman, Joseph, Joshua Kunitz and Louis Lozowick, *Voices of October* (New York: Vanguard Press, 1930)

Freydkina, L., *Dni i gody Vl. I. Nemirovich-Danchenko, letopisv khzni i tvorchestva* (Moscow: Bserossiyskoe, Teatralvnoe Obshchestvo, 1962)

Fricker, Karen, '*Medea* Bows out on a Parisian High', *Irish Times*, Weekend Review, 29 March 2003, p. 7

Fülöp Miller, René, *The Mind and Face of Bolshevism* (London and New York: Putnam, 1927)

Geddes, Norman Bel, *Miracle in the Evening: An Autobiography*, ed. William Kelley (New York: Doubleday, 1960)

Girardet, Raoul, *L'Idée Coloniale en France 1871 à 1962* (Paris: La Table Ronde, 1972)

Gliksohn, Jean-Michel, *Iphigénie de la Grèce antique à l'Europe des Lumières* (Paris: Presses universitaires de France, 1985)

Goldhill, Simon, 'The Audience of Athenian Tragedy', in P. Easterling (ed.), *The Cambridge Companion to Greek Tragedy* (Cambridge: CUP, 1997)

Gorchakov, Nikolai A., *The Theatre in Soviet Russia*, trans. Edgar Lehrman (New York: Columbia University Press, 1957)

Gorelik, Mordecai, *New Theatres for Old* (New York: Samuel French, 1941)

Gourfinkel, Nina, *Le théâtre russe contemporain* (Paris: Editions Albert, 1930)

—— 'L'apport du théâtre étranger au début du XXe siècle', *La Revue des Lettres Modernes*, 3 (April 1954): 3–15

—— 'L'apport du théâtre étranger au début du siècle', *La Revue des Lettres Modernes*, 4 (May 1954): 18–31

—— 'La politique théâtrale russe et le réalisme', in *Le théâtre moderne, hommes et tendances* (Paris: CNRS, 1958)

—— 'La théâtrologie soviétique,' *Cahiers Théâtre Louvain*, 9 (1968–69): 15–20

Gray, Paul, 'Stanislavski and America: A Critical Chronology',

Drama Review, 9 (Winter 1964): 21–60

Gregor, Joseph and René Fülöp Miller, *Das Russische Theater* (Zurich, Leipzig and Vienna: Amaltheaverlag, 1928)

Hall, Edith, 'The Singing Actors of Antiquity', in P. Easterling and E. Hall (eds), *Greek and Roman Actors: Aspects of an Ancient Profession* (Cambridge: CUP, 2002), pp. 3–38

—— 'Introduction: Why Greek Tragedy in the Late Twentieth Century?', in E. Hall, F. Macintosh and A. Wrigley (eds), *Dionysus since 69: Greek Tragedy at the Dawn of the Third Millennium* (Oxford: OUP, 2004), pp. 1–46

—— 'Aeschylus, Race, Class, and War', in E. Hall, F. Macintosh and A. Wrigley (eds), *Dionysus since 69: Greek Tragedy at the Dawn of the Third Millennium* (Oxford: OUP, 2004), pp. 169–97

—— 'Barbarism with Beatitude', *Times Literary Supplement*, 21 February 2003, p. 19

—— (forthcoming), 'Aeschylus' Clytemnestra *versus* Her Senecan Tradition'

Hall, Edith and Fiona Macintosh, *Greek Tragedy and the British Theatre 1660–1914* (Oxford: OUP, 2005)

Hall, Edith, Fiona Macintosh and Amanda Wrigley (eds), *Dionysus since 69: Greek Tragedy at the Dawn of the Third Millennium* (Oxford: OUP, 2004)

Halperin, D. M., J. J. Winkler and F. I. Zeitlin, *Before Sexuality. The Construction of Erotic Experience in the Ancient World* (Princeton, NJ: Princeton University Press, 1990)

Harrington, J. P., *Modern Irish Drama* (New York: W. W. Norton, 1991)

Heaney, Seamus, 'The Cure at Troy: Production Notes in No Particular Order', in M. McDonald and J. M. Walton (eds), *Amid Our Troubles: Irish Versions of Greek Tragedy* (London: Methuen, 2002)

—— *The Burial at Thebes* (London: Faber and Faber, 2004)

Henderson, Jeffrey, 'Greek Attitudes Towards Sex', in M. Grant and R. Kitzinger (eds), *Civilisation of the Ancient Mediterranean*, 3 vols (New York: Scribner's, 1988)

Holst-Warhaft, Gail, *Dangerous Voices: Women's Lament and Greek Literature* (London: Routledge, 1992)

Hoover, Marjorie, *Meyerhold: The Art of the Conscious Theatre* (Amherst: University of Massachusetts Press, 1974)

Hornblower, S. and A. Spawforth (eds), *The Oxford Classical Dictionary*, 3rd edn (Oxford: OUP, 1996)

Houghton, Norris, *Moscow Rehearsals* (New York: Harcourt, Brace and Co., 1936)

Ingham, Bernard, *Wages of Spin* (London: John Murray, 2003)

Innes, Christopher, *Avant Garde Theatre 1892–1992* (London and New York: Routledge, rev. edn 1993)

Johnston, W. M. (ed.), *Encyclopedia of Monasticism* (Chigago: Fitzroy Dearborn, 2000)

Katsaïtis, Petros, *Iphigenia*, ed. E. Kriaras (Athens: Institut français d'Athènes, 1950)

Keane, Terry, 'Allow Me the Last Word on John Waters' World', *Sunday Times*, 18 June 2000

Kennelly, Brendan, *Cromwell: A Poem* (Dublin: Beaver Row Press, 1983)

—— 'Louis MacNeice: An Irish Outsider', in M. Sekine (ed.), *Irish Writers and Society at Large* (Gerrard's Cross: Colin Smythe, 1985)

—— *Euripides' 'Medea': A New Version by Brendan Kennelly* (Newcastle-upon-Tyne: Bloodaxe Books, 1988)

—— *The Book of Judas* (Newcastle-upon-Tyne: Bloodaxe Books, 1991)

—— *Euripides' 'The Trojan Women': A New Version by Brendan Kennelly* (Newcastle-upon-Tyne: Bloodaxe Books, 1993)

—— *Sophocles' 'Antigone': A New Version by Brendan Kennelly* (Newcastle-upon-Tyne: Bloodaxe Books, 1996)

King, Beatrice, 'Vladimir Nemirovich-Danchenko, Greatest Figure in 20th Century Theatre', *Anglo Soviet Journal*, 4 (1943): 153–60

King, Jeanette, *Tragedy in the Victorian Novel* (Cambridge: CUP, 1978)

Kleinhardt, W. '*Medea* – Originalität und Variation in der Darstellung einer Rache', Ph. D. diss., Hamburg University, 1962

Knowles, Dorothy, *French Drama of the Inter-War Years 1918–1939* (London: George G. Harrap and Co., 1967)

Knox, B., *Word and Action: Essays on the Ancient Theater*, (Baltimore, MD: Johns Hopkins University Press, 1979)

Komisarjevsky, Theodore, *Myself and the Theatre* (New York: E. P. Dutton and Co., 1930)

Kotzamani, Marina Anastasia, '*Lysistrata*, Playgirl of the Western World: Aristophanes on the Early Modern Stage', Doctoral Dissertation, Graduate School of the City University of New York, 1997

Kristeva, Julia, *The Powers of Horror: An Essay on Abjection*, trans. Leon. S. Roudiez (New York: Columbia University Press, 1982)

Kubo, M., 'The Norm of Myth: Euripides' *Electra*', *Harvard Studies in Classical Philology*, 71 (1966): 15–31

La Bute, Neil, *Bash: Latterday Plays* (New York: Overlook Press, 1999)

Larson, Orville, *Scene Design in the American Theatre from 1915 to 1960* (Fayetteville and London: University of Arkansas Press, 1989)

Law, Alma H., 'Meyerhold's *The Magnanimous Cuckold*', *Drama Review*, 26 (Spring 1982): 61–86

Lee, Veronica, 'The Anger of Heaven is Nothing to the Anger of Men', *Independent on Sunday*, *Life* section, 9 February 2003

Lefkowitz, Mary, *Women in Greek Myth* (Baltimore, MD: Johns Hopkins University Press, 1986)

Lenin, V. I., *The Emancipation of Women* (New York: International Publishers, 1978)

Lenormand, Henri-René, *Théâtre Complet*, vol. IX (Paris: G.Crès, 1936)

—— *Les Confessions d'un auteur dramatique*, vol. 2 (Paris: Michel, 1953)

Lewis, Sian, *News and Society in the Greek Polis* (Chapel Hill: University of North Carolina Press, 1996)

Loomba, Ania, *Colonialism/Postcolonialism* (London: Routledge, 1998)

Loraux, Nicole, *Les enfants d'Athéna* [1981] (Paris: Seuil, 1990)

Lounatcharsky, Anatoli Vassilievitch, *Théâtre et révolution* (Paris: Maspero, 1970)

Luschnig, Karl, 'Time and Memory in Euripides' *Iphigenia at Aulis*', *Ramus*, 11 (1982): 99–104

Lysistrata, a new adaptation in two acts translated from the Greek by Gilbert Seldes, in Burns Mantle and John Gassner (eds), *Treasury of the Theatre*, vol. 2 (New York: Simon and Schuster, 1935)

Lysistrata, ed. with an introduction and commentary by Jeffrey Henderson (Oxford: Clarendon Press, 1987)

MacDonald, Ann-Marie, *The Way the Crow Flies* (London: Fourth Estate, 2003)

McDonald, Marianne, *Euripides in Cinema: The Heart Made Visible* (Philadelphia: Centrum Philadelphia, for the Greek Institute, 1983)

—— *Sing Sorrow: Classics, History, and Heroines in Opera* (Westport, CT and London: Greenwood Press, 2001)

McDonald, Marianne and J. Michael Walton (eds), *Amid Our Troubles: Irish Versions of Greek Tragedy* (London: Methuen, 2002)

—— (trans.), *Euripides' Andromache* (London: Nick Hern Books, 2001)

—— (trans.), *Sophocles' Electra* (London: Nick Hern Books, 2003)

—— (trans.), *Euripides' Electra* (London: Nick Hern Books, 2004)

McDonald, Marianne and Martin M. Winkler, 'Michael Cacoyannis and Irene Papas on Greek Tragedy', in M. Winkler (ed.), *Classical Myth and Culture in the Cinema* (Oxford: OUP, 2001), pp. 72–89

MacDowell, Douglas M., *Aristophanes and Athens* (Oxford: OUP, 1995)

Macgowan, Kenneth, 'American Note-book Abroad', *Theatre Arts Monthly*, 6 (October 1922): 299–312

—— *Footlights Across America* (New York: Harcourt Brace, 1929)

Macgowan, Kenneth and Robert Edmond Jones, *Continental Stagecraft* (London: Benn Brothers, 1923)

Macintosh, Fiona, *Dying Acts: Death in Ancient Greek and Irish Tragic Drama* (Cork: Cork University Press, 1994)

—— 'Tragedy in Performance: Nineteenth- and Twentieth-century Productions', in P. E. Easterling (ed.), *The Cambridge Companion to Greek Tragedy* (Cambridge: CUP, 1997), pp. 284–323

—— Introduction: 'The Performer in Performance', in E. Hall, F. Macintosh and O. Taplin (eds), *'Medea' in Performance 1500–2000* (Oxford: Legenda, 2000)

Macintosh F., P. Michelakis, E. Hall and O. Taplin (eds), *Agamemnon in Performance 458 BC to 2004 AD* (Oxford: OUP, 2005)

MacKinnon, Kenneth, *Greek Tragedy into Film* (London: Croom Helm, 1986)

MacKinnon, Kenneth and Marianne McDonald, 'Cacoyannis vs. Euripides: From Tragedy to Melodrama', in N. W. Slater and B. Zimmermann (eds), *Intertextualität in der griechisch-römischen Komödie* (Stuttgart: M&P Verlag für Wissenschaft und Forschung, 1993), pp. 222–34

McMullan, Anna and Cathy Leeney (eds), *The Theatre of Marina Carr: '...before rules was made'* (Dublin: Carysfort Press, 2003)

Mader, Joe, 'Iffy *Iphigenia*', *San Francisco Examiner*, 2 June 2003

Magarshack, David, *Stanislavsky: A Life* (London: Faber and Faber, 1986)

Mahon, E., 'Women's Rights and Catholicism in Ireland', *New Left Review*, 166 (November–December 1986)

Markov, Pavel Aleksandrovich, *Rezhissura Vl. I. Nemirovicha-Danchenko v muzykalnom teatre* (Moscow: Vserossiyskoe Teatralvnoe Obshchestvo, 1960)

—— *The Soviet Theatre* (New York: B. Blom, 1972)

Martin, Jean, *L'Empire Triomphant 1871–1936*, vol. 2, *Maghreb, Indochine, Madagascar, îles et comptoirs* (Paris: Éditions Denoël, 1990)

Matskin, A., *Portrety i nablyudeniya* (Moscow: Iskusstvo, 1973)

Mellert-Hoffman, Gudrun, *Untersuchungen zur 'Iphigenie in Aulis' des Euripides* (Heidelberg: C. Winter, 1969)

Mercier, Vivian, 'Irish Literary Revival', in W. E. Vaughan (ed.), *A New History of Ireland: Ireland under the Union II, 1870–1921*, vol. VI (Oxford: OUP, 1996)

Merriman, Victor, 'Greek Tragedy Loses the Plot', *Sunday Tribune*, 1 April 2001

Merwin, W. S. and George E. Dimock, *Euripides, Iphigeneia at Aulis* [in the series *The Greek Tragedy in New Translations*] (Oxford: OUP, 1978)

Meyerhold, V. E., *Meyerhold on Theatre,* trans. and ed. with a commentary by Edward Braun (New York: Hill and Wang, 1969)

—— *Écrits sur le théâtre*, ed. and trans. Béatrice Picon-Valin (Lausanne: La Cité, L' Age d' Homme, 1975)

—— *The Theatre of Meyerhold: Revolution on the Modern Stage*, ed. and trans. Edward Braun (New York: Drama Book Specialists, 1979)

Michelakis, Pantelis, *Achilles in Greek Tragedy* (Cambridge: CUP, 2002)

—— review of Suzanne Aretz, *Die Opferung der Iphigeneia in Aulis: Die Rezeption des Mythos in antiken und modernen Dramen* [2002], in *Bryn Mawr Classical Review,* online at http://ccat.sas.upenn.edu/bmcr/2002/2002-01-05.html

Michelini, A. N., *Euripides and the Tragic Tradition* (Madison: University of Wisconsin Press, 1987)

Mirsky, D. S., *A History of Russian Literature*, ed. F. J. Whitfield (New York: Routledge and Kegan Paul, 1949)

Monks, Aoife, 'Private Parts, Public Bodies: Cross-Dressing in the Work of Deborah Warner and Elizabeth Lecompte', Doctoral dissertation, Trinity College Dublin, 2002

Moran, Sean Farrell, *Patrick Pearse and the Politics of*

Redemption: The Mind of the Easter Rising, 1916 (Washington, DC: Catholic University of America Press, 1994)

Moskvin, I., *The Soviet Theatre* (Moscow: Foreign Languages Publishing House, 1939)

Mossman, Judith (ed.), *Oxford Readings in Classical Studies: Euripides* (Oxford: OUP, 2003)

Mueller, Martin, *Children of Oedipus and Other Essays on the Imitation of Greek Tragedy 1550–1800* (Toronto: University of Toronto Press, 1980)

Murray, Oswyn, John Boardman and Jasper Griffin (eds), *Greece and the Hellenistic World* (Oxford: OUP, 1988)

Nakhoph, J. M., 'E kleronomia tou Aristophane', in Aristophanes, *Meletes*, trans. from Russian into Greek by M. Garides (Athens: Mokhlos, 1957)

Nemirovich-Danchenko, V., *My Life in the Russian Theatre*, trans. John Cournos (London: Geoffrey Bles, 1937)

New York Times Directory of the Theater (New York: Arno Press, 1973)

New York Times Theatre Reviews 1920–1970, 10 vols (New York: *New York Times* and Arno Press, 1977)

Ni Anluain, Cliodhna (ed.), *Reading the Future: Irish Writers in Conversation with Mike Murphy* (Dublin: Lilliput Press, 2000)

Oakley, J. H. and R. H. Sinos, *The Wedding in Ancient Athens* (Madison: University of Wisconsin Press, 1993)

O'Brien, Edna, *'Iphigenia': Euripides,* adapted with an Introduction (London: Methuen, 2003)

O'Brien, M. J., 'Orestes and the Gorgon: Euripides' *Electra*', *American Journal of Philology* (1964): 13–39

O'Kelly, Emer, 'Tales of Greek Inevitability', *Sunday Independent*, 1 April 2001

O'Rawe, Des, '(Mis)translating Tragedy: Irish Poets and Greek Plays', in L. Hardwick, P. Easterling, S. Ireland, N. Lowe and F. Macintosh (eds), *Theatre: Ancient and Modern* (Milton Keynes: Open University Press, 2000), pp. 109–24

Paech, Joachim, *Das Theater der russischen Revolution* (Berlin: Scriptor Verlag, 1974)

Page, Denys, *Actors' Interpolations in Greek Tragedy: Studied with Special Reference to Euripides' 'Iphigeneia in Aulis'* (Oxford: Clarendon Press, 1934)

—— (ed.), *Select Papyri III*, Loeb Classical Library series (Cambridge, MA: Harvard University Press, 1970)

Paris-Moscou 1900–1930, Exhibition Catalogue, 2nd edn (Paris: Centre Nationale d' Art et de Culture, Georges Pompidou, 1979)

Parker, R., 'Sacrifice, Greek', in S. Hornblower and A. Spawforth (eds), *The Oxford Classical Dictionary*, 3rd edn (Oxford: OUP, 1996), pp. 1344–5

Paulin, Tom, *Seize the Fire: A Version of Aeschylus' 'Prometheus Bound'* (London: Faber and Faber, 1990)

Pearse, Patrick, *Collected Works* (Dublin and London: Phoenix Publishing, 1917)

—— *Collected Works*, 5th edn (Dublin: Irish National Publishing Company, 1924)

—— *Selected Poems: Rogha Dánta*, ed. Eugene McCabe (Dublin: New Island Press, 1993)

Pearson, Anthony, 'The Cabaret Comes to Russia; the Theatre of Small Forms as a Cultural Catalyst', *Theatre Quarterly*, 9 (1980): 31–44

Perrier, Jean-Louis, 'Le théâtre, apôtre de la diversité culturelle en Irelande', *Le Monde*, 14 October 2002

Peter, John, 'Making War, Not Love', *Sunday Times*, Culture section, 16 February 2003, pp. 18–19

Pitcher, George, *The Death of Spin* (Chichester: Wiley, 2002)

Plays, trans. Kenneth McLeish, 2 vols (London: Methuen, 1993)

Pomeroy, Sarah B., *Goddesses, Whores, Wives, and Slaves; Women in Classical Antiquity* (New York: Schocken Books, 1975)

—— *Women in Classical Antiquity* (New York: Dorset Press, 1975)

Purkiss, Diane (ed.), *Three Tragedies by Renaissance Women* (London: Penguin, 1998)

Raphael, Frederic and Kenneth McLeish, 'Aeschylus' *Suppliants*', in *Aeschylus Plays: One* (London: Methuen, 1991)

—— 'Aeschylus' *Libation-Bearers*', in *Aeschylus Plays: Two* (London: Methuen, 1991)

Redmond, John (ed.), *Themes in Drama VII: Drama, Sex and Politics* (Cambridge: CUP, 1985)

Rehm, Rush, *Marriage to Death: The Conflation of Wedding and Funeral Rituals in Greek Tragedy* (Princeton, NJ: Princeton University Press, 1994)

Reid, Jane Davidson (ed.), *The Oxford Guide to Classical Mythology in the Arts* (New York and Oxford: OUP, 1993)

Reinhardt, Karl, 'Die Sinneskreise bei Euripides', *Eranos*, 26 (1957): 79–317, reproduced in his *Tradition und Geist* (Göttingen: Vandenhoek and Ruprecht, 1960), pp. 223–56, and in English translation in J. Mossman (ed.), *Oxford Readings in Euripides* (Oxford: OUP, 2003), pp. 16–46

Riches P., 'A Taste of Strawberries: Pilgrimage to the Two Monastic Dependencies of Simonopetra in Southern France 14–17 June 2002', in *Friends of Mount Athos: Annual Report 2002*, pp. 61–6

Rudnitsky, Konstantin, *Russian and Soviet Theater 1905–1932*, trans. Roxane Permar, ed. Lesley Milne (New York: Harry N. Abrams, 1988)

Russell, Robert and Andrew Barratt (eds), *Russian Theatre in the Age of Modernism* (New York: St Martin's Press, 1990)

Sarraut, Albert, *La mise en valeur des colonies françaises* (Paris, 1923)

Sayler, Oliver, *Inside the Moscow Art Theatre* (Westport, CT: Greenwood Press, 1925)

Schlegel, A. W., *A Course of Lectures on Dramatic Art and Literature*, trans. John Black, 2 vols, 2nd edn (London: J. Templeman and J. R. Smith, 1840)

Scullion, S., 'Nothing to Do with Dionysus: Tragedy Misconceived as Ritual', *Classical Quarterly*, 52 (2002): 102–37

Seaford R., *Reciprocity and Ritual: Homer and Tragedy in the*

Developing City-State (Oxford: OUP, 1994)

Seldes, Gilbert, *The Seven Lively Arts* (New York: A. S. Barnes, 1924)

—— 'Adapting *Lysistrata*', *Theatre Guild Magazine* (October 1930): 60–2

Shannon, Geoffrey, *Divorce: The Changing Landscape of Divorce in Ireland* (Dublin: Round Hall, 2001)

Siegel, Herbert, 'Self-delusion and the *Volte-face* of Iphigenia in Euripides' *Iphigenia at Aulis*', *Hermes*, 108 (1980): 300–21

Slater, N. W. and B. Zimmermann (eds), *Intertextualität in der griechisch-römischen Komödie* (Stuttgart: M&P Verlag für Wissenschaft und Forschung, 1993)

Smith, Wesley D., 'Iphigenia in Love', in G. W. Bowersock, W. Burkert and M. C. J. Putnam (eds), *Arktouros: Hellenic Studies Presented to Bernard M.W. Knox* (Berlin and New York: de Gruyter, 1979), pp. 173–80

Smolin, D. (trans.), *Lysistrata*, trans. George S. and Gilbert Seldes, in *Plays of the Moscow Art Theatre Musical Studio* (New York: Brentano's, 1925)

Sommerstein, Alan H. et al. (eds), *Tragedy, Comedy and the Polis* (Bari: Levante Editori, 1993)

Sourvinou-Inwood, C., *Tragedy and Athenian Religion* (Lanham, MD: Lexington Books, 2003)

Soyinka, Wole, *The 'Bacchae' of Euripides: A Communion Rite*, in *Wole Soyinka: The Collected Plays* (Oxford: OUP, 1973)

Spivak, Gayatri, 'Can the Subaltern Speak?', in P. Williams and L. Chrisman (eds), *Colonial Discourse and Post-Colonial Theory* (New York: Harvester Wheatsheaf, 1993)

Sprigge, Elizabeth, *Sybil Thorndike Casson* (London: Gollancz, 1971)

Stallybrass, Peter and Allon White, *The Politics and Poetics of Transgression* (Ithaca, NY: Cornell University Press, 1986)

Stanislavski, Constantin, *My Life in Art*, trans. J. J. Robbins (London: Methuen, 1980)

Stephenson, Heidi and Natasha Langridge (eds), *Rage and Reason: Women Playwrights on Playwrighting* (London: Methuen, 1997)

Stoudt, Charlotte, 'Wartime Myths', *Village Voice*, 20 July 2004

Synge, J. M., *The Playboy of the Western World* (Cork: Mercier Press, 1974)

Taafe, Lauren K., *Aristophanes and Women* (London: Routledge, 1993)

Taplin, Oliver, 'Sophocles' *Philoctetes*, Seamus Heaney's, and Some Other Recent Half-rhymes', in E. Hall, F. Macintosh and A. Wrigley (eds), *Dionysus since 69: Greek Tragedy at the Dawn of the Third Millennium* (Oxford: OUP, 2004), pp. 145–67

Taylor, Don, 'Introduction' to his translation of *Iphigenia at Aulis*, (London: Methuen, 1999), pp. vii–xviii

Teevan, Colin, *Iph. . . After Euripides' 'Iphigeneia in Aulis'* (London: Nick Hern Books, 1999)

—— *Iph. . . A New Version from the Greek of 'Iphigenia in Aulis'*, 2nd edn (London: Oberon Books, 2002)

Unsworth, Barry, *The Songs of the Kings* (London: Hamish Hamilton, 2002)

Van Steen, Gonda, '"The World's a Circular Stage": Aeschylean Tragedy Through the Eyes of Eva Palmer-Sikelianou', *International Journal of the Classical Tradition*, 8 (Winter 2002): 375–93

Vermeule, E., 'The Boston Oresteia Krater', *American Journal of Archaeology*, 70 (1996): 1–22

Vlastos, G., *Socrates, Ironist and Moral Philosopher* (Cambridge: CUP, 1991)

Walton, J. Michael (trans.), *Medea*, in *Euripides Plays: One* (London: Methuen, 2000)

Ware T., *The Orthodox Church* (London: Penguin, 1993)

Waters, John, 'Problems in Excusing Medea's Murders', *Irish Times*, 19 June 2000

West, M. L., *Ancient Greek Music* (Oxford: Clarendon Press, 1992)

White, Victoria, 'Irish Theatre Begins to Change as Audience Becomes Increasingly Diffuse: Women Writers Finally Take Centre Stage', *Irish Times*, 15 October 1998

Wilde, Oscar, *Complete Works of Oscar Wilde,* introduced by Vyvyan Holland (London: Collins, 1971)

Wilkinson, John, *Iphigenia* (London: Barque Press, 2004)

Williams, Bernard, *Shame and Necessity* (Berkeley: University of California Press, 1993)

Williams, Martin, 'Ancient Mythology and Revolutionary Ideology in Ireland, 1878–1916', *Historical Journal,* 26 (2) (1983): 307–28

Winkler, Martin M. (ed.), *Classical Myth and Culture in the Cinema* [1991], rev. edn (Oxford: OUP, 2001)

Worrall, Nick, 'Meyerhold's *The Magnificent Cuckold*', *Drama Review,* 17 (March 1973): 14–34

Worth, Katharine, 'Greek Notes in Samuel Beckett's Theatre Art', in E. Hall, F. Macintosh and A. Wrigley (eds), *Dionysus since 69: Greek Tragedy at the Dawn of the Third Millennium* (Oxford: OUP, 2004), pp. 265–83

Worthen, William B. (ed.), *The Harcourt Brace Anthology of Drama,* 3rd edn (Boston: Thomson Heinle, 2000)

Zeitlin, Froma, 'The Closet of Masks: Role-playing and Mythmaking in the *Orestes* of Euripides', *Ramus,* 9 (1980): 51–77; republished in J. Mossman (ed.), *Oxford Readings in Euripides* (Oxford: OUP, 2003), pp. 309–41.

—— *Playing the Other: Gender and Society in Classical Greek Literature* (Chicago: Chicago University Press, 1996)

—— 'The Argive Festival of Hera and Euripides' *Electra*', *Transactions of the American Philological Society,* 101 (1970): 45–69, republished in J. Mossman (ed.), *Oxford Readings in Euripides* (Oxford: OUP, 2003), pp. 261–84

Zyl Smit, E. van, 'Contemporary Witch – Dramatic Treatments of the Medea Myth', D. Litt. diss., Stellenbosch University, 1987

Index

Index